LEARNING TO SAY GOODBYE

ALEXANDRA DIONISIO

1

©Alexandra Dionisio 2025

This is a true story drawn from my own life. Certain names and details have been changed to protect privacy, but every feeling, every turning point, remains as I remember it.

Published by LTSG Publishing
Printed in the United States of America
First Edition, December 2025
ISBN 979-8-9935944-0-8

To the children and families who welcomed me into their homes
- your courage and love are the heart of this book. Thank you for
trusting me with your stories; identifying details have been changed
to honor your privacy.

To "Jordin" and the hospice team - nurses, social workers, chaplains,
and volunteers - your steadiness and tenderness taught me what
service looks like.

To my husband, Andrea, and our daughters, Gia and Giulia - thank
you for your patience, humor, and endless faith in me.

To my friends and early readers who offered clear eyes and kind edits
- I'm grateful for your truth and care.

Special thanks to Ursula for her generous reads and wise edits; to my
writing coach, Vanessa, whose heart and soul, deep understanding of
grief, and gift of "Image Moments" shaped these pages; and to Kathy
- your friendship and steadfast support mean the world to me.

To Mona, for relaying the word that became my compass: Trust.

To Kathrin, my forever friend and north star.

May this book honor each of you.

CHAPTER 1

"Kathrin is dead."

I hear the words whispered by my father - words that, once spoken, split my world. They drop through the phone like boulders, sending ripples that sweep away the very structure of my life. My legs buckle; the once-solid floor gathers me in as I drown silently in my office. A loud swooshing sound rushes up behind me, tossing me like a leaf caught in a giant wave, throwing me onto the floor gasping for air. Sound drains out. My chair, the desk with the laptop I had been working on, the glass walls of my office, the sprawling windows overlooking the Arabian Gulf, and the jewel-like buildings along its pristine beaches - all fall away until only a white nothing remains. My reality shrinks to the ground I'm crumpled on, my eyes fixed on the dusty wire of a long-forgotten paperclip peeking out from underneath my file cabinet.

The force of my father's words catapults me out of my body. I'm half a beat behind reality, living in a parallel hush, as if sound ceased to exist. I can feel the hard surface of the vinyl flooring under my knees, the subtle lines of the fake wood imprinting on my hand. My other hand claws the phone like a lifeline I can't drop for fear of being swept away. For a moment, I marvel at the complete emptiness around me. I stare at the body on the floor - my body - knuckles straining white against auburn hair, as I grip the phone, while another part of me observes from above. Around and inside me: a milky, soft emptiness. Maybe this is what it's like to stand in the space between reality and nightmare. The fog parts, allowing me a glimpse of the floor, the paper clip, the edge of the cabinet, and - something else. A sound? A voice.

… my father.
… I think.

Word fragments flutter against my ears like moths, leaving only a trace of understanding: "… accident … I'm sorry … hate … bearer of bad news …" His voice fades as my brain wraps itself in cotton, a built-in mercy, that mutes the claws of heartbreak. Thoughts rise like bubbles and burst before I can hold them. I squeeze my eyes shut, trying to catch one. At last, a phrase stutters to the surface, coughing like an old engine, repeating over and over without meaning.

Kathrin is dead.
Kathrin is dead.
Kathrin is dead.

Impossible. We just spoke. When? WHEN?? Why can't I remember? I chase the last time I heard her voice, as if the stamp of a date could undo the sentence. The word ricochets around my skull

- when, when, when - until language thins to noise. When, when, when, … wheeeeen …wheeeennnnnn

STOP!

I throw myself in front of this avalanche of thoughts and shepherd my mind back to the question it keeps losing. What was it again? Confused, I stumble through word fragments - What was I just thinking about? It is on the tip of my tongue …. Oh yes, there it is: "When." Triumph surges, but it's hollow. What does "when" even mean? Why is it important? Brain fog clouds everything, but then it hits me. Another boom - low and final - rolls through me:

Kathrin is dead!

Denial raises its head and hisses a loud "No!" Impossible! She can't be! She is the constant threaded through every room of my life, infusing every memory from childhood to adulthood with her presence, her friendship, her love. My life is infused with her perfume and the scent of the chocolate-covered caramels we ate after nights out dancing. She has been there for it all: teenage angst, high school dramas, heartbreaks, movie nights, and shared Sweet and Sour Chicken at our favorite Chinese restaurant, our weddings, the birth of our children. She is the one I can always rely on, no matter the hour or reason. One call or text shrinks the distance between Vienna and Dubai to virtually nothing, as we are there for each other, - listen, talk, laugh, commiserate about trivial arguments with our respective husbands, gossip about work, or simply check in.

But "dead" means gone, so NO, this cannot be! I am here; therefore, she must be too. We are two sides of the same coin, two hearts, one mind, swaying to the same rhythm, just on opposite sides of the world. Soul sisters in every sense of the word - we have been since we were kids. After all, we're not at an age where people die. I just turned forty-one, but I feel more like twenty-eight; growing up is not a linear process, and from my perspective, death is a lifetime away.

That logic buys me a breath - the first one in ages. Oxygen fills my lungs with cool relief, expanding them, snapping the clamps of dread around my chest. My surroundings rush back into view. I can feel my knees still pressing against the floor, phone against my ear, out of habit more than out of necessity because I don't even know if my father's still on the line. I think I hear his voice, but cannot make out the meaning of the words. Without looking, I wave my arm behind me, searching in vain for my desk chair, which had rolled against the floor-to-ceiling window just out of reach. Instead, I get a hold of my desk, pull myself up from the floor, but not before flicking the paperclip with a sudden sense of vengeance, so it disappears completely under the cabinet.

With a deep exhale, I straighten up, pull my shoulders back, chin up - breaking the threads of despair that are ready to pull me down and tie me up in a neat little bundle of pain.

Arschbackenzusammenkneifmentalität! I command myself. One of those insane monstrosities of the German language, where multiple words of unrelated meaning are threaded together like beads on a string, creating a mismatched but strangely accurate image. A mindset more than a word, literally translates to "pinch-your-butt-cheeks-together-mentality,' as in: pull yourself together and get over it. Wise words from my mother ....

My mother ....
My mother is dead.

That I know to be true. She died 4 years ago after a relatively short but painful battle with cancer, my first personal encounter with Death. Of course, this was not the first time someone I loved had passed away, but when my grandfather died, I was too small to remember much more than sitting on my mother's lap and seeing the emotions etched on everyone's faces. They tried to shield me from the harsh reality of death by showering me with love and affection through curtains of tears. And it worked: the false sense of happiness lured my 4-year-old self to more pressing matters, such as hunting a runaway crayon from my mother's handbag across the shiny, slightly bumpy linoleum floor, trading the prickly sting of disinfectant for the soothing scent of wax, bright color, and art.

My grandmothers' deaths came later, while I was studying abroad. Their passing was sad but expected, a natural part of life's cycle, learned through biology and history. Living beings are born, live, grow old and die. But my mother was different. At sixty-six, she wasn't old, despite my daughter's insistence that life was black-and-white when her grandmother was young, just like old movies. Until then, my mother's life followed that simple birth, live a long life, grow old, and die -timeline. Well, minus the old age part. Death skipped a few chapters with her.

And then my dad called.

It's always a phone call that changes everything. That afternoon, the Dubai heat pressed in, and a pair of Indian Myna birds argued in the palm tree outside the kitchen window. I loved those pesky little birds with their loud screeches and clever minds. But that day, their noise drowned out the voice on the phone. My father did not say she was dying; those words were never spoken. Instead, the truth hid between the lines, shaking me. My mother had been sick since April, a string of misdiagnoses and complications piling up. Yet we never discussed the what-ifs. My parents, both physicians, prided themselves on clear, honest communication with patients, but with her illness, they clung to vague hopes, avoiding the possibility of a terminal outcome. As if the mere mention of death would make the cancer cells thrive, triple, and quadruple. As if allowing myself to discuss my deepest fears would open the door to a death sentence, and I, personally, would be responsible if my mother didn't recover. Holding all the what-ifs inside was too much. I'm optimistic - sometimes excessively so - my glass is always half-full, and I couldn't care less if that bothers others. It is my glass to fill after all. But watching my mother cycle in and out of the hospital, seeing her brave smile on Skype, smiles hiding the depth of something I could only guess was fear, trepidation, and pain, I wondered: was she hiding it from me or from herself? As much as I wanted to believe all would be well, the control freak inside of me needed to know the options.

What if …

I wanted to be prepared for all eventualities while holding my glass steady at half full. But just in case, let's talk about what happens if the diagnosis was wrong again. What if it's cancer? What if it can't be cured? Just give me a moment to talk about what could happen. What I could say that would make a difference. What I need to say. What I need to hear. But I play along, respecting her path, though it choked me with unspoken questions. But isn't it my job to question the status quo? When is it my turn to step out of the role of a daughter and into the role of an equal? Not mother-daughter, but two women; talking openly, human to human, with love and fear in our hearts, baring our pain? I hate to be complicit in these lies we tell ourselves in order not to rock the boat. But I play along, my father's voice in my ears, "We need to be gentle with her. She has a hard time with this, but you know your mother. She does not want to talk about it. She will be fine. Just keep things light-hearted."

And I do.
And so does he.
Until the call. Well, actually, beyond the phone call.

I am standing in the kitchen of our home in Dubai, a dish towel draped over my shoulder, phone in one hand, frying pan in the other. "Shhhhhhhhhhh!" I yell, slamming the window shut. "Sorry, Paps, those damn birds. I could not hear myself think. Give me one more second." I say towards the phone. With a loud sizzle I stir the vegetables and turn my attention to the voice on the other end of the line. "Hi! Sorry about that. I'm making dinner for the kids. They're at the park with Melanie. It's been one of those days. Giulia had an upset stomach last night and has been cranky all day." I sigh. "But now I am all yours." The silence stretched, broken only by his soft voice, "I think you should come home." That is all it took. Those words cut through me like a knife. My fears had not been unwarranted after all. My glass starts to wobble, spilling hope left and right. I knew. I just knew!

With that sudden realization everything around me switches off. This is it! I feel my life pivoting. Change is coming. Everything becomes quiet and far away, as if I am looking through a long tunnel, only seeing what is right in front of me, but even then, it is distant, unreachable, dim, out of focus. The only sound I can hear is my own heartbeat filling my head, drowning out everything else. My life is becoming something I watch from the outside, like a silent movie. Silent because this is the first time I encounter the cotton-protection-mechanism of my brain. All sounds are muffled, and nothing - no words, no emotions, no physical contact seems to get through this barrier of isolation.

The vegetables char unsupervised in front of me. I hang up, scrape the pan, and start over - on autopilot. I'm in function-mode, extremely efficient in organizing everyone and everything around me. My need for control is the engine that drives me, that pushes me to move faster and faster through the tunnel of my shrunken reality. My mind runs a mile-a-minute, chasing down to-do lists, filling every breath with an electric current of frenzy. My movements are rushed, hard, as if in fast-forward, losing their fluidity, replaced by rigid automation. I finish dinner, plate the food for the kids, and leave them with their nanny Melanie to supervise. The dish towel is still draped over my shoulder as I sit at my desk, booking my flight, making shopping lists, to-do lists, and planning everyone's life for the next week, possibly longer.

Thank God for the luxury of having a live-in nanny. Melanie has become part of our little family over the years, adored by the girls for her Tagalog songs and gentle care. Without her, I could never drop everything and leave. But she has my back. Whatever my husband can't do, she will take care of. Focused on Melanie's singing, Giulia does not protest the next forkful of beans.

Minutes, hours, days blend into one: I fly to Frankfurt, catch a train from the airport to Saarbrücken, our little town near the French border. I find the apartment key under the doormat, pack supplies for my mother in hospital, make sure we don't forget anything to make her more comfortable, take care of my father, and make sure we are all fed, while keeping the household in decent shape. After all, my mother does not appreciate it when the kitchen is left in disarray, and even though she is not here, her presence still fills every nook and cranny of my parents' warm and inviting home.

The apartment is all carpets, soft cushions, warm-wooded antiques, and the gentle ticking of old clocks. There are soft aquarelles on the walls next to oil paintings, holding on to their golden frames with a stiff upper lip. The Sterling Silver key tray glistens on the table near the front door, where my mother's car keys sit pouting next to an open, wrinkled-looking pack of Fisherman's Friends.

Walking into the hospital room, in contrast, feels like taking a cold shower. The smell of stale cafeteria food emanating from a nearby cart loudly argues with the prickly scent of disinfectant over who can better cover the odor of sickness and apathy. The defeated clicking of my father's leather shoes echoes along the long empty hallway to my mother's room, the metronome to the squeaky soles of my high-top sneakers against the linoleum floor.

She is awake, sitting upright, and greets me with a huge smile, as if the hospital room, the bed, and the medical equipment nearby are mere stage settings to a perfectly ordinary scene. Nothing unusual to see here.

Everything is fine.

I must have left the woman at the door, because the person sitting down in the wooden chair next to my mother's bed is the obedient daughter, who answers my mother's questions about her flight, the girls, and her husband. The daughter, whose concerns about her mother's health are brushed aside with a quick "It's all going to be fine." The daughter, who is too caught up in the parent-child dynamic to speak up.

Don't rock the boat.

Once we leave the hospital, my dad and I walk in silence. Truth settles between us like an unwelcome guest. We know. But this unacknowledged truth keeps us apart, filling the space between us with a cold, tangible silence, as I struggle to figure out who is walking next to my dad now: the daughter or the woman? Who does my father need me to be? Does he need the safety of our comfortable father-daughter relationship, or does he need an equal, a shoulder, a confidante, someone to help him face what's ahead?

I have no idea.
So, I do it all.

I flicker from one identity to another, daughter, woman, daughter. Seamlessly and sometimes with a dizzying speed, shedding identities like skins. I scan his face for cues - who do I need to be now? Which version of myself does he need?

The tightrope walk between identities is exhausting! It fills me with a constant fear that I am getting it wrong. That I am not enough. Not enough of a daughter to give my dad the feeling of purpose and accomplishment of being a good dad, in a moment when everything else seems to be going wrong. And not enough of a woman to carry some of his burden, when our little world is about to implode. As my mother grows more translucent and quiet, she is moved to the palliative care unit of the hospital, and with it the clear line between woman and daughter blurs, leaving a new being behind. Not a woman, not a daughter, but a mess of both. Too weary and drained to adapt myself to the needs of others. It is all too raw.

My dad and I hardly leave my mother's side, taking turns spending the nights at the hospital. We find little rest, wiping her brow, wetting her lips, filling the room with idle talk in an attempt to keep the shadows of death away just a little bit longer. The room is cold and drafty, the cot's thin blanket no comfort or respite whatsoever. But I can't sleep anyhow, out of fear of waking up alone. The soft light behind my mother's bed is barely bright enough to allow me to read to her, but I do so anyway, until my eyes hurt from the strain and the tears that occasionally roll down my cheeks.

My mother's decline hits me hard. Seeing her suffer like that, holding her limp hand during those final moments, stands in such a stark contrast to the life she had lived; a big personality with an even bigger laugh. Sixty-six is not an age to die - or so we thought. My dad walks out of the room for a quick bathroom break, or to shake off some of the dread that has piled onto his shoulders. I pull my chair close to her bed and draw idle circles over the soft skin of her hands. I am out of stories to tell to fill the silence, so I switch to humming. That is about as musical as I can get, as I don't have a musical bone in my body. But I manage a few nursery rhymes that she used to sing to me as a kid. They feel wrong though, out of place, so I switch to old German Schlager music, songs we used to sing together in the car when I was little. The melodies ebb and flow from the depths of my memories, notes bubbling over my lips without me paying much attention to them. Until one song in particular captures my attention, the hum turning into words in my head that sound like life is having a good laugh at my expense:

> *Mit sechsundsechzig Jahren, da fängt das Leben an*
> *Mit sechsundsechzig Jahren, da hat man Spaß daran*
> *Mit sechsundsechzig Jahren, da kommt man erst in Schuss*
> *Mit sechsundsechzig ist noch lange nicht Schluss*

The hum dies on my tongue, choking me. I hope she did not hear that or make the connection. Guilt tightens my insides into cold clumps.

> *"Life starts with sixty-six,*
> *at sixty-six, you enjoy it,*
> *at sixty-six, you are just picking up speed,*
> *at sixty-six, life is far from over."*

She is not moving, no sign that she heard me at all. I feel like throwing up. The song mocks me, louder the more I try not to think of it. I fall silent and am relieved when the door opens, and my dad walks in again. Outside, a few lonely snowflakes push their noses against the window.

My mother never gave up hope. Until her very last breath, she never once admitted defeat in the face of Death. Her infamous *"Arschbackenzusammenkneifmentalität"*, so ingrained in her very essence, wouldn't let her be vulnerable and open to the possibility of the end. Unfortunately, what was perceived as strength all her life, now turned into something that bars us all from getting closure. If you keep up hope to the last minute, you cannot allow yourself to say goodbye; you cannot say those final words of love and appreciation that can be a source of comfort and acceptance for the ones left behind. So much is left unsaid, words that hang in the air like clouds, that grow heavier and heavier as the days go by. But it is her decision to ignore the fatality of the situation, and neither of us dares to defy her. We do not dare to upset the precarious balance of empathy and our own selfish need to hear those final words of love, as if they have some magical power. What could that last exchange mean? What could I say that would make a lasting impression on her fleeting soul? Would goodbye lessen the wounds or light the path ahead? I will never know.

I love you.

I'm scared to live without you - your wisdom and encouragement, your memory of who I was, your hopes for who I'll become - and for Gia and Giulia without their Großmama. I'm scared for Papi. Her death will crush him. How is he going to cope all alone here with me being so far away? What are we going to do?

Please forgive my rebellions, the times I hurt you.
I am sorry for not cleaning up my room, for coming home late, for not calling.
I want more time.
I love you! Please! Don't go!

All left unsaid.

All we could do was stay close, talk to her, in the hopes that our voices still reach her and make the passage easier, allowing her to let go. After all, this is HER moment - her hour, her way - and who am I to question how she chooses to do so? I'm still here; I'm still alive and blessed - or cursed - with having to work on my feelings and learn to deal with my grief.

Death scared the hell out of me. I had never been with anybody at this final stage of their life. As inevitable as it is, the fear of the unknown leaves us - the people left behind - without words. The moment my mother passes away, I'm holding her hand. There it is, resting in mine, warm and soft, her gold rings on her fingers, as if she is just sleeping, ready to wake up at any moment. Even as a young child, my mother always reminded me to make sure my nails were well kept, because you never know when you have to go to the hospital for an emergency, and how embarrassing it would be to show up with long, dirty nails. The memory makes me smile as my glance falls on my mother's perfectly manicured hands with coral nail polish.

My eyes move from her hands to her chest, then to her face, hanging on her mouth to detect a breath. Her lips are pale, dry, and cracked in the middle, reminding me with the shake of a stern finger that I am not doing enough. I swipe Vaseline over the rough skin until it shines in the soft light. We have moved past the ice-chips-stage already; gone are the hours when Mami could swallow. The Vaseline and a small bowl of water are the only creature comforts left. That and the morphine. I dunk an oversized cotton swab into the cool water and watch the drops disappear on her tongue, bringing no visible relief. We have feared this moment for a while now. For two days, every inhale has come with the soul-shattering death rattle - deep, wet, unrelenting, as if she were drowning in front of me.

The doctors and nurses tried to soothe our worries, as we hung on every word they said, as if somehow their presence would bring an end to her suffering. Every time the door to her room opens, and the soft light from the hallway throws an expanding rectangle onto the polished hospital floor, extending to her bed, bringing with it the gentle steps of soft-soled shoes, our eyes, and our hopes lift. "She cannot feel it," they say. "It sounds a lot worse than it is," and "This is very normal at this stage." "THIS IS NOT HELPING!" I scream in my head. *I don't want you to placate me with words! I want you to stop this nightmare!* I yell, pulling my hair, flailing my arms, throwing myself onto the floor in a tantrum, reminiscent of my five-year-old self, all the while sitting still as a statue in the hard chair next to my mother's side.

But now all is quiet. The room is still; my father crosses one leg over the other, clears his throat, and we settle into another hour of waiting. I look out the window, the view obscured by my own jagged reflection. The thick black winter curtain outside lifts reluctantly to a muted gray, hiding behind the black silhouettes of bare trees and buildings. I get up to open the window, hoping that the cold air will bring some relief, but even the air refuses to enter the room. The rattle has stopped a while ago, and what we perceived as a relief is just a natural progression towards the inevitable. Now there are breaks. Long breaks. Between each breath. We hold our own in unison, the expanse between breaths holding us as a family. Is this it? I lean forward, searching for a breath, aching for the slightest movement of her chest.

Longer.
Longer.
Nothing.

A petal from the pink roses on her nightstand falls in slow motion. Still nothing. Then, there it is - finally! A soft inhale. Oh, the relief that floods through me. It feels soothing, cool, and vibrant, but fleeting. Just as another exhale flows out between her parted lips and then ...

Waiting.
Searching her face, her chest.
You are not doing enough.
Calling forth that long-awaited movement.

A sign.
Anything.

As her breath ebbs, we are there together: my dad on one side, me on the other holding her hands: Our little family - together for the last time. And then, from one second to another, she is gone - no struggle, no sound to announce the change - nothing. I could just feel that her spirit had left. The window of the hospital room is still ajar, to a cold winter's air holding vigil outside. There were even some flurries earlier, blurring the gray sky, but now it is crystal clear and sunny. My mom used to say, "It is always sunny when angels travel." I like to picture that her spirit flew out the window, free at last, flying in its full glory through the sunshine, towards the light.

What is left is not my mother anymore - hard to describe, but it feels nothing like her. Her essence, her being, is gone, leaving behind a shell that looks like her, but also bears no resemblance anymore to the mother I knew and loved. I am still holding her hand, frozen in a never-ending moment. I do not dare to let go. I cannot. I think there are tears blurring my vision, dripping on the sheets, as her hand cools under my touch. Time stands still. Blurred. Silent. What could be minutes or hours is interrupted by a sound I have never heard before: A strained sob followed by a deep guttural groan; the sound of a broken heart shattering on the other side of my mother's bed. I am scared to look at him, but I cannot help myself. My eyes tiptoe over the bedspread, that is still and tidy, tucked in at the foot of the mattress. They follow the shiny metal railing down to the linoleum floor, along the speckled pattern to his cognac-colored leather shoes and the red-and-blue striped socks. My dad loves his colored socks. Today, they slouch around his ankles, a pale crescent of skin showing where jean meets sock. Even his legs look dejected.

My father crumbles in front of my eyes. His strong shoulders slump, his coloring changes, his appearance desaturates to muted shades of a transparent quality. With the flip of a switch, his light

21

has been dimmed. Was there always this much white in his hair, or did this single moment age him inside and out?

I was lucky to have parents who were still so much in love. Not the new kind of love that pulsates and flutters, giggles, and blushes, but the kind of love that has weathered and withstood, matured, and deepened. It had been built solid, brick by brick, cracks of disappointment and resentment cemented over. The foundation bearing layers of moss along the lighter scars where work and common interests fixed the breakage. They still fell asleep holding hands. They kissed each other hello and goodbye and checked in with one another before making decisions. Their bond was symbiotic. In their younger years, they were the stereotypical stunning couple: he, tall, dark and handsome, with a calm, centered authority. My mother, blonde, slender with busy hands and clicking, confident heels, and a laugh that opened hearts. She was always a source of comfort and wisdom to everyone around her, ready with a cup of coffee, an open ear, and motherly advice. She had this magnetism, this welcoming aura of acceptance that attracted people to her. It happened more than once that I came home to find my mother's cigarette smoke pooling around the kitchen counter, two empty plates littered with cake crumbs, the smell of coffee that had dried in dark rims on the inside of my mother's rose-patterned porcelain cups. Two faces turned towards me in unison as my entrance interrupted my mother and one of my close friends, entangled in a deep web of conversation. But this was very typical - she always had an open ear for all of my friends. My mother was loved and admired by almost everyone I ever brought into our home, for she was genuinely interested and always able to impart her analytical yet very heartfelt advice. (I say "almost" because it definitely excludes the occasional boyfriend of my teenage years, who was unfortunate enough not to meet my mother's approval.)

Unfortunately, this was something our own relationship had lacked. I yearned for her warm, nurturing support, unbraided from expectation and free of hints of disapproval or criticism. But I think we were too similar in many ways, and she could not be as objective with her own offspring as she was with my friends. I always perceived her comments as driven by her desire for me to be better - to do better, to choose better - whether it was about love, studies, or work. Objectivity was not her strong suit in that regard, but maybe I was just expecting too much. Of course, she always wanted the best for me, but her definition of "best" was usually met with skepticism from my side. Gifted with the maternal genetic imprint of stubbornness, I displayed a strong urge to go my own way and do things just a bit differently than everyone else. That's what made it hard for us to see eye to eye. Time will tell, as my own daughters grow: will I be able to nurture their wild spirits and creative minds in a way that allows them complete freedom without judgment on my part?

I pull my eyes away from my father. A strand of blond hair is stuck to my mother's forehead, and I lean over, my hand hesitates a moment before I dare touch her face. Her skin still has a hint of warmth, but lacks her spirit. With a soft brush of my fingers against her skin, I wipe the hair back into place. My hand hovers, craving proximity but fearing Death. Barely touching the fabric, I smooth down the creases in my mom's nightgown and straighten the edge of her blanket over her chest.

The relationship with my mother was deep and powerful - just like my mom herself. She had spent most of her career running the on-site health clinic and emergency room at the nearby Ford factory, where she treated patients for everything from work accidents to routine occupational health issues. In this male-dominated environment, she fought a long and uphill battle until she was part of the factory's management team, highly valued for her wisdom and knowledge as well as her passion for the over 6000 employees she supported. Back when "equal opportunity" was barely a phrase, she made it real, step by hard step. My mother was always a strong supporter of women's rights in the workplace and fought every step of the way up the ladder.

Consequently, she raised me to be a strong, independent woman who stands up for her goals and protects her family with any means possible. I like to think that she would be proud of me now if she could see me and watch her granddaughters blossom. But our relationship was also difficult and delicate - a precious equilibrium that required a lot of energy to be upheld, and I dreaded the moment the smallest pebble would cause the scales to tip. It never unleashed a storm, but rather an icy silence, laced with the passive-aggressive slamming of cupboard doors and drawers; a side of hers reserved solely for the ones most loved and rarely witnessed by others.

This complex mother-daughter bond shaped my teenage years. Despite my parents' hopes for a large family, I was an only child. They made sure it never felt like a disadvantage. I missed the built-in companionship of siblings, but I learned to be self-sufficient and content in my own company. My childhood was sheltered, and I lived for the future - hungry for the freedom of adolescence. As I reflect on my early years, they seem like beads on a necklace; one season connected to the other by the flow of my life: winters of roasted chestnuts, snow, sledding; long warm summers roaming fields and forests; horses; endless afternoons outside with friends. Nothing to upset the monotony of small-town life. We did not move anywhere, there were no drastic changes or tragedies - life was peaceful and secluded.

I adored my parents. They were strict, but full of love and affection. Now that I am a mother myself, and can compare, I can say in all honesty that I was an easy child. I never caused much trouble - not as a baby, as I was mostly sleeping and never cried much - and not as a young child or pre-teenager. In hindsight, I was pretty boring and never posed much of a challenge.

.... Until the teenage years hit. Suddenly, I felt this longing to grow - to be more independent and to finally find my voice. Growing up without siblings meant I had never learned to spar, to stake a claim; that lesson would take years. I was surrounded by kids who seemed more determined, more decisive, and fearless. I admired - and resented - that edge. I craved the independence and the audacity to speak my own mind and timidly started to draw the first faint lines in the sand of my *Elternhaus*[1]. This was the time to test my boundaries, and the target of my early rebellions was - due to the simple reason of proximity and availability - my mother, who was usually home in the afternoons while my father worked at a safe distance until the evenings. We sparred over grades, chores, tone, curfews, the wrong kind of friends, and the right kind of friends.

But again, what seemed a big deal to me then can now only be described as a "*Sturm im Wasserglas*", a "storm in a teacup", as it was mild in comparison to the teenage revolts I have witnessed amongst my friends and family since. But through all these hormonal tides and teenage dramas, I always relied on the love and support of my closest friend for my mental sanity: Kathrin.

Kathrin was everything I aspired to be. She had a rebellious older brother (who sometimes let us orbit his parties), and she herself was funny, beautiful, and skinny, with just the right amount of curves in just the right places, while I was still waiting to fill out an A-cup. She was smart, with grades that should have put us leagues apart, yet she never judged me for the effort it took me to not even come close. Visually, we were polar opposites: her long dark curls and big brown eyes were a stark contrast to my blonde hair, blue eyes, and fair skin that burnt rather than tanned. Years of ballet gave her posture I tried - and failed - to emulate. Life, ever fair, made her a little clumsy, which often sent us into fits of laughter when she tripped over nothing and flung her handbag skyward.

But we were also identical in many ways. We shared a sense of humor and a taste in books, music, movies, and chocolates - thank-

---

1   *Elternhaus, German, "parental home".*

fully, never in boys. She was always there to listen, laugh, and empathize. And nobody understood the nuances of my parents' love as much as she did. She talked me off ledges, patched broken hearts with laughter and candy, and turned every vacation into an adventure. We were inseparable and brought out the best in each other. She was more on the quiet and reserved side, whereas I was the more outgoing and courageous one, yet together we were formidable; a true force to be reckoned with.

... Kathrin
- wait ... Kathrin is dead!

I am still here, slowly becoming aware of my surroundings again: my office, separated from my colleagues only by a thin glass divider and a door that is always open. I pull myself off the floor, realizing the phone is still clenched in my hand. I can hear my dad's heavy silence on the other end, his breathing bearing witness to the pain he is going through himself. Making the call that collapses my world - again - can't be easy. My heart goes out to him, and I feel the pain of separation, that old guilt that's been my constant companion since I left home for the first time at the age of 15.

I remember my parents taking me to the airport. It was January, and cold air rushed with the crowds through the long tunnels of Frankfurt's airport. I had a big suitcase and a camping backpack. My parents had exchanged German currency for $200, which I carried in a travel wallet hanging from my neck, together with my passport and flight tickets. My eyes flickered from sign to sign, from face to face, too hurried and fidgety to linger anywhere for long. I had flown only a few times before at the most, and never alone. My mother embraced me so tightly, as if she wanted to soak up the feeling of me in her arms with every fiber of her being, blinking tears away. She was strong, my mother, but also very vulnerable.

And at this moment, I realized for the very first time the endless depth of her love. I saw the struggle in their eyes: terrified and anxious about letting their baby go, but happy for the steps I was about to take - away from a very provincial life in a small town with an even smaller small-town mentality, towards the big unknown: six months in Denver as an exchange student. Those six months did exactly what my parents hoped: they lit a hunger for learning and gave me a confidence far beyond my old horizon. But once this light was sparked, the hunger for more kept pulling me away from home, weakening the strong roots I had formed in my hometown. I think those first six months were the hardest for all of us. The torrent of new experiences and impressions drowned out the homesickness I felt during quiet moments, but for my parents, time stretched like chewing gum until they could fold me back in their arms at the end of that summer. Still, I never fully settled back into our small town. The next few years flew by: first relationship, preparation for the final high school exam, and finally the long-anticipated high school graduation. Now I was finally free to follow the path my parents had put me on years ago - to go off and explore where fate would take me: Florence, Paris, New York, Berlin, Dubai.

I am forever grateful to them for this unselfish act of letting me spread my wings, which took me further and further from home. With every move and every new chapter in my life, I could feel their pride, always laced with a subtle undertone of sorrow and regret of not being there in person to witness it. After the initial shock of the empty-nest syndrome, my parents had grown to enjoy their own independence again, but especially once they became grandparents, the distance became a burden - separation, missed milestones - the quiet tax of globalization.

I am acutely aware of how fortunate I was to have had the opportunity to leave my hometown behind and spread my wings. But many friendships that had defined my youth had now all but disappeared. The strain of the distance was too much for most of these bonds - stretched beyond their capabilities, we found ourselves left with little in common, awkward silences just a symptom of the different paths we had taken. The one constant, despite distance and time, was always Kathrin. We never let a week go by without talking at least three to four times, texting even more frequently. But our friendship started at such a young age, when communication was on a level beyond purely verbal.

Our parents had been colleagues and friends. Not close friends, but they belonged to the same circles: all doctors of various specialties who worked in our relatively small city and, due to their various roles within the community, shared common interests and values. It was a cold Saturday morning in early spring. I know that because the first tips of the snowbells made their way through the black soil next to the garage. Lazy clouds pulled themselves over the hills on the horizon, their bellies heavy with rain to come. My mother opened the door to a burst of cold wind and clicked in her high heels towards the car, the car keys jingling from her hand, rushing me to follow. The air smelled wet with hints of rotting leaves and pine from the garden. I held the heavy front door with my foot before the draft pulled it shut. "Not so fast! Put on your warm jacket, the red one," the words tumbled out from under my dad's black mustache as he pulled his own leather jacket from the hook high up on the wall of our cloak room. It smelled of leather and safety, a scent I loved. Sometimes, when I was home alone with my nanny in the afternoons after school, before my mom came home from work, and the hours stretched lazily on the couch, waiting for something to happen, I would sneak into the entrance hall and stick my face in the jackets and coats hanging there. My dad's leather jacket or my mother's fall coat, the beige one, with the silk scarf peeping out from the pocket, smelling of her perfume. Sometimes I even found loose coins or a candy tucked away - tiny treasures in the lining of our life.

I went on my tippy-toes and still could not reach my red jacket, so he unhooked it and held it open for me in a grown-up gentleman's gesture that made me giggle. (Despite my mom's insistence it smelled of "sweaty snow-child," to me it smelled like nothing at all.) My dad bent down, pulled my long braid free, wound a scarf around my neck, and zipped me up. With a playful pat on the bottom, he sent me scampering after my mom.

It was quite normal to spend Saturday mornings downtown on a leisurely shopping run. First stop was usually the fruit and vegetable store, its crates arranged in delicious, colorful rows, the extra *Pfennig*[2] buying the quality regulars expected. Leaving my dad and me with the heavy bags, my mom would chirp, "Let me just have a quick peek in here," and vanish into a boutique with white, featureless mannequins in the window. Back then, those detours were torture; fashion meant nothing to me at six. My absolute highlight was a trip to the butcher, where the rotund man behind the counter with red cheeks and an impressive belly always handed me a Vienna Sausage or a slice of *Lyoner*[3] before turning to my mom. "What can I tempt you with today, *Frau Doktor*?" I tugged her coat, mouth full. "*Lyoner*, Mami! Buy some *Lyoner*!" The butcher winked at me.

Before heading home, we often had lunch at one of the local restaurants along the cobble-stoned town square. During the warmer months, chairs, tables, and umbrellas spilled everywhere, turning the square into a stage where everyone was both performer and spectator. In winter, when the cold wind whipped under our coats and the air was heavy with rain, the square, void of any outdoor seating, seemed to double in size. It was lined by warmly lit window displays of the surrounding boutiques, interspersed with cafes and restaurants, which now beckoned their patrons with lonely chalkboard signs of daily specials.

---

2   *Pfennig - German. An old German currency before the introduction of the Euro, equivalent to pennies.*

3   *Lyoner is a variation of a ring-shaped Bologna sausage, typical for the Saarland region in Germany.*

"Where should we go for lunch?" My dad asked, a smile playing around the ends of his mustache, anticipating my answer. "Stiefel, Stiefel!" I squealed, jumping so a puddle leapt onto the adjacent cobblestones. "*Zum Stiefel*," a rustic restaurant owned by the local brewery, was my favorite - especially in winter, when a heavy felt curtain separated the gusty doorway from the dining rooms. You stepped through the cold and then, in a single breath, into a warm, welcoming world smelling of heartwarming, home-cooked food, and the malty sweetness of freshly brewed beer.

The windows of the old corner building, set with antique wavy glass and speckled with air bubbles, were adorned with green wooden shutters that were always open. Above the entrance hung an old-fashioned brass sign from an ornate cast-iron rod, bearing the image of a worn boot and "*Zum Stiefel*" in old German calligraphy. The furniture was solid wood with benches along the walls and white tablecloths. The floors alternated between terracotta tiles and well-worn wooden floorboards. I remember the smooth feel of those wooden floors quite well. I preferred them over the tiles. Wood was warmer than tiles when sitting on the floor, especially near the door, where cold air snuck in with newcomers. When adult conversations drifted beyond my patience, I'd slip under the table. There, soft light filtered through the tablecloth, and the muted voices of my parents and their friends created a private little cave. I would spend a long time coloring the kids' menu or playing with the toys my mother had deliberately packed into her treasure trove of a handbag.

My dad helped my mother out of her thick coat and, in one swoop, picked up my red padded jacket with the blue piping and hung it on the nearby coat hanger, his maroon leather jacket on top. I tiptoed behind him and slipped beneath several layers of coats until only my winter boots and cream stockings were visible. I love the feeling of the heavy coats covering me. They smell of perfumes and gossip. There are padded coats with their smooth surface, their static pulling my hair out of its braid, next to a fur jacket that smells a bit musty and tickles my nose. Nudging myself deeper into the underbelly of the coat stand, my face brushes over the curly surface of a long black Astrakhan coat, steeped into the grandmother-scent of 4711[4]. The heaviness of the coats reminded me of going to the Christmas Market with my parents; cocooned in the crush of bodies where coats and the hems of jackets were moving in waves all around me, I would be cozy and warm despite the freezing weather, but scared of losing my mother's hand in the crowd. I slipped out of the coats before my parents even noticed my absence, and when I got to the table, Kathrin's parents had arrived with hugs, shoulder slaps, and a flurry of greetings. Her older brother, a tall, lanky, blonde boy with curls and glasses, stood off to the side, looking disinterested. "Psst!" I looked around for the sound coming from somewhere nearby. Kathrin sat crouched under the table, lifting the tablecloth like a stage curtain, in invitation, and I crawled into our table cave.

This is my first memory of Kathrin and me together: two little girls, barely three months apart in age, having the most wonderful adventures under that table. Her brown hair was much shorter than mine, and she wore a beige knitted turtleneck sweater with roses and red and brown rain boots. We were princesses fleeing an "evil prince" (her older brother, who wanted nothing to do with our plot). Other days, we were thieves - true masterminds who secretly stole treasure in the form of forks, napkins, or saltshakers from the table-top, unbeknownst to anyone above, of course (or so we thought). Meanwhile, the adults tolerated our chubby little hands sneaking up from underneath the tablecloth and usually placed a few "treasures" toward the edge so we wouldn't spill drinks or topple plates.

---

4   4711 is the world's original Eau de Cologne - a fragrance from Cologne, Germany, dating back more than 230 years.

"Girls, we are ready to order. Should we get you some *Schnitzel* with French Fries or *Dibbelabbes*[5] from the children's menu? *Apfelschorle*[6] for both of you?" Kathrin's mom always knew the right things to order.

The sweetness of this memory permeates my soul, leaving me with the warm feeling of safety and a yearning for a time when life was so much simpler, happier, and free of pain.

... pain ...

A sharp breath claws up my throat. I break through the surface of those memories and land roughly back in adulthood, back at my desk - the heavy Dubai air pearls on the outside of my office window in wandering diamonds of condensation. My hand is still locked around the phone. Ice-cold reality rushes over me, and I realize that my chest is heaving, strangled by a tight grip of emotions too awful to even address.

I manage to whimper between the sobs, which now work their way up from my chest, making it impossible to speak. "Papi ..." - a single word carrying a thousand others: "Please let this not be true! Not Kathrin. Not again." In that instant, I am his little girl again, and we are both standing at the mouth of a dark tunnel of heartbreak he knows too well.

Despite the whirlwind of pain, confusion, and numbness, I can also see his pain. He has weathered enough sorrow; I try -ridiculously - to spare him mine. *"Arschbackenzusammenkneifmentalität"* is so ingrained that even from the deepest state of sorrow, I am trying to pull myself up again. For him.

I am not very successful, though.

---

5   *Dibbelabbes a delicacy from Saarland; potato hash with bacon and green onions oven-baked in a "dibbe", a form of Dutch oven or heavy cast iron pan.*

6   *A mix of apple juice and sparkling water*

Tears streak my face. The guttural sounds escaping me must carry beyond the perceived isolation of my office. Just as my office walls are transparent, my emotions are visible to all my colleagues. I need to get out. NOW. I pull all the shattered pieces of my heart together and walk the gauntlet of desks and concerned faces. I'm still clutching the phone to my ear. It is my prop, my shield I can hide behind, while tears run down my face. I can only think one thing: "Please don't talk to me, please don't talk to me, please don't!" I keep my eyes fixed on the floor, not giving anybody the opportunity to approach to comfort. I make it to the bathroom. The cool tiles soothe my forehead, and my knees shake so hard that I slide down along the wall, where I find comfort in a corner, curling into a tight ball of tears and pain.

"I don't understand, Papi."

As I try and fail to master my emotions, my mind refuses the facts. "Car crash." "Uli and Maximilian ok." The fragments twirl like leaves in an icy cold wind, refusing to settle. My body heaves with sobs, animal and raw. "I'll call you later, Papi" is all I manage before I let my body take over and collapse, gasping between sobs that feel like they're tearing out my heart.

Two gentle voices pull me back into the now and force my brain back into action - a warm hand on my shoulder. Concerned faces swim into view, seemingly on the other side of the glass walls I'd left behind in the office; far away and distant. I blink through tears. Their words blur "Mhhh mmmm, mmh, mhhh? Mmhhh mmhh," like the Swedish Chef from the Muppet Show. I can see lips moving, head tilted, long blonde hair fanning over her shoulder. My eyes search for something solid. There is a butterfly. A tiny silver butterfly dangles on a chain around her neck, forever suspended above that inch of shiny skin between her bosom. The cold bathroom light reflects off its wings. "Bosom," what a strange word. Do people still use it? I feel my mind slipping again. Another voice - calm and remembered - pushes in: "Remember your breathing techniques from when the kids were born. Breathe through the pain; in … pause … out … pause …" I turn inward, as I feel my ribcage rise and fall with the wave of each breath; let each exhale widen a little isle of quiet.

I need to focus; I need to figure out what happened. Surely, I misheard. Maybe he was confused. That must be it! Not an ideal scenario either, but preferable in its lack of finality. I grasp the helping hands offered by my colleagues huddled around me, and straighten, mortified by this feral grief in a place where I am usually composed. I force my mouth into a smile that feels like a grimace, splash my face a little bit too vigorously with cold water, and head back to the safety of my office. I look like a mess: swollen eyes, blotchy skin, my blouse wet from tears and water, hair sticking out in confused angles, and a large ball of tissues squeezed in my fist. But I walk with determination in my step, my heels clicking with borrowed confidence down the hall.

Ok, time to approach this from a logical standpoint.

I sit back at my desk on the 30th floor, my eyes on the horizon, taking in a view I am privileged to see every day: the line where the crystal sky meets the Arabian Gulf is sharp, darker than the rest of the sea. Closer, Palm Jumeirah glitters like a jewel; yachts slide past massive villas and hotels lining the shore, Sheikh Mohammed's Island just off to the right. The scene is painted in brilliant blues and turquoise with dashes of white and tan. Despite the towers on either side, my view is unobstructed; only a thin layer of humidity frames the lower quarter of my window. It's another perfect winter day in Dubai. The stark beauty jolts a memory of September 11, 2001, when Andrea and I, still unmarried, woke up to a stunning New York morning with bright blue skies and deceptive clarity - a day that changed the lives of millions of people in an instant. As the parallel forms, the knot in my stomach tightens.

With two clicks, I open Google and type "Vienna car accident." My fingers rush each letter as if they're about to write something I can't take back. I hold my breath, index finger hovering in hesitation over the "search" button. This is not what I want to do on a Monday morning - or ever, for that matter.

I withdraw my hand. My palms are sweaty. Instead of clicking "search," I pick up the metal ruler from the pencil holder. The sharp corners bite into my palm, as I bend it this way and that; the sting grounds me in the now. I can't take my eyes off the screen. Do I want to open Pandora's box? I could just call Paps back and make sure I misunderstood. But that scares me even more; deep down, I know that I'd hear the same words again, and there's no un-hearing them.

As I look at my computer, I become acutely aware of every single key: the slightly rounded corners of the black, shiny buttons, bearing both English and Arabic letters. Just as Steve Jobs intended, every aspect of this keyboard is pleasing to the eye. It is absurd, but my mind found a few precious moments of serenity in this subtle perfection. I knew this was the calm before the storm, an instant of respite before acknowledging the harsh reality.

What I want is someone to tell me that everything is alright and make the pain go away. Instead, I default to what I've practiced for years: on the outside, a strong, independent woman who can hold her own. The problem with being "strong" is that people rarely ask how I am actually doing. I've proven again and again that I am just fine. In crisis, when others panic, I keep everything going - or so I like to believe.

But what others read as strength is a coping mechanism. Falling apart is not an option. I am terrified of losing control by surrendering to fear and uncertainty, even for a moment. It takes too much effort to dig myself out of that hole, so I throw myself into work instead; an incessant torrent of energy spent on emails, phone calls , and meetings means no time at all to pause and reflect on the state of my own heart.

I've inherited more from my mother than I realized. Her refusal to give up hope must have grown out of the same need for control, the same coping mechanism of strength. And that didn't end too well. Maybe "sucking it up" isn't perfect, but I don't know what else to do. I don't think this is a door I can open just yet. Who knows where it would lead? And right now, I still need my scaffolding of strength to get me through whatever lies ahead. What happens if grief asks for the one tool you won't put down?

From the perspective of my now slightly wiser years, I know for a fact that strength in the face of adversity and chaos is nothing more than a band-aid - a quick fix to avoid dealing with the actual issue, masked by the calm, collected appearance of control. But there is nothing wrong with band-aids! In fact, they're extremely useful; they let you carry on despite the wound. But they're temporary. At some point, the dressing must come off, and the cut beneath tended to before it festers into something worse.

CHAPTER 2

NYC 2001

My wounds had festered before - especially after 9/11. "Where the heck are you going?" Andrea blocked my way to the metal front door of our apartment. "I can't sit here anymore and do nothing. I am going to the office to check in. I need to get out of here! I literally can't breathe anymore. And if I hear one more "you can't," I am going to explode!" I threw my messenger bag over my shoulder and pushed my electric scooter past Andrea out the door.

The company I worked for then had its office inside the über-trendy Chelsea Market in the Meatpacking District of Manhattan. Less than 24 hours after the attacks on the World Trade Center, the open warehouse space within the market building had turned into a control center for the rescue efforts on Ground Zero. Donations poured in - protective gear, water, food - and restaurants rallied to open their kitchens to volunteers who made sandwiches and packed lunches for the rescuers. Firefighters, Police, and FBI used the space as their command post and a brief refuge on their way in and out of the chaos of lower Manhattan.

I'd been restless since the enormity of it all became clear. Sitting at home, watching the nightmare on TV from the comfort of my couch, felt unbearable. We were close enough to see the towers fall from our street, while wide-eyed people, covered head to toe in gray dust, walked past us in stunned silence. I could feel the emotional ripples of loss and pain this attack had caused. It made my skin crawl and filled my insides with tiny popping sensations, as if the rising pressure needed a venting valve. People were panicking, grief-stricken, and in shock, yet I was not doing anything to help - it was killing me. With a grim determination, I leafed through the Yellow Pages, tearing the thin paper in my hurry to find numbers for the Red Cross and other help organizations. But all I got was the standard "If you are not a registered emergency helper with the Red Cross, there is nothing you can do. Just stay at home, Ma'am."

That was the one thing I could absolutely NOT do! Caged and frustrated in our tiny apartment, I focused on what I could do: call - again and again - to reach our families. "I can't get a line!" I yelled, slamming the phone onto the couch. Finally, one by one, familiar voices trickled through, tethers to a world that seemed far removed from ours; a parallel universe where airplanes stayed in the sky and people did not jump from skyscrapers before they collapsed. It was hard to shut off that night - the TV or the running commentary in my head. I kept looking at my shoulder, waiting for the personifica-tion of this voice to make itself known. But my shoulder remained empty. It kept me pacing up and down, made me jump up from the couch as soon as my body settled down. Nothing was able to shut it up, except a few hits of a joint passed to me by Andrea late at night, when the sirens outside and the voice inside finally quieted down.

"I'll just be a short while," I called back at Andrea before the ele-vator doors clanked shut behind me. "Morning, Curtis." I nodded at our portly doorman, dropping the "good" like a hot potato. Usually,

I'd stop for a chat, see how his kids were doing, or get an update on the weather before getting a glimpse of it through the large window, but today every word was too much. Outside, the streets held their breath; a few apologetic cars hugged the curb, tiptoeing through a city that had come to a standstill. I wasn't going to work - no one was - but I needed to move. The smoke of the buildings hung heavy in the air. Now there was a new smell as well - a sweet-sour, chemical smell of burning God-knows-what, laced with something else that I could not pinpoint, which permeated everything, and only sudden changes in wind direction would ease the stench for a short time. I could not help but wonder what exactly was burning there. Thinking of all the lives lost and people still buried in the inferno that was raging in the heart of the city made my throat tighten. I suppressed the urge to vomit. Little did we know that this smell would linger for weeks and months to come. I gunned the scooter down the middle of the empty road, avoiding potholes and slipping through red lights, open slashes of wide empty roads on both sides.

Within minutes, I reached the Chelsea Market building, jumped the curb, and pushed the scooter through the heavy brass-framed glass doors, bypassing the bike rack with remnants of violated bike locks and a lonely front wheel, its spikes rusted. The Chelsea Markets, with its stripped-down brick architecture, polished concrete floors, exposed metal beams, and historic feel of an old, refurbished biscuit factory, never failed to fascinate me. I felt privileged to work here, in this historic building, where worlds and times seemed to collide. I loved hearing the hearty New Yorker-, Brooklyn- and Long Island accents, as the shopkeepers had lighthearted discussions across the hallways. But today, the usual array of scents wafting out of the shops - flowers, bread, wine, chocolate, and seafood - was muffled under a dome of shocked hyperactivity. I pushed my scooter along the hallway, my sneakers squeaking on the polished floor. The place buzzed with productivity, spurred by incredulity - as if sheer movement could suture the wound carved into our city.

I nodded a short hello to the Head of Security, hurrying past me; his walkie-talkie crackled in a manner that made him pick up speed. "Raymond, what's going on?" I called after him before his tall, broad frame disappeared around the corner. He stopped, turned, and took a gulping breath as if downing a jug of cold water while I caught up with him. He scowled at my scooter. "What have I told you about bringing that thing inside?" He frowned. "But never mind now." He towered over me and a thin layer of sweat shimmered on his dark, bald head like dew. His brown eyes, that usually sparkle with mischief, were rimmed in red, peeking out cautiously from deep, hollow caves. "We're collecting supplies for down there." He nodded in the general direction of South, meaning the area that is now called Ground Zero. "First-Responder center out back; donations where the gallery used to be - past the soup shop and the Lobster Place. Wanna help? Bimmy's needs hands." He's already moving as he points, leaving me and my scooter floating in his wake of determination.

Needless to say, I never made it to the office that day. I joined the line in Bimmy's kitchen, one more set of hands in a human conveyor for sandwiches and wraps bound for the crews working around the clock. Being one of many soothed my frayed nerves and gave my restless hands something to do. "Food made with love" was the tagline of the restaurant, and this was never truer than today. Every person along the dented metal table was fiercely focused, filling the bread with more than just ingredients. The repetitive motions of stacking sandwiches reminded me of the chugging of a steam engine: bread, meat, veg, condiment, love - repeat. Lost in the rhythm, I briefly forgot where I was and why. Carlos and Izzy, two of the regular kitchen crew, quickly adapted to all the newbies and showed us how it's done. Their hands moving faster than anyone's, setting the rhythm for the rest of the crew to follow. Each sandwich was wrapped and added to a growing pile, then whoever was closest ferried the "food of love" to the main collection point. Tray balanced, I dodged through the hallway and was struck by the difference in the faces I saw - sad, exhausted, with lines etched into the features that were not there a mere twenty-four hours earlier. Someone had set up rows of benches and tables in the building's open area, where firefighters and police sat in exhausted silence, dust caked into their gear, walkie-talkies crackling with distant sirens.

Lower Manhattan was in total lockdown, effectively shutting down traffic to allow only emergency vehicles access to the restricted area. One of the market trucks had clearance to run supplies directly to the heart of Ground Zero, or as close as the debris allowed. The truck was manned by six guys I recognized by sight, not name, and they looked like this wasn't their first run. They're dusty and tired-looking, but they had a fire of determination in their eyes that sparked something inside of me. I had to be on that truck! I lifted the tray of sandwiches over my head, and one of the guys grunted a thanks as he took the tray and stacked it among boxes and crates in the center of the cargo bed. As if summoned by my thoughts, a large hand reached down. "Hop on!" Raymond's stony face held the ghost of a smile. He hauled me up onto the tailgate, slid over, and made space on the rim of the open pick-up truck. Next thing I knew, the wind was stinging my eyes as we drove down, closer and closer to the smoking pyre of what was left of the World Trade Center.

My jeans, sneakers, and a thin hoodie offered none of the protection I should've probably had in a situation like this. But none of us seven was dressed for the part. Someone passed me a hard hat and a dust mask from the stack of supplies, which I pressed into my chest like a yellow security blanket. Around me, the guys stared at the billowing smoke ahead with a fierce intensity, their faces set, jaws clenched, lips tight. Other emotions flickered - determination, anger, empathy, and sadness - then blew away on the wind. We were all regular people, not "certified" anything. I could still hear the voice of the Red Cross lady on the phone. "If you're not a registered emergency helper with the Red Cross, just stay at home, Ma'am."

Ha! Ma'am my ass!

This was OUR city, whether we were born here or not, and the raging fire that's burning on Ground Zero burns within us as well. It propelled us to do things we would have never thought possible. I carried boxes containing 6 gallons of water each with ease, even though one gallon in a shopping bag would usually hurt my hands. Over and over, we loaded and unloaded the truck as fast and efficiently as possible, working in silent resolve, pulling the trolley with a heavy load over uneven surfaces, and somehow kept moving - strength we wouldn't have had on any other day.

We advanced as close as we could and parked in front of the evacuated Stuyvesant High School. "Let's move!" We all jumped from the truck, unlocked the tailgate, and started unloading the boxes and crates. "Ok, we need water and supplies at each command post. Hand whatever is needed to anyone you meet on the way." Our driver seemed to know what he was doing, but I felt lost trying to figure out where to bring the boxes assigned to me. We only had two hand trolleys on the truck; a group of three guys peeled right with a loaded trolley, while the others went off by themselves, each carrying large stacks of boxes. This left me with a trolley piled high with boxes containing gallons of water and smaller bottles. "You got it?" the driver asked. "I'm good," I replied with more confidence than I felt. "Just wait for the guys to come back from over there." He pointed somewhere over my shoulder, where the others were disappearing behind a fallen façade - glass and concrete everywhere. The driver jumped back in the truck, made a U-turn, and headed back the way we'd come.

"I'll meet you back here in a bit!" He called out the window before disappearing in a cloud of dust. Were they expecting me to just wait here? Hell no. Alone, I put both hands on the cart and pulled. Nothing. It did not even move. "Fuck!" I looked behind me, but the others were out of sight and earshot. "I got this! I am not going to stop!" Adrenaline and shame coursed through my veins. I was sure the guys would think I was the weak link. I couldn't prove them right. With a big breath, I braced and pulled with my whole body. Finally, the cart moved, bounced over a rock, rolled a bit, and got stuck again. Another deep breath, brace, and pull. I learned quickly that it is all about momentum. It seemed impossible, as there was no organized system in place yet; sharp dust and smoke were biting my eyes and debris was piled high on the roads. I was grateful for my sunglasses and the dust mask - a makeshift protection which proved invaluable but also miserable. I don't know if it was the sun, which was still quite strong this early in September, or the heat of the fires burning in and around the pile, but breathing under the mask turned brutal fast. Sweat ran down my forehead, stinging my eyes, and leaving gray rivers of caked dust on my face.

The powder-like dust clung to my skin, creeping into my ears, every crevasse, coating every hair, blocking every pore. The inside of my nose dried up, burning with every inhale. Mixed with sweat, the dust turned into stinging mud that felt like it was sucking every drop of moisture out of my body. Soon my mouth was desert-dry, and I had the urge to spit every few minutes. The dust-crusted mask made it hard to breathe. I stopped the cart for a short break, leaning against the heavy boxes. My fingers cramped and stiffened, and I fidgeted with the elastic of the mask, craving a breath of unrestricted air. "Don't take it off!" A passing fireman put a gloved hand on my shoulder. He had appeared out of nowhere, a ghostly gray figure, camouflaged with the debris around us. "We don't know what we're breathing here." His voice was muffled behind a thick rubber mask that covered his nose and mouth. The rest of his face looked like a stone statue, crusted under a thick layer of dust. As thanks, I handed him a bottle of water from my cart. "Thanks, hon," he mumbled, unclasped his mask, closed his eyes, and poured half the water over his face, washing muddy rivulets down until a flushed skin tone appeared. He poured the rest into his open mouth just to spit it out, retching. I gave him a second bottle, which he drank in one go before throwing the empty bottles onto a nearby pile of rubble, quickly reattaching the mask. He tapped his heavy helmet in greeting, nodded, and moved past me with heavy steps.

I got in front of the trolley again. Breathe, brace, pull. Every few steps, I looked back over my shoulder to find the path of least resistance while still heading in the general direction where the others disappeared. I was getting used to the weight and the resistance, and adrenaline fueled my progress. "Whoa, sweetheart. Weren't you supposed to wait with that?" Raymond rushed towards me with big steps, trying to take the trolley. "No, I got this. We do this as a team." I shifted my grip, giving his large hands space to hold, and together we hauled the trolley forward. Raymond looked down amused, but said nothing. No one questioned my place after that.

The blood-filled blisters on my raw hands bore testament to the work we'd done; something I didn't even notice until I washed the thick coat of mud and dust off my hands that night, staring in disbelief at the angry sores on my fingers and palms, only to forget them again the next day as soon as I climbed back on the truck.

There were four command posts set up in different quadrants along the perimeter of destruction. Some were reachable, while others posed more of a challenge since we had to cross treacherous ground or pass through or around partially collapsed buildings. We were in a state of constant alert, surveying the ground for sharp objects, bodies, or - though unlikely - signs of life, while listening for the feared sound of three short alarm tones, signaling immediate evacuation of the area due to a possible collapse.

We stuck together the first half of the day, unloading and carrying supplies to areas that were easier to access. Later, we fanned out to cover several spots at once. I made my way along the west side of the fallen buildings. I was told to deliver my supplies to the back of the World Financial Center, a building just to the west of the World Trade Center, past the makeshift morgue, and on to the temporary command post. Landmarks were useless in the eerie setting. There was no street or pavement, only the uneven surface of gray rubble, knee-high in places. The street was void of life. Leaves of paper lay as if fallen from a giant tree, some fluttering in the wind ahead, rushing off in a hurry.

Twisted metal leaned casually against the wall, surrounded by shards of glass. The jagged shell of a facade hugged the broken carcass of a car, crushing it in an embrace so hard that it fused the two into an unrecognizable heap of metal and concrete. I looked around, trying to orient myself. The plumes of smoke ahead to the left marked where the towers had stood, the street ahead completely blocked by rubble. I had to find a way around the pile to reach the command post and drop my supplies. To my right, the glass doors to the World Financial Center stood wide open, revealing a dark and forbidding entrance hall beyond, the cracked glass held open by an uneven carpet of dust, debris, and papers. I'd been here before - over a year ago - when it was bustling with lunch crowds: bankers in suits, women in elegant office attire rushing about, their heels clicking over the polished marble floor. The large L-shaped building hugged the waterfront, and even though I had not seen it in person, I was sure there was an exit out toward the water. The thought of polished floors and the possibility of a smooth passage with my trolley was all it took. I gave the trolley a hard pull to dislodge the stubborn wheels, then dragged it toward the door. A bright red heart at my feet caught my eye. There, among the orphaned papers, grime, and dirt lay an I♥NYC pin. The needle of the pin had remnants of felt attached to the back, as if it had lived on a cubicle wall until it exploded outwards, carried by fire and wind, landing here.

I ♥ NYC

Nothing felt truer. As New York City lay broken around me, its heart cracked wide open by an act of terrorism, my own heart bled love for this city. I picked up the pin, sending a silent prayer for the person it had once belong to, and pinned it to my hoodie.

The building was quiet and dark, the only movement coming from a flickering 'Exit' sign near the elevator banks. I navigated through the dark hallway and clicked on my keychain flashlight - never once used until now - and followed the bobbing dim circle of light. My shoes crunched over rubble; echoes rattled the marble and my nerves. A reflection of light on water brought me to a halt. The hallway ahead was flooded and the dim glow of the flashlight made the water shimmer like black velvet - beautiful and menacing. Only a few yards of the ankle-deep water stood between me and the winter garden, a possible exit to the waterfront. I knew that finding my way around the building, through the rubble, would be nearly impossible. My hands burned, and the cool metal of my trolley stuck to the open sores. The smooth floor inside offered a welcome respite from the struggle outside. Weighing my options, I stepped into the cold water, resisting the urge to dip my aching hands in search of relief. I knew that my feet would pay the price later, being con-fined in soaked sneakers for the rest of the day. Halfway through the water, I froze in my steps. The unnerving sizzle of electricity from broken wires dropped an iceberg into my stomach. My heart slammed out of my chest. Panic gripped me and its icy hand stirred a fear for my life. In this split second, I realized that nobody - apart from my truck mates - knew where I was. My parents, who were vacationing in Italy, seemed a million miles away. ..... and Kathrin! Oh, she'd be pissed with me right now.

But this is NOT where my story would end! Not here! Not today!

Fear loomed over me, like a solid shape, coiling a rope around my body, grinning in perceived victory. I touched the pin on my hoodie, steadied, and took one step, then another. The sizzling stopped. My heart pounded - not panic anymore, but exhilaration. I'd beat Fear! Adrenaline flushed my body, giving my step an urgency and making my hands and knees shake, but I had won! In the midst of catastro-phe, joy flickered - then a cold flash of guilt: How could I feel so alive when the world around me was falling apart?

Reaching the end of that hallway felt like a rebirth. I left the treacherous water behind and pushed into the winter garden, or what remained. The domed glass ceiling lay under debris; beams that once framed glittering panes of glass were blackened with ash. Metal from the WTC had crashed through the far side of this cavernous ribcage, opening up a ragged hole, exposing the void where the towers stood. Some of the glass windows across the ceiling had been shattered by projectile rubble, which covered the floor, chairs, and tables of the abandoned coffee shop in front of me. A lump rose in my throat. Sunlight fell through the dust in solid shafts. My mind projected images of the Winter Garden's former glory over the aching reality in front of me, like an old-fashioned slide projector, with a rogue image stuck on top of another. What was once a sparkling jewel of glass and light, with palm trees reaching eagerly towards the ceiling, in an attempt to mirror the awe-inspiring height of the Twin Towers looming directly above, was now brutally diminished to a haunting shadow of its former glory. I blinked, and the memory dissipated, leaving an aching nostalgia behind.

I jerked the trolley forward, underestimating how fast the wheels would move across the smooth floor, and bumped into one of the coffee tables. A glass of orange juice left behind by a customer, whose peaceful breakfast had turned into a nightmare, shivered - the top inch a murky gray of ash. The half-eaten pastry, napkin, and plastic spoon were covered in dust. I couldn't look away. Once bright and nourishing, now mute under a layer of grief - frozen in time.

CHAPTER 3

DUBAI 2016

Now, sixteen years later, I sit at my desk in Dubai. I realize that grief works much like those ashes on the orange juice. It settles on my soul, freezing me in a state of shock and disbelief. It shuts out any other feeling in its all-encompassing cloak of pain and fear - fear of the future, of being alone, of not coping without the person I've lost. Every plan we had made for a future together, every scenario I had taken for granted, is now a mockery in the face of loss. My mind races along the dark passageway of my future, passing all the important milestones, now covered with still water. Milestones I once wished for now seem not only meaningless but insulting in their unreachable brightness. Even the possibility of getting out of this darkness feels unfathomable.

I look up as I feel my colleagues' eyes on me like pins on skin; they prickle and burn. The moment I meet their stares, they lower their eyes to their desks, guilt flushing their cheeks. Only Seif, my friend and owner of the company, holds my gaze with tenderness. I can't keep it, not even for a second. The care he shows pricks my eyes with tears.

For the first time in my life, as I sit at my desk, I experience light as something physical in the sense that there is a distinction between the light I can see and the light I feel within me. It's as if the absence of my inner sparkle can dim the physical light around me. Even the glow of my computer screen seems dimmer as I keep staring at the Google search button.

As I finally gather the courage to click, bracing myself to jump into the unforgiving reality of online news sites, I feel …

… Nothing.
… No sadness, no fear, no grief, no loneliness, no shock.
… Nothing!

The cold knot, where my heart used to be, won't let me feel, as my eyes fly over the screen. *"Fatal car crash on the A21: Highway closed for hours."* It is like any other story - tragic, distant, something far away that shouldn't touch me. Looking back now, I'm stunned at how my mind protected itself from the images before me. Maybe the moral standards for accident photographers in Austria differ from what I'm used to, but these pictures reveal a horrific accident in such stark reality that it takes my breath away. The car is almost completely obliterated - impossible even to tell the make. That anyone could have survived is a miracle. But my dad said Uli and Max are alright.

Didn't he? He said that. He must have. I cling to it like a mantra - Kathrin's husband and the baby are okay! They're okay!

What is left of the car seems almost fused to the sound barrier running along the highway, metal beams sticking out at impossible angles through and around the car, as if someone had lifted the vehicle, flipped it, then thrown it against the barricade. I switch into autopilot, scrolling through the images that show the rescue operation from beginning to end - each worse than the last - as hordes of firefighters swarm the wreckage. There is just no way that I can connect this nightmare of twisted metal with my Kathrin. It does not fit! No way!

... until it does!

There, on the side of the road, lies the baby pram. I recognize it immediately: the dark blue fabric, its cognac-colored leather handle and the toy hanging from the side, which I bought for Maxi not too long ago. It looks like someone just took it out of the trunk and placed it neatly on the side of the road - a tiny hint of order in the chaos.

Kathrin studied Law while I went to Design School - a perfect illustration of our differences. She studied the laws I sometimes pushed and tested, though never seriously; smoking weed was firmly on the wrong side, something she'd never even considered doing. I admired her rootedness, her steadfast path, even if Law wasn't her truest passion - she saw it through. While I moved cities and countries, craving change and chasing the next challenge, she stayed homebound, deeply woven into an extensive circle of friends and family, cultivated and nurtured over decades of living in the same place. I had lost my roots from constant movement; I envision them under my arm in a small green enameled terracotta pot, with a white stripe, a drainage hole, and a tiny crack, letting me uproot and reset-tle wherever the wind blows. And one root in that pot is Kathrin.

She is a source of constant love and support; every conversation leaves me better than I was before. Our friendship is water, fertilizer, and sun. What more does a plant need to flourish? The connection we have is so genuine and deep, so life-affirming in its essence, that the thought of losing her never once crossed my mind!

On days that I feel hormonal or anxious, worst-case scenarios do cross my mind. The big "What if....?" looms like a blood moon over a troubled mind. They usually revolve around losing my husband, my dad, or God forbid, the children. As soon as those thoughts arrive, I push them down forcefully, aware that they originate from a place of happiness and the fear of loss. But they NEVER, EVER revolved around Kathrin! Not once! Our friendship felt lifelong, and I never doubted that we'd grow old together. How naive we were of life's unpredictable turns and twists.

One of the last gifts I received from Kathrin was a little bracelet - a tiny silver plaque on a plum-colored string, with the engraving "Together 100." Tears sting my eyes as I now look down at this last promise, wrapped around my wrist. The smooth metal is warm against my skin and so light that I don't even feel its presence. Protectively, I cup my hand over it, binding the bracelet - and the promise - into place. Kathrin knew that the losses I experienced during the past years had changed me. First, my mom; then my brother-at-heart, Alireza; and, just 8 months later, one of my good friends and bridesmaids, Milly, who left her husband and two small boys behind. Every time Kathrin was there to hold me up, put me back together when I fell apart. She knew when to listen and when to say just the right words to pull me out of my grief. I don't know how to grieve without her.

We had this crazy dream that we spoke about often. We would grow old and grey together. 100 years old. Because, statistically speaking, women outlive their husbands. So, if all else failed, we'd still have each other, live in a quaint little nursing home, and continue to wreak havoc together from the comfort of our walkers. "Together 100" was our safety blanket when life got a bit too scary and real.

Now, the bracelet holds a deeper, darker significance. It mocks me - a cruel reminder of how helpless we are in the face of our human existence. How presumptuous to plan the future when nothing is guaranteed! The only thing we truly have is the moment - this breath, this very second. Everything beyond that is hope. Everything beyond this very moment is not guaranteed and does not exist. But all we do is plan and live for the future; a future that might never come. And fate sits in a tree and mocks us as we walk by, so eager to reach the next bend in the path, climb the next hill, reach the next destination.

I separate myself from the heartache crackling over my skin and slip into the more comfortable emptiness of functioning on autopilot. I close my laptop and pack my things to leave the office. As I walk out, I stare at the floor in front of me, avoiding eye contact with my colleagues, whose empathetic faces are too much for me to bear right now. It takes all the strength I have just to put one foot in front of the other. The cool floor of the office yields to the marble of the elevator, with countless shoes fading in and out of my field of vision. A pacifier drops, wailing multiplies and echoes in the small space. Doors open, feet rush out, kicking the pacifier this way and that before it lands on the metal threshold. It balances and teeters before it disappears down the abyss. More wailing. More feet. Doors close. Feet shuffle. Doors open and spit me out into the parking garage's suffocating midday heat. Sandy concrete floor with yellow markings guides me to my car, the door thudding shut behind me.

I'm unsure how I descended three ramps, cleared the garage, passed several traffic lights, and reached halfway home, but here - 10 minutes' drive from the office, on the overpass from Media City to Sheikh Zayed Road - I crash back into the present. She is here.

SHE IS HERE!
KATHRIN IS HERE!

My hands are on the steering wheel, the prayer beads in UAE national colors are swaying from my rear-view mirror, and goosebumps rise up on my arm, each leaving a tiny shadow in the bright sunlight of midday. I can feel her sitting in the passenger seat next to me, the way she has done countless times in the past. I almost swerve the car as I look next to me to make sure I am not hallucinating. Of course, the seat is empty. But I can feel her presence and hear her laughter. "Stop being so dramatic. This is not you! You know better!" she reminds me. I almost laugh out loud. "HA! Easy for you to say, you are not here anymore!" I can feel her answer, "Are you sure?" She pauses as if waiting for my mind to catch up. "I am not going anywhere. Together 100 does have a new meaning now! Think about it!" And with those words, the moment passes, and I am alone in the car once again.

Well, not really alone.

Something lingers - a faint presence that has not left me since, as if a part of Kathrin has manifested itself and is now somewhere around me, almost like a faint scent that I can barely smell; something so delicate that I am not even sure which one of my senses I am using to detect it. But it is there! For a heartbeat, the veil lifts and the lightness of our friendship slips in. I feel almost airy, taller, happier - yes, "happier"! Maybe it was the fact that I was on autopilot, that for a few minutes, I had turned off my pain and was purely functioning as I was navigating my car through traffic. Maybe this was the empty canvas Kathrin needed to project her energy onto. I want to hold on to it - to her.

I glance at the empty seat next to me and then at the bracelet on my wrist. So, it was not an empty promise after all! Together 100 just did not mean what I thought it would. Something deep inside of me knows that we will always be connected. Together 100 and beyond. And this feeling seems strangely familiar, but I cannot quite put my finger on it. Almost like the hint of a thought - a delicate and fragile little thing, thin as a wisp of smoke, floating through my brain. I try to catch it, but always come back empty-handed. I know it is trying to remind me of my spiritual roots, a belief system I have all but forgotten over the past years.

I have forgotten so many things!

Life in Dubai and motherhood shifted my focus outward, meeting family needs while neglecting my inner self. As I sit in my car on the side of the road, I feel disconnected from reality, as if I am allowed just a few minutes in this tiny capsule of detached space and time, where - just for an instance - I can glimpse the path ahead and know what I will have to do.

"You know better!" she had said. I need to remember what I have learned in the past to get through this loss and the long months ahead. For a moment, her laughter has once again filled my heart with a certainty: There is more after death.

I have received some beautiful spiritual messages in the past, and every time they have filled me with a sense of hope and happiness - a light in a sea of turmoil and unrest. The latest one had been just four years ago.

CHAPTER 4
SAARBRÜCKEN 2012

It was a few days after my mother's death. Germany at the end of October matched our spirits - cold, gray, and wet. Rain pelted our car as my dad and I were driving toward my aunt's house. I fluffed the light fabric of my scarf, filling the space between the collar of my leather jacket and my neck to block some of the cold from creeping into my clothes. The engine hadn't warmed yet. "Do you want the radio on?" I asked just to puncture the numbness. My dad just shook his head, a small huff lost in his mustache. I withdrew my hand from the radio knob and turned to look outside again. Silence coiled up my legs, higher and higher until it restricted even the sounds my breath makes. I rested my forehead against the cool glass of the passenger window and watched the raindrops rush along.

I didn't dare look at my dad, marooned in his own grief, so I just stole furtive glances here and there. His knuckles were white on the steering wheel, his stare focused but empty. The immensity of my mother's loss filled the car. It wasn't just my own pain, but my father radiated such a profound sense of sorrow that it almost choked my heart. At any moment, he could have stopped the car, turned around, and I would have understood. I set a hand on his arm as a gesture of encouragement. No reaction. His arm was rigid, no twitch, no nod, no eye contact. Dejected, I pulled back. I don't think he even noticed.

For years, my parents had a difficult relationship with my aunt. Words hardened, misread, and left to calcify - silence did the rest. For years, I was stuck in the middle of this relentless cold-weather front that had spread across the two sides. I loved my aunt and had a close relationship with her since childhood, grown out of our shared passion for art - hours spent with watercolors, oils, and pastels at her living room table, crumbs from assorted cookies mingling with paint as summer breezes billowed curtains and revealed bright dahlias in the garden.

As the conflict grew, I refused to take sides and became Switzerland: neutral ground for both parties, and unwilling to even comment. I treaded lightly around my parents, evading mentions of phone calls or visits to avoid fueling the fire. Silence and avoidance served me well, uncomfortable but acceptable.

Death changes things. Dynamics shift, and finally, people are willing to make the first step. The realization of time running out is often a great motivator to put hurt feelings, pride, and the past behind and reconnect. My aunt had reached out and visited my mom during the last moments of her life - a gesture that I was grateful for. Even though my mom was not conscious at this point, I want to believe that she knew, ready to forgive and move on - in her case literally.

I looked at my father, who had stepped away from the bed to give my aunt some space to say goodbye. I could see from his face and body language that he felt torn - torn between loyalty to his old grievances and the scene unfolding in front of us. I touched his arm to soothe the boil of emotions. He shrugged me off, turned his back to the bed, and stared at the trees outside the window, eyebrows furrowed. We knew that Mami was slipping away, and the helplessness in those last days was absolute. Lashing out would have been an easy relief. It would have even been understandable. But it would have crushed the fragile threads forming between him and his older sister.

Knowing that my own little family was waiting in Dubai for my return and that the time with my dad was limited, my motivation to support this peace process wasn't entirely selfless. My life and my job were waiting for me, and eventually my dad would be alone with his grief. Grudges, resentment, and anger do not make for good company. Even a slim chance at reconciliation eased my guilt and anxiety about leaving him alone again.

Three days after my mother passed away, we drove to my aunt's house. The majestic trees along the sides of the road leaned into each other for support, forming a dark tunnel; leaves funneling the rain down to pelt our car with even larger drops, as if to jolt us out of our stupor. Chestnuts, still in their spiky green casing, roll towards the gutter, dislodged prematurely from the safety of the canopy. My tears have dried, but I pull a scrunched-up tissue from my jacket pocket and turn my head, pretending to look at something outside, while blotting my runny nose.

My parents' apartment spat us out with relief, as if glad to be alone. The dense silence within those walls felt solid these past days, muffling every sound and emotion into gray indifference. Every day was packed with landmines: her scarf, her shoes, her handwriting on a note. We needed to plan the funeral, pick an urn, and put an announcement in the paper - each an impossible task. "Herr Doktor Grüneberg, which font would you like to use for the death announcement?" the funeral director asked. My dad stared at the options laid out across the table, indecision paralyzing. My arms felt like lead as I lifted one of the paper samples. The more decisions, the tighter my chest locked, casting everything in cement, cracked only by the sharp ring of the phone.

My dad looked at me, as if needing a reminder to answer. "Hello?" he said, the bravado thin. I couldn't hear the voice on the other side, but he stood still, eyes on the horizon where low-hanging clouds met the rooftops. "Ok, we'll be there." He pulled air forcefully through his nose - not a sniffle, but a signal that the conversation was over. "Bye," He hung up, stared out the window for another minute. "Looks like we are going to your aunt's for lunch tomorrow." He decided so fast his internal emotional compass never had time to swing. It wouldn't have mattered anyway - overloaded by grief, it was paralyzed.

As our car drew closer to my aunt's house, we entered uncharted territory, and neither of us knew how the next few hours would play out. It was just past noon, yet the headlights of oncoming traffic splintered into bright fragments against the windshield until the wipers washed them away with a monotonous swish, swish. I searched the cupholder for some gum, but found only a few loose coins and my mother's ever-present pack of Fishermen's Friend. Scorched by the memory, I pulled my hand back and glanced at my dad. He didn't notice.

Outside, the houses scooched apart, making room for larger gardens, framed by hedges and low walls. They hunkered down, as the rain blurred the straight lines of windows, doors, and walls. Water rushed off the roofs and bubbled from overflowing gutters, clogged with chestnut leaves. We rounded a sharp corner, and the trees fell away behind us, along with the darkness and the rain. A patch of sky burst open into a radiant blue, framed by wispy edges of gray, where the sun shouldered the clouds aside. Streaks of solid light sliced down, making streets, cars, and gardens gleam like freshly polished crystal. The sunlight sparkled, reflected by millions of droplets all around us. Everything looked new and full of promise. As if slapped in the face, I sat up straight and inhaled, as if for the first time. The clouds lifted outside and within, and I feel hope stir.

"PULL OVER! PULL OVER! NOW!!!"

My dad nearly swerved as I yelled at him. He still seemed stuck in the weather I had just emerged from, but he pulled over without complaint, the coins in the cupholder jingling in surprise at the sudden change of direction. I was out of the car before it fully stopped. "Look up!" I cried, pointing to a row of houses ahead. And there, centered right over my aunt's house, arched the most spectacular double rainbow I had ever seen! The sky behind was steel gray, and in its gloominess, the perfect backdrop for this proud band of color.

The timing couldn't have been more perfect; it was the jolt needed to pull me out of my numbness. There was no denying this was a sign from above - a nod of approval from my mom. My aunt's house sat right in the rainbow's center, and any doubt regarding this rekindled relationship evaporated. A giggle bubbled up from my stomach, almost hysterical, as tears filled my eyes. I turn to my dad, laughing and crying at the same time. "It's Mami! That's from HER! That's HER rainbow!" I laughed out loud and ran over to him, throwing my arms around his neck, so that he had to brace himself against the door. He was pragmatic, not one for signs, spirits, or life after death, but something touched him at that moment. Maybe it was my exuberance or the undeniable synchronicity of events, but whatever it was, it painted a slight smile on his face as he looked up.

I took a deep breath, filled my lungs with the crisp, fresh air, and drew the rainbow inside, painting my soul in pastel colors. With one last look, I climbed back into the car, still smiling through happy tears. The atmosphere had shifted. The gloom had lifted, and I leaned over to turn on the radio without asking this time. My dad didn't stop me. Undoubtedly, there was a long road and many dark days ahead, but what we had just witnessed felt like the first ray of hope.

CHAPTER 5

DUBAI 2016

Strange how, through all the grief of losing my mom, Alireza, and Milly, I had forgotten this - wrapped too tight in pain to seek hope. Yet, here on the side of Sheikh Zayed Road, raw from incomprehensible loss, I feel it again: pastel hues of hope - a giggle somersaults out of me.

"You are losing it." A grave voice reaches my ear from my left shoulder. I pull down the visor and open the mirror. My shoulder critic sits there, his legs drooping over my collarbone, his face a mask of tears. "I am not." I retort. "She was here, clear as day! Well, maybe not 'clear as day' but real enough." My shoulder critic tucks his legs under, pulls out a small compact, and starts to applying a thick layer of white makeup to his face. He is wearing a wrinkled business suit that looks like he just stumbled out of a bar and smells like it, too. Wet skin does not take well to makeup, so the result of his efforts is rather blotchy-looking, as he draws thin, arched brows and rims his eyes with exaggerated black lines. He paints two thin vertical lines extending from the center of his left eye. He then blots his cheeks with a gold-speckled shade of peachy pink that looks suspiciously like my favorite NARS blush. He finishes the look with a black tear painted on his right cheek, even as real tears smudge his eyeliner into ugly black streaks. He looks at me dejected as our eyes meet in the mirror. His streaked face makes him look old and wrinkled like a raisin.

My shoulder critic has been with me for as long as I can remember, born perhaps from only-child loneliness, or simply a part of me, like an arm or leg. He appears unbidden and then disappears again for long stretches of time, but when he is around, he is always dressed to express rather than impress, wearing whatever he likes without being bound to social expectations, from a fairy costume one day to a three-piece suit the next.

He kept me company when I was little, when long afternoons stretched out before us with sun-drenched fields and patches of forest to explore. He came with me when we climbed over the rickety fence of our neighbor's garden to steal apples or plums - in fact, I seem to recall it was his idea. We laughed and rolled in the grass together, plotted hiding places. Whenever I doubted myself, he encouraged me, comforted me when I was sad, and gave me courage when I was scared. We were adventurous, daring, and never alone. He was the embodied freedom of youth.

And he wasn't always a critic. He used to be silly, carefree, and had a wonderful imagination. Sometimes we would lie hidden in the deep grass at the bottom of my parents' garden, the place I used to call the Fairytale Meadow. It was full of wildflowers, waist-high grasses, and fat bumble bees that stumbled nectar-drunk from one bloom to the next. He would tell me stories of strange creatures and elves, as we wove tiny baskets out of grasses and chased grasshoppers.

But then I grew up, and with it came a new energy into my life: insecurities and self-doubt. He picked up on careless remarks thrown at me by classmates or friends, words that stuck like gum. He picked them out of my hair, one by one, and chewed on them, so that they would not burden me. They made his stomach hurt. He always said he could handle a bit of pain out of love, but over time they changed him. He became cranky, distrustful, and even angry at times, losing weight to become scrawny, with skinny, very pale legs and pronounced knees, which is probably why I rarely see him in shorts. The shoulder critic was born.

"You ok?" He looks anything but, but I ask just to break the silence. He clenches his lips shut, merging the two black ovals he's painted there. Then his lips move, but no words come out. He looks up at the sky for help, one hand on his throat, then draws his lips into an exaggerated downward motion, his cartoon-like brows meet at a sharp angle, and his shoulders drop. Silence has always been his coping mechanism around grief. In fact, when my mom died, he was absent from my life for months. For a while, I thought he was gone for good. Or maybe grief casts a chasm between us that is too wide to bridge. With a soft plop, he is gone.

I look at myself in the mirror. I am pale, almost gray - my own tear-streaked face and runny mascara a less cartoon-like expression of the same emotion. I lick my thumb and wipe the black smears away, remembering how my mom used to do the same thing sometimes when I was little: lick her thumb to wipe some dirt off my face. Yuck! I loved my mom, but that was gross.

My earlier irrational giggle has all but evaporated, leaving behind a cold spot where the glimmer of hope was just sitting a moment ago. I close the visor with a slap. Receiving signs is a strange mix of hope and a smidgen of fear of losing my mind. But the hope has drifted into the background. It isn't time for healing just yet. First, I must pass through the immediate pain of my broken heart. For now, it drones out any chance of inner peace and reflection. I know this: as long as I am in acute turmoil of grief, there is no place for quiet contemplation. Hope still hovers somewhere out of reach, but

I am caught in a rat race of fear, loneliness, anxiety, pain, regret, and anger. How can I be open to the subtle messages when my darkest fears are yelling at me.

The week leading up to the funeral is rough. I take a few days off work to figure out how to exist in this new reality. But after the first day, I long for the simplicity of leaning into my left brain. The soothing monotony of the workflow feels like the right kind of distraction. At home, I have nothing but time under my fingernails. I am jonesing for something to block out the pain; to shake me out of this suspended state my mind is caught in.

I tried going to the gym. After my mom died, I sweated my grief onto the mat. I punched and kicked it out during Muay Thai sessions. The harder I went, the better I felt. The grief bled through bruises into my skin that I carried like warrior paint. I worked out every day and pushed myself to a point where my brain ceased to function. But now, the gym is a minefield of well-meaning hugs that reduce me to tears. I cannot deal with it. I booked a sparring session, but crumpled into a sobbing heap after 5 minutes. Miserable.

The afternoon sun saunters into the stairwell of our house, drunk, slurring that there are still too many hours in the day. A sigh shudders out of me; I long for the inky forgetfulness of sleep. "Mamiiiii!! Melanie is taking us to the park." My two blonde screeching banshees, nine and six years old, stampede past me up the stairs, braids and skirts flying. "Where is my water bottle?" Gia demands. "Gia took my Shopkins and does not want to give them back! Giaaaaaaa!" Giulia's voice rises to the amplitude of a car alarm. My frayed nerves tingle. Deep breath.

Propelled by the sheer noise, I rush to the living room, scanning the table and sideboards for the missing bottle. Nothing. My eyes snag on a silver picture frame half-hidden by philodendron leaves: Kathrin, Gia, and me at her wedding. Feels like yesterday. I can hear her laughter. Birch branches swayed above us, casting nets of sun and shade. Gia, barely a year old, chubby in my arms, her plump diaper bottom rested on my folded arms. She had looked up, mesmerized by the play of light and dark, ignoring the photographer, who immortalized two best friends, foreheads touching above my baby, her goddaughter, a carefree moment of pure joy.

I feel like throwing up.

I nudge the frame behind the plant as if hiding it could stop the pain. Guilt makes me pull it out again, and I prop it up against the nearby lamp. My eyes are swollen and gritty.

"Madam, have you seen Gia's water bottle?" Our nanny's soft voice is padding around me at a safe distance. She has been lowering her voice around me since the phone call, treating me as if I might break. She might be right.

"I got it." I huff, unnecessarily short. In truth, I've got nothing: no water bottle, no patience, no control of my feelings. I mentally scan images of our house stored in my short-term memory bank, each room, each shelf. There - half-hidden under a couch cushion. "Giaaaaaaaaa, give me my Shopkins!" Giulia's voice amplifies to unbearable levels as she flies past me again, following her older sister at the heels.

"ENOUGH!" Grief thunders out of me, stopping my daughters mid-stride, eyes wide, breath held. The drunken shadow of the sun in the stairwell shrinks into a solid mass - Giulia's chin wobbles. Melanie tucks them under her wings like Mother Goose and ushers them out, the bottle still sticking out from under the cushion. A minute later, the front door closes with an ever-so-gentle thud as they leave for the park. Silence floods the house and finds me still staring at the photograph.

The shadow, intimidated, tiptoes towards evening. I stand until the call to prayer pulls me out of my stupor. Upstairs in our bedroom, I rummage behind my sweaters. My usual ability to cope with my daughters' simple quarrels has worn thin. I know that my outburst wasn't about their misbehavior, but my lack of coping mechanisms. I need to get back to the office. I suck at this. My grief makes me a bad mother. Most days, I can hide that I am not fully here, even from myself, but my family only has a part of me. The other part is lost somewhere, broken and discarded by the side of the road, like an empty pram.

A hot new feeling wells up through my chest, leaving a vile, bitter taste in my mouth: self-loathing. At this moment, I hate myself for my lack of patience and presence. They deserve a mother who is engaged and loving, not someone who explodes at the slightest pretense and cries behind closed doors. I cling to every hug like a life raft - but shouldn't it be the other way around? Shouldn't they be the ones soaking up MY love? They are still so little. They cannot understand. Hating myself almost soothes my grief; it is a feeling that I can direct. I direct it at that part of me failing as a mother.

My fingertips brush against something hard, and I pull out a cigarette pack from its hiding place behind my sweaters. I am not a smoker. There was a brief period after high school when I did have the occasional cigarette. But not with any serious commitment. After my mom died, I picked it up again for the same reason I do now: filling my lungs with toxic smoke helps me direct my anger at myself. It didn't last long then. Maybe a month. But I bought this pack the evening of the call. Whenever I feel close to losing it, I sneak out on our bedroom terrace for a smoke. Hiding this self-destructive vice fits my narrative of anger - at myself, at life, at the accident, at Kathrin for dying. Anger takes the edge off grief. And cigarettes take the edge off anger. Win-win, except for the nasty smell of shame and self-loathing the smoke leaves behind.

The sun is still nailed to the same spot above the rooftops when I step out on the terrace, desert sand scrunching under my flip-flops. I'd hoped it would be closer to setting by now. Days are short in Dubai during winter, but not short enough. The last verses of the call to prayer sway in the palm fronds. The shadow, more relaxed now, leans against the wall and soaks up the fading warmth.

If time would just pass already - it's the living through it that hurts.

The girls come home a few hours later, tired and sweaty. To over-compensate for my outburst, I wrap them in bear hugs, and we walk up the stairs to the bathtub, one chubby sticky hand in each of mine. Their bubbly tales of friends, swings, and scooters wash over me, dislodging the lingering odor of grief. "We ate a picnic dinner in the park!" Giulia explains the grease stains on the front of her dress and wipes at them with grimy hands. "Oops!" Her big green eyes look up at me under a thick curtain of black lashes, scanning my face for a reaction. Guilt punches me in the ribs again, and I cover my wince with a smile. "No worries, *Amore*[7]. I'll stick that straight in the wash." I pull the soiled dress over her head and blow a raspberry on her tummy.

The evening prayer is the last hurdle of the day. I recite the same German phrases with the girls every night, a tradition from my childhood. I remember my parents sitting at the edge of my mat-tress, hands folded, repeating the same words. My dad's hands car-ried the medicinal scent of his office soap and sanitizer, too pungent to be washed away before dinner. My mom smelled of her perfume. Opium by Yves Saint Laurent is a heavy scent as it is, but years of use had desensitized her nose, and where one spritz might suffice, she needed three. Even her pearls guarded her scent protectively long after she was gone. I had wrapped them in a plastic bag to preserve it, but like a thief, it escaped. One day, I opened the bag and found only a quiet strand of pearls without stories to tell.

---

7   *Amore - Italian. "Love," often used as a word of endearment*

Tonight, work is keeping Andrea late in the office, so it is just us girls, scooched together on Giulia's lower bunk bed. Orange light from the streetlamp filters through the filigree arabesque woodwork over the window. I unclip a forgotten metal barrette with purple flowers from Giulia's head and smooth her hair behind her ear before she snuggles in. A single hair is stuck in the hinge, and I dangle it like magic a few inches from her face, making her laugh. I slip the clip into the back pocket and fold my hands.

The words of the prayer are like pebbles, worn smooth over generations, warm and comfortable in the bed between us.

"Dear God, make me godly,
so that one day I can go to heaven.
Amen.
Dear God, please protect
Mama and Papa,
Gia and Giulia, ..."

What follows is a list of names of our family members and close friends. In the original prayer of my childhood, we concluded:

"... and please protect everyone
dear to our hearts.
Amen."

But the girls began making subtle changes after my mother passed away. We could no longer include her name. In their minds, the dead are in heaven and no longer in need of God's protection. So, we made prayer Version 2.0, moving her name to the end: "

... and Omama, in heaven with the angels."

Unfortunately, we had to add quite a few names over the last four years: not only my mom, but Alireza, my dad's dog Paul, and then, because they wanted to be fair, my dog Tina as well, who had passed away when Gia was just a baby. When their names float off our lips at night, it fills the room with familiarity and warmth. I can almost feel their memory as indentations on the mattress.

But now I must change the order of the prayer once again. Taking Kathrin's name from the front of the list and putting it at the end, in *"heaven with the angels,"* makes my tongue trip. Giulia pushes her folded hands under mine, wriggling her fingers to coax a smile. She may not understand the gravity of death, but she knows enough to try and cheer me up. Concentration narrows my vision to the pink flowers on the duvet, blurring.

Despite all efforts, I drop the flow of the prayer. By omitting Kathrin's name from the beginning, it loses its structure and crumbles like ashes over my tongue. I'm disoriented and can't remember where to pick up the words. Gia, always the empath, feels my struggle and continues with a serious tone:

"… and Omama, Kathrin, Ali,
Paul and Tina,
In heaven with the angels.
Amen"

"It's ok, Mami." Gia leans forward and cups my face in her hands, a gesture too grown-up for a nine-year-old. Her moss-green eyes part a curtain of long dark lashes, scanning my face for the pain rising in my throat. The reading lamp paints her face with soft strokes, highlighting the peachy skin on her cheeks and forehead, bathing the right side in deep blues. She plants a kiss on my cheek and pulls me into a tight hug. I dip my grief in the golden curls tumbling over her princess nightgown, inhale the sweet berry scent of her shampoo, and come up for breath, feeling lighter. With the soft pitter-patter of bare feet, Gia climbs up the wooden ladder to her bunk. I pull her blanket over her shoulder as she nuzzles her nose into her pink bunny. Giulia is already asleep when I kiss her goodnight and turn on the nightlight, blowing a few extra kisses toward Gia on my way out.

My hand clings to the door frame, unwilling to let go. The shimmer from the nightlight tugs at my shirt, waning in brightness and emotional support the further I go. Defeated, my hand drops and I step into the cool air of the silent, dark home around me, interrupted only by occasional sleepy mumbles muffled by blankets and cuddle-toys - reminders that I'm not alone after all.

I don't turn on the light, trusting my toes to feel their way down the cool stone ledges of each step until I reach the living room. Silver dapples of moonlight swim in the pool outside, then flicker like fish across the black chandelier, diving into the silver-framed mirror before hiding behind the shadow of the curtains.

I sink onto the last step and lean my head against the wall. My eyelids succumb to gravity, giving my red, swollen eyes a moment of respite. With one deep exhale, I drop expectations and the duties of motherhood next to me on the stairs, breathing in the silken strands of unfiltered grief. Finally, I can let the pain wash over me without guilt or restraint. Yet the tears only scratch the back of my eyelids - unshed. I've cried them all already.

With a soft ping, my phone screen illuminates the sideboard. I pick it up, peering through sandy eyes at the message on the lock screen.

"I am on my way, Amore. Leaving the office now. You ok?"

My index finger hovers, not knowing what to say. Until a few days ago, I waited for Andrea to come home every evening, so we could chat over dinner or watch TV. Now all I crave is solitude. I won't even have time to sneak another cigarette. He would smell it.

Grieving is a lonely process. Until now, life has spared Andrea the heartbreak of loss: his parents, his sister, niece, nephew, cousins, friends - all healthy. Even his grandparents are still alive. And as much as he tries to comfort me, there's a disconnect. Knowing grief in theory, from a safe distance, is nothing like experiencing it physically - not only once, but four times. He hates to see me suffer, and his hugs come in abundance - deep, soulful wraps that connect to the heart. Under normal circumstances, I would melt into them. But after four losses, I feel broken. I don't know if I have the strength to put myself back together when I emerge from those hugs.

Now each hug feels entangled in expectation - to make the pain stop, to hasten recovery. Every time I feel his gaze, I know he's waiting for signs of improvement, putting all his energy into this goal. He cooks for me, takes over chores, brings me my favorite chocolates, and lets me sleep in.

Feeling better?
Nope!

I hate to disappoint him. Deep down, I know the hugs help, but they are a drop in an empty bucket that will take a long time to fill. Over three losses, I've pulled myself together - for him, for the kids - so they'd feel that their efforts were working, that I wasn't broken. And I know I'm doing it again. "You ok?" is hoping for *Yes*. I want to say yes. For him.

Arschbackenzusammenkneifmentalität.

The question is: whom am I lying to? Him or myself? I leave the message on delivered, turn the phone off, and head to bed.

The days until the flight to Vienna drag their feet, time turning into a blur of hours and minutes, smashed together with the unpredictable brushstrokes of a toddler. Other times, minutes would thin into long, transparent things that wove themselves through my hair, impossible to dislodge. I would spend hours combing through them one by one, braiding them into a construct that resembled time. Then suddenly hours leap and I find myself sitting in the same spot as earlier, shadows pointing accusingly in the opposite direction, my growling stomach the only proof that time hasn't stood still.

I look at myself in the mirror and frown. Halfway through my make-up routine, eyeliner in hand, one eye done, I stalled in a sequence of movements that should be second nature. Why even bother? I drop the eyeliner and lean forward, peering intently at my unlined eye. Fuck it. "I am not going!" I call out towards the bedroom, where Andrea lies with his laptop. "Of course, you are." He replies without looking up. "I cannot! Look at me. I look like shit. There is not enough makeup in the world to hide those bags. Plus, I am in no state to go anywhere. I'll just pull everyone down." Self-pity stains my voice and blotches my face, making me even more pathetic - if that is even possible.

"Go! It will be good for you to get out. Livia would be disappointed if you missed it." Andrea rolls onto his side, pushes the laptop aside, and looks at me standing in the doorway. "Look, the kids are in bed, and I've got it handled. Go. If you don't feel like it, you can sneak out early. But at least try."

Livia has put together another Book Salon, a smaller version of the more extensive literary conferences she once organized with her late husband. Andrea is right. I should go. Under normal circumstances, I'd already be there, helping her set up, and offering support. This is the second event that she's organized alone since her husband died two years ago. She had always been the driving force and was determined to keep it going. Over the past six years, she's become a close friend - a bright shining star whose energy is palpable. Our losses brought us closer; she speaks my language of grief and never shies away from my tears. I promised I'd be there. But honestly, mingling, socializing, and listening to inspiring talks is nowhere on my list of priorities tonight. I just want to curl up and hide.

"Fine!" I turn back to the mirror and give my other eye its much-needed liner. The felt tip runs smoother than usual over my swollen lid, and I end up with a longer wing than intended. Too lazy to fix it, I extend the other line as well, a more dramatic look than planned. Oh well. I shrug at myself in the mirror and grab a discarded hoodie from the chair. "Can you make sure to put the food in the fridge before you go to sleep?" I raise my voice, distracting Andrea from the fact that I am rummaging through my closet for my hidden cigarettes. "Ahhaaaa." is the only answer I get, his focus back on the screen. I slide the cigarettes into my hoodie pocket and, with an envious glance at our cozy bed, wave Andrea a dispirited goodbye.

As I walk downstairs, I pause to look out the window at the mosque across the street. Compared to Dubai's opulent mosques, this one is small and humble, but at night it glows in warm orange tones, highlighting the intricate designs on its dome and the minaret. Out of the corner of my eye, I catch a small glowing spark on my shoulder. My little critic sits cross-legged, a tiny shisha[8] bubbling beside him. He closes his eyes, inhales with gusto, a thin tendril of apple-scented smoke spiraling towards me. He is dressed in a long taupe linen shirt and cuffed shorts revealing knobby knees, layered necklaces of beads, silver chain links, and black leather. Even his wrists are adorned with stacks of bracelets that clink as he moves. "You think you are the only one who smokes around here?" he says with a raised eyebrow and blows a thick cloud of smoke into my face. "Let's go!" He demands, pointing his skinny arm toward the front door. Caught, I continue downstairs without a word.

---

8   A shisha is a water pipe used for smoking flavored tobacco, where the smoke is filtered through water before being inhaled.

Fifteen minutes later, I enter a courtyard of sound and light, infused with the scent of *Oud* [9] and trays of appetizers. Not recognizing anyone, I cling to the juice handed to me by a passing waiter, as if the glass justifies my presence. I'd prefer a proper drink, but this is Dubai, where alcohol is confined to bars and hotels.

"Bellaaaaa[10]! I am so glad you made it!" A whirlwind of auburn hair twirls toward me. Her voice is full of energy, her eyes darting everywhere, scanning details that still need attention before the speakers arrive. Her Italian accent is always stronger when she is happy, and despite the stress and nerves leading up to the event, she seems happy - frazzled but happy. I lean into her generous hug, grateful for the dim lighting that hides the fact that my smile is struggling to reach my eyes.

Once again, Livia has outdone herself. Despite failing sponsors and unreliable support - typical for the region - she has transformed the outdoor space with the simple addition of fake grass, bean bags, cushioned seating areas, and strategic lighting into an inviting hub. Men in white and women in black traditional Emirati dress stand in monochrome groups while young people in bright clothes weave towards the bean bags. The sweet scent of e-cigarettes drifts past, reminding me to sneak to the parking lot for a quick smoke while I have the chance. My fingers toy with the half-empty pack in my hoodie, but Livia pulls me along before I can escape.

"There is someone you need to meet!" she insists, ignoring my protests as we snake our way through the crowd, her arm hooked in mine. Probably better this way; otherwise, I might have lost my nerve and left the venue altogether.

---

9   *Oud - Arabic. A luxurious Middle Eastern scent made from resin-saturated agarwood.*

10   *Bella - Italian. Word of endearment used among friends or lovers, translates to "beautiful."*

Dressed in black, Livia radiates control, giving brisk directions to people with clipboards and schedules. These minutes are precious - the frantic pre-event rush - yet here she is with me. Then a woman waves from the crowd, and Livia steers me towards her. She barely has time for an introduction before hurrying off again. "Alex, this is Mariam - Mona to her friends. Mona, this is Alex. You girls need to talk," and she's gone, off to finalize sound and lights.

I'm left standing before a woman in her mid-thirties, a colorful headscarf loosely draped. Her warmth is palpable, her beauty tangible, rather than superficial. Under normal circumstances, I'd handle a random introduction fine, but tonight I feel adrift and cannot find my social footing. "Hi," I say more awkwardly than I am used to. Mona's smile is wide, her hand extended. "Hello." I stumble through polite small talk until she suddenly pauses, eyes intent. Her deep brown eyes, framed with kohl, gaze straight through the façade of make-up and polite smiles I've built. The silence stretches. I want to look away, wriggle free, but her eyes hold me - not judged, not exposed, just seen. Despite myself, the dam bursts, and tears spill down my cheeks. Here I am, in the middle of the conference seating area, the event about to start, having a major meltdown in front of a complete stranger. But instead of shame, I feel relief. Without hesitation, Mona envelops me in a nurturing hug. I sink into the motherly warmth - a hug without expectations, without pressure to "feel better." Just a pillowy embrace that holds me as I am falling. I let go completely, floating on waves of acceptance.

"She is here," Mona whispers, warm against my ear.
My heartbeat stops.

"She is right here next to you. I can feel her. She wants you to know everything is alright." With a jolt, I slam back into reality. I straighten, blinking furiously to look at Mona.

What the heck!?!?

Time freezes. There is no question who Mona is talking about. Kathrin! A shiver races down my arms and spine, unleashing fresh tears. Mona's words hit me like an electrical current, vibrating through me.

As if on cue, the event begins. Darkness falls like a velvet curtain, and a spotlight illuminates Livia on stage. Applause rises, pulling Mona and me out of our bubble. Her embrace slips away as she shifts her gaze forward. The loss of that connection leaves a void -cool, quiet, giving my thoughts space to catch up. Even with my eyes on the stage, nothing registers. My mind is fixed on one word: Kathrin.

She is right here next to you. Mona's words echo like shouts in a tunnel. I scan the heads in front, the faces beside me, as if Kathrin might be sitting there. Of course, I see nothing but strangers. Still, Mona said she was here. What did she mean? How could she know? Did Livia tell her?

As I debate these thoughts, I brace myself for the inevitable commentary. My shoulder critic must be chomping at the bit to chime in. It is one thing to weigh thoughts internally; it is quite another to have Mr. Know-it-all interject. As if summoned by my thoughts, he snarks:

"Do you hear yourself? What are you talking about? Kathrin? Who are you kidding? Your grief is an open book to everyone who sees you! It's written all over your face! No mystery about that! Look at those swollen eyes, the way you cry the moment someone looks at you. Are you really buying this supernatural mumbo-jumbo?"

I refuse to meet his eyes, staring blindly at the stage. Some days I despise him - such a mean little shit! I just know it was true. I felt it!

Nothing else needs to be said. Those words carried a deeper connection to my truth, no matter what this little asshole thinks. Kathrin was there at that moment! My reaction wasn't just to Mona's words; it was to a sensation beyond my usual senses - just like the moment in the car on the day of Kathrin's accident. It had the same vibration.

Again, my critic pipes up, palms open, fingers stretched wide.

"How did she know? Seriously! Of course, Liv' told her! That Moooooona woman didn't just pull that out of the air!" He drags out her name in a mocking bellow.

No. Highly unlikely. Livia had been lost in her own world, consumed by this event. No way! With a dismissive swipe, I brush his arguments aside - discussion over. I'm done entertaining his negativity. Instead, I turn back to the stage, catching only the last sentences of the first talk before applause rises. I hadn't heard a single word.

> WhatsApp messages:
> 00:14 am
> Livia: Thank u so much for coming today. Sorry I couldn't spend more time. Did u enjoy the talks?
> 00:15 am
> Me: Loved it! u did amazing once again. Sorry couldn't stay longer. ☹
> 00:15 am
> Livia: Mona texted. She wants your number. Said u guys had a great chat and there was more she needed to tell u. U ok if I pass it on?
> 00:15 am
> Me: OMG, Mona! She said some crazy stuff. I was bawling my eyes out - great first impression :o She said she felt Kathrin there!!! I totally lost it.
> Did you tell her????? About Kathrin, I mean?

00:17 am
Livia: Mona is very special. She gets "messages"
- she helped me so much after G died. U should
talk to her again. And no, I didn't say anything.
Wanted to see what happens when u meet.
00:17 am
Me: ... (three dots appear, then vanish - I'm left
without words)

The shriek of my alarm clock rips through the still bedroom at 4:00 am. I'd been awake, waiting, my hand ready to pounce, fighting the blanket's grip before switching it off. I had hoped to connect with Mona before the funeral. Our strange encounter and Livia's message made it clear that we had barely scratched the surface. She might not have the answers I seek, but my intuition told me we met for a reason. I was clinging to the hope she could help somehow, that talking to her would give me strength to get through the days in Vienna, where Kathrin's family and friends were gathering for the final goodbye. But it didn't happen. She texted me the day after the Salon, but my work was insane; I had to leave no loose ends before the flight. And in the evenings, I was too drained to do anything and too distraught to sleep.

I peel myself out of bed and stagger to the bathroom for a quick shower. I said goodbye to the kids the night before, so this morning I just nuzzle a few kisses into my husband's neck; half-asleep, he pulls me close. On my way out, I tiptoe into the girls' room, breathe soft kisses onto their foreheads, tuck Gia's bunny back under her arm, and slip downstairs where my suitcase waits.

"As-salamu alaykum.[11]" I greet the Uber driver, sinking heavily into the seat as he loads my luggage. My aches, every bone and muscle screaming. The nights since the call have been hell. Grief and

---

11   As-salamu alaykum - Arabic. "Peace be upon you," used as a greeting.

insomnia are inseparable companions and, in their union, a formidable adversary.

"Would you like some water, Madame?" The driver holds up a plastic bottle and smiles at me in the mirror. "No, thank you. I'm ok." I turn my face to the window.

Every night since the call has been the same. I go to sleep early, read a few pages, and then turn the lights out. My husband drifts off beside me in minutes, his steady breath comforting. But despite exhaustion, I can't sleep. I toss and turn for hours until my muscles ache from fatigue. There is not a single position I can find rest in. I get up and do some light stretches to relieve my aching body. The walls of our bedroom close in on me, making it hard to breathe. As quietly as possible, I open the balcony door and drink in the fresh air. Above me, stars sparkle stubbornly against the Dubai sky that is always glowing, pulsating with life below. The projection clock throws the time casually against the dark ceiling of the bedroom; an unobtrusive red glow announces 3:30 am. Stress and panic set in. The urgency to get some rest pushes my heart rate up, making it worse. Eventually, I fall into a dreamless, sleep-like state. Like a switch being flipped: one second, I am struggling to calm my breath, the next moment I am jerked awake by my alarm clock. No gentle drifting, just darkness ripped open. My body resists rising, clinging to the suspended void of dreamless half-sleep, preferable to pain. But today the alarm rang at 4:00 am, and I headed to Vienna on zero sleep.

I am dreading this trip. I am scared of walking into Kathrin's apartment, with her jackets hanging near the door, her keys in the little bowl on the windowsill, her energy everywhere. I'm scared of the emptiness her absence has left behind.

The driver turns on the radio, soft Arabic music nudging at my silence. Outside, violet, rose, and tangerine hues splash the clouds as the sun rises. Dubai's skyline, which always strives to be bigger, better, and more beautiful, pales next to the natural symphony of light. Towers streak past, silhouettes ignited by dawn, flames of reflection paying homage to the true queen of Dubai, as she rises gracefully out of the desert, rays reaching unchallenged across the city. My thoughts travel with the clouds, leaping ray to ray, freed from grief for a few moments. Daydreaming becomes flight; a few minutes of peace where nothing else counts but this very moment.

The taxi pulls to the curb, and I walk into the vast departure hall of Dubai's airport on autopilot. Its spotless marble and soaring domed ceiling barely register as I keep my eyes low, following cracks in the floor past a determined pair of leather shoes and the flirty click-clack of elegant high heels toward the check-in counter.

"As-salamu alaykum," I greet the Emirates agent, handing her my passport. Her dark eyes gaze down at my passport along a finely shaped, elegant nose. Her red lipstick holds her lips in a permanent half-smile, which she now directs at me.

"I see you are flying into Vienna today. Beautiful city!" she says, filling the silence as the computer loads. Her black hair knotted neatly at her neck, one rebellious strand fluttering in the air-conditioned draft beneath her pillbox hat.

"Work or pleasure?"

I freeze. How do I answer that? It's not work. But it's not pleasure either. Displeasure? Duty? Heartbreak? "Neither," I mumble, intending to leave it there - but truth tumbles out. "I'm going to my best friend's funeral, she ..." Tears cut me off.

I rummage through my bag for sunglasses. Not there. Panic seizes me. The tears won't stop. My face burns, sweat trickles down my spine. I dump everything on the counter: my book, the little Ziplock guarding my allotted amount of liquids, five packs of tissues, wallet. The pile grows with my shame. Am I panicking about my missing glasses or about my unexpected emotional outburst? WHERE ARE THEY? I cannot go to a funeral without them. I need that shield to hide behind. The thought of going without that security blanket is unfathomable.

"I am so sorry!" the lady behind the counter says, visibly uncomfortable with my outburst. She tucks her stray hairs back under her hat, regaining a solid air of unapproachability. Mortified, I sniffle a quick "It's ok." behind my tissue. It's ok? No! It is definitely not ok. Why do I always say that when someone offers condolences? It is not ok! But I say nothing, swipe all my belongings back into my bag, grab my boarding pass, and escape toward the passport control. The travelator whisks me past groups of travelers, gaggles of Emirates crew, heels clicking in unison, hair immaculate, rolling their hand luggage towards a private entrance. Thanks to the early hour, there is no line at the passport control. I step forward, placing my passport and ticket on the marble counter. Under the cold, prying gaze of the officer behind the desk, I avert my red, swollen eyes, trying to disguise my emotions as a common cold, emphasized by a cough here and there.

Instead of heading to the airport lounge, I make a beeline for the duty-free shops. I need sunglasses! I dodge a group of kids tugging stuffed camels from a shelf, before their nannies herd them away, the sad-looking toys abandoned on the floor. The backlit display of sunglasses sparkles at me. Nearby, an elderly Indian lady in a gold-trimmed sari reaches for rhinestone-studded glasses, her arms jingling with bangles. The tinkling draws me in, her hennaed fingers moving gracefully as she studies herself in the mirror. She wobbles her head appreciatively, then disappears behind a rotating rack. Free from distractions, I scan the shelves. Fate seems on my side: I find the perfect pair on the very first try. Big and black, ombré glasses, perfect to hide behind, while still looking somewhat glamorous. The pair even has a little hot pink accent on the rim. My color! I love them. Price tag? Irrelevant. Normal spending rules don't apply when you're about to bury your best friend.

I am about to pay when the bright pink of a lipstick catches my eye. My pink - the one Andrea and I used for our wedding color and that later became my signature, popping up in my accessories and jewelry, wherever I needed something to brighten up my wardrobe. I don't usually wear lipstick, maybe a gloss now and then. But these aren't normal circumstances, and a bit of color might help. Hot pink lipstick for a funeral. Kathrin would pretend to be scandalized but secretly indulge me! I've always been the daring one. So, who cares about what's acceptable for a funeral!

Something rebellious stirs as if the thought of a bright color is bordering on indecent. One could argue that a bright pink lipstick would be out of place on such a somber occasion, but I don't give a shit right now. Heat rises inside of me. I need to have it! It feels like I'm flipping the bird to this whole fucked-up situation.

I don't want to bury my best friend.
I don't want to say goodbye ... again!

Anger boils hot through my veins. I want to scream. FUCK THIS! Why didn't she wear a seatbelt? She ALWAYS wore her seatbelt. Kathrin was so rule-bound, particular, strait-laced - and now this? No way. Yet here she is ... dead. Because she was not wearing her friggin' seatbelt!

Fury stabs through me. What was she thinking? Every moron wears a seatbelt! WHAT THE ACTUAL FUCK!

Sadness evaporates into rage. I grab two lipsticks and slam them with my credit card onto the counter beside my sunglasses. The saleswoman gives me a look, but I don't care. The rage feels good. It courses through my veins like gasoline, making my skin buzz. I snatch the glasses before she can bag them, rip them from their box, and shove them on my nose. The world dims. Better.

I still have time, so I head for the lounge bar. It is 8 am, but I don't care. Airports are suspended in time; a place where you just live in the moment, hovering between time zones and jet lag, where mornings and evenings blend into one. I order a shot of tequila and down it the moment the bartender pushes the glass towards me. I order another one, and the rage subsides into a tight knot of flames in my stomach, then dissolves into silence. The angry voice in my head retreats, watching me with a mixture of embarrassment and pity. My insides are scorched earth, a reminder of how broken I am.

I pull out the lipstick and stare at my reflection behind the bar. The woman staring back looks pale, out of sorts. Her sunglasses are absurd indoors. She applies a tentative coat of hot pink with a shaky hand, smacks her lips, inhales deeply, and straightens her spine. Leaving a tip, she heads to her gate.

The lipstick works. It lifts me, casting a shield of confidence. Like a costume, it hides the broken me. My posture shifts, my stride steadies. By hiding my grief I can feel a fragment of who I was before - safe, fearless.

Superficial? Yes.
Necessary? Absolutely not!
But it feels good.

Fueled by alcohol and lipstick armor, I raise my eyes to the travelers around me. Families with kids, Emirati men in spotless *kandooras*[12] trailed by women in black *abayas*[13], handbags glinting. The heady scent of Oud lingers. Two teenage girls bob to music from an iPad. - A memory takes me by the hand and pulls me out of the airport and into my parents' bathroom.

---

12   *Kandoora - Arabic. A traditional long robe worn by men in the Arabian Gulf.*

13   *Abaya - Arabic. A loose over-garment, worn traditionally by Muslim women, covering the whole body except head, feet and hands, combined with a Sheila, the matching head scarf.*

Kathrin, barely 19, leans into the mirror and applies brown eyeshadow from the small Chanel compact she "borrowed" from her mom. She wrinkles in concentration. "Is this too much?" she asks. The air is heavy with perfume, hairspray, and anticipation. The weekend lies before us like an all-you-can-eat buffet, full of choices: movies, dancing, and possibly a flirt or two. My bare feet are bouncing up and down on the soft rug as I dance to the music blasting from the radio. Instead of answering, I shimmy to her side, throw an arm over her shoulder so we're cheek to cheek in the mirror - her brown curls against my blond bob, her brown eyes meeting mine. She is wearing my silver hoops, which look better on her than they do on me. "You look faaaabulous!" I grin. Lucio Dalla's "Caruso" flows out of the speakers - my mixed tape spinning into our shared love of all things Italian.

Right after high school, I spent 6 months in Florence, the best six months of my life. Kathrin visited often; we collected memories: tiny matching tattoos on our wrists, hers a rebellious first, done with terror at her parents' reaction; or the time we placed cucumber slices on our eyes in preparation for a night out and ended up with bright red eyes, unable to leave the house. Turns out they were zucchini. As the heart-wrenching song filled the room, I grabbed my hairbrush. On cue, we leaned in, belting into the prickly microphone:

"Te voglio bene assaje
Ma tanto tanto bene, sai
È una catena ormai
Che scioglie il sangue dint'e vene, sai"

Little did I know that this song, years later, would be impossible for me to listen to without dissolving into tears.

That night, our enthusiasm makes up for the lack of vocal ability as we sway and sing around the bathroom, not even noticing my mother in the doorway, smiling indulgently.

"I see you girls are having fun already. We're off to bed. Make sure to be home by 2 am," she reminds us.

Kathrin and I exchange a conspiratorial glance, stifling a giggle as the door shuts again. To be home by 2 am we'd need to be in a cab by 1:40 am at the latest. Sometimes we flirted with that cut-off, pushing for just one more dance, but rarely broke curfew. More often, we ended the night sprinting out of the club, jackets half-on, squealing with laughter on the way to the taxi stand. Scenes like this defined those days. Life hung above us like heavy branches of ripe fruit. High school was behind us, and in front of us lay a cornucopia of possibilities.

Those were the days.

Getting dressed up together was one of our fundamental bonding experiences. Often, the anticipation mattered more than the night itself. Arm in arm, hand in hand, we walked into clubs with the blind confidence of the young. Life hadn't scarred us yet, and it showed. How I long for those nights. The weightlessness of carefree living seems like the most precious gift. I wish I had known to cherish it as the priceless memory it would become.

I drop my hand luggage by an empty seat facing the boarding gate - forty-five minutes to go. I plop myself onto the chair, the rubber soles of my sneakers squeaking against the marble floor in protest, the leather of the chair sighing under my weight. A unicorn Beanie Baby dangles from the backpack of a little girl beside me, its blank stare meeting mine. The air hums with the usual airport noise: announcements rising above the drone of voices, then dropping back. Behind my sunglasses, my eyes sting, gritty and swollen.

My eyelids grow heavy. Colors and shapes blur past, too busy for me to notice. I close my eyes, floating in the space between external reality and the mess inside me. I feel myself floating, untethered and free, propelled by the warmth that the tequila has left behind.

The sharp, chemical smell of artificial lemon from the nearby ladies' room snaps me back. Across from me, an elegant woman in her fifties reads a paper through horn-rimmed readers, her suit jacket sharp, knee-length pencil skirt, red soles flashing as she crosses her legs. Who travels like that? On a six-hour flight? I glance at my own scuffed high-tops, their laces having settled into a comfortable permanence, easy to slip on and off.

Nowadays, I rarely dress up. Given the choice between a dress and a pair of jeans, I pick jeans. Add my high-tops, casual off-the-shoulder shirt, and just a hint of lip gloss. But back then, Kathrin and I loved to dress up, swapping clothes like gossip. What's mine was hers, and the other way around. But jeans and high-tops would not do this time around. A funeral demands a black dress. I have the perfect one - bought two years ago for my mother's funeral.

... Oh, that dress.
As beautiful as it is, it carries guilt.

I remember the day I bought it. After my dad's call, I was in shock. He didn't spell it out, but I felt it in my bones: this was serious. I booked my flight immediately, pacing the house like a caged tiger. Should I pack? Clean the kitchen? Check food supplies? Pack. Yes, pack. I pulled out a few t-shirts and jeans, searching my closet in vain for anything warmer. After three years in Dubai, my wardrobe wasn't built for the cooler temperatures of a German October. Happy for the excuse to get out of the house, I went to the nearby Mall of the Emirates. Shopping would help. For hours, I roamed the shops aimlessly, my mind constantly with my parents. Mami had been in and out of hospital, now recovering at home - but my father's voice carried a fear I'd never heard before. *"I think it's time for you to come home for a while."* They had always downplayed any illness or hidden it from me until after the fact.

But this time I knew it was bad. Really bad!

Eventually, I reminded myself: I just needed something warm. Straightforward. But due to the brain fog clouding my head, I had just wasted several hours wandering about. I had no patience to rifle through the sales racks at Debenhams, but also did not want to spend a fortune. Why am I even wasting my time shopping? Extreme times call for extreme measures. And with that, I head to Harvey Nichols.

The British luxury department store was beyond my budget but perfect for a splurge. And just now I need a little pick-me-up. I loved its elegance: the flattering lighting, the feel of cashmere and silk under my hands, as I trailed along the displays. Heading towards the sweaters in the back of the store, a black dress caught my eye. Perfect: long sleeves, fitted with a sweetheart neckline, and a soft fabric that promises to hug my body in all the right places. I didn't allow my mind to think it, but deep down I knew: this was for the funeral. Without trying it on, I grabbed it and rushed over to the register. As the clerk wrapped it in satin paper, I grew impatient, desperate to escape. Receipt in the bag, I sprinted out. All thoughts of buying winter clothes were out the window. At home, I shoved it deep into the closet, like a dirty secret. When it is time to pack for my flight, I stuffed the shopping bag straight into my suitcase; too ashamed to even acknowledge it. I knew it was perfect for many occasions, but guilt haunted me. Buying a funeral dress while my mother was alive felt like disloyalty - cold, macabre. I acted on fear instead of hope. How heartless I must have seemed.

Three weeks later, I wore it at her funeral.

Now, standing in line with my boarding pass, the dress waits in my suitcase in the plane's belly. I haven't worn it since. Now it is branded "the funeral dress." I doubt I ever will wear it again. It smells of tears.

CHAPTER 6

VIENNA 2016

Nine hours later, the taxi drops me unceremoniously in front of an oversized wooden door in Vienna's 9th district. Without leaving his seat, the driver pops the trunk, and I pull out my suitcase. The boot hasn't even closed before he speeds off, leaving me on the sidewalk, the bag at my feet. An unfriendly cold wind whips down the street and grazes my cheeks with icy hands. I find Kathrin's last name on the panel next to the door, ring, and then gaze up at the elegant 19th-century Biedermeier[14] building. The six-story façade with its pillars framing the door and the ornate pilaster on top is the center of the block, tucked neatly between corner buildings on either side. It seems only yesterday that I was here, visiting for a few days during the summer. With that memory comes the ghostly image of Kathrin

---

14 *Biedermeier architecture (1815-1848) emphasizes simplicity, comfort, and restrained classical elegance*

and I, dragging Maximilian's pram through this door, laughing, the echo of her sandals still in my ears.

The door buzzes. I push the memory aside, take a breath, and step inside. The heavy door slams shut with a metallic thud, my steps echoing in the empty hall. Rows of dark green mailboxes line the wall. Kathrin's is the second-to-last; I can see her hands as they unlock the front flap, pull out a wad of letters and brochures, and stuff them into the folded cover of the pram. Her silver bracelet twinkles, and the memory dissolves. I knew that I would see her everywhere. Her presence fills the very air I breathe.

I pull my suitcase down the gloomy hall, the rat-a-tat-tat of the wheels against the small floor tiles my only companion. The elevator clanks and shudders, groaning its way up six floors. The sound is not loud enough to drown out the memories of Kathrin's voice soothing Maxi. He'd been tired after our walk, the seams of his olive-green summer shorts stretched over the bottom, calling for a diaper change. His tiny, plump feet had been kicking in frustration, and his voice rose to a shrill screech as the elevator doors closed behind us, the sound amplified by the metal walls of the tiny cabin. Kathrin bent over him, her wavy brown hair fell in silky waves towards her son as he stretched his hands up, reaching for something to pull. Kathrin gave him her keychain as a distraction, and with a happy gurgle, he shook it, amused by the metallic clinking sound. I worried he'd drop them into the elevator shaft the second the doors opened.

As if on cue, a cold draft nips my neck as the doors slide to the side, and I step onto the small landing. My knuckles whisper against the apartment door, ignoring the metal knocker in the center, its bite too jarring for this arrival. I don't want to be here. My head turns longingly towards the elevator, just as the door slides shut. Everything looks familiar with the quality of a déjà-vu. But it feels wrong, like being sucked into a parallel universe. Memories press against me from every wall, and I haven't even stepped inside.

Shards of ice break off from my heart and fall straight into my stomach. Part of me hopes nobody answers. What do I say? ... to Uli? ... to Maxi? Oh God, Maxi. He can't even understand! He is only two - well, not even! He will be two next month. Oh God! His birthday! The far-reaching consequences of Kathrin's death and her absence from his life knock the wind out of me, and I steady myself against the doorframe.

Arschbackenzusammenkneifmentalität!!

I have to be brave for Maxi. But how, when his eyes are hers? And soon he won't even remember her.

There are footsteps approaching behind the door. Locks click. The door swings open. My breath stalls. Uli in a gray V-neck, white collar poking out, hair unkempt, dark circles under his eyes. I am not used to this disheveled version of him. He has his cell phone wedged between his chin and shoulder, and waves me inside with one hand, the other arm resting in a sling. As I step over the threshold, he throws me an apologetic smile and walks back into the depths of the apartment to continue his phone call. Before he disappears into the other room, the knot of the sling and I have a stare-down in the hallway. How can it be that Kathrin is gone and the only visible sign of the accident is a sling?

I close the door quietly, not to wake the memories. And as predicted, Kathrin is everywhere. Her jeans jacket is slung over a chair, her shoes under the radiator, the left one on its side, as if she had just stepped out for a moment.

The apartment hums with life, the opposite of the void I found at my parents' house after my mother's death. Kathrin's presence permeates the air like the scent of a perfume, and the tension I had felt on my way here slides off me like an old coat. For a moment, I pause and inhale the familiar scent only her home holds. Inexplicably, I feel comforted by the familiar pictures on the walls that greet me like old friends. The apartment embraces me, even the furniture leans in for a gentle caress when my hand trails along the polished wood of the antique sideboard on my way to the living room. Her presence is so tangible that it hugs my soul.

Maxi's little face peeks out from the living room. I rush towards him and lift him into a twirling hug, squeezing him tight as I nuzzle his neck. He still has the smell so particular to small children - not baby, not grown, but sweet and heartwarming. His little arms are wrapped around my neck, and he giggles as I smooch kisses near his ear. He wriggles free and toddles back to his playmat, eager to show me his blocks. His blond hair is longer than last time; unruly curls framing a bruise and cut on his forehead. I brush a strand aside, but he shakes it back protectively over the wound. The winter sun peers through the window, watching him before it slips below Vienna's rooftops.

I lower myself down onto the playmat and soak in the familiar surroundings. The couch cozies up against a white floor-to-ceiling bookcase, bursting from its seams. The spines of old friends are lined up in tight rows. Kathrin and I had a passionate love for fantasy novels growing up, and the black spines of the Wolfgang Hohlbein books are easily recognizable among the rest, just as they are on my bookshelf back in Dubai. My eyes travel over several books by German authors I don't recognize, and land on a series of Rita Falk books, most of which are in my collection as well. They had traveled to Dubai by mail or in suitcases, for birthdays or Christmases, and each one of them bore an inscription on the inside cover in Kathrin's handwriting. The charming stories of the cranky detective *Kommissar Franz Eberhofer,* with his heavy Bavarian accent and a passion for Southern German cuisine, are woven through the last five to six years of our friendship. We even cooked the recipes printed on the last pages of each book. Kathrin's dad is from Bavaria, which is why these stories held a special place in her heart - and in mine. In fact, as I read the books, the voice of the detective that I hear in my head sounds very much like Wolfi, Kathrin's dad. With a stab, I realize that from now on I will have to buy my own Rita Falk books. Or maybe I won't. I don't think I can read them again.

Plastic clatters. Maxi upends his red Fisher-Price sorting bucket, pieces tumbling across the mat in front of him. *"Nochmal!*[15]*"* his big eyes look up at me, eyebrows raised in an invitation, no, a demand to join him. How can I resist? The sorting bucket feels like an heirloom. I had one growing up, the girls had one, and I had gifted this one to him a year ago. The sound the pieces make as they fall through the lid takes me right back to when Gia and Giulia were small.

"Hey, sorry about this. I had to arrange the flower delivery for the cemetery." Uli says, dropping the phone on the table. We embrace in silence, longer than usual. His shoulders shake, and I blink my tears away until we part.

Despite the grief, it soothes my soul to be here, and for the first time since the phone call, I can feel myself relax. Whenever grief rises, I look at Maxi. His innocence is heartbreaking and healing at once. He pulls me out of sorrow, into the small world of blocks and toy cars. His curls, flushed cheeks, sparkling eyes - they tether me to life, if only for moments.

The metal door knocker announces new arrivals. With a solid draft of cold air and the smell of the outside, Kathrin's parents, Bärbel and Wolfi, step in. I hear muffled voices in the hallway as they shrug out of layers of coats and scarves. Instead of draping them over Kathrin's on the chair, they make the extra effort of hanging them in the mirrored closet. The hallway light flicks on against the settling shadows of dusk, and the warm light spills the paper-cut silhouettes of Maxi's grandparents into the living room. Bärbel's perfume is a step ahead of her and embraces me in a whirl of childhood memories. Seeing them is breaking me open all over again. Their

---

15 *Nochmal - German. Again. Children's favorite word, especially when trying to get adults to repeat a game.*

clothes do their best to hold them upright, but they look sunken. It is not so much the weight loss that strikes me, even though that is substantial in itself. No, rather it is a loss of substance, of density. They seem translucent, as if flickering between two realities.

With a thud, Bärbel's handbag drops to the floor. The loss we share has its own gravitational pull, drawing us together in a long and tearful embrace.

My lifelong friendship with Kathrin has welded us into a constellation that includes both of our families. We orbit around each other, drifting closer and closer over the years. My relationship with Bärbel had deepened since my mother's death, as we moved from simple European cheek-kisses as a greeting to longer, heartfelt hugs that carried deeper meaning. Now, when I hug her, it feels like I am hugging Kathrin, a part of her at least. And I am sure she finds the same connection in me, as we stand now in the middle of the apartment, clinging to each other.

Wolfi shifts his weight from one foot to the other and pats my shoulder instead of joining in the hug. His eyes barely touch mine, too afraid to rest on anything that reminds him of Kathrin. He clears the emotions out of his throat and turns to Maximilian, who lifts a book to his grandfather. "Oh, what do you have there?" Wolfi's voice breaks and crumbles over the open pages, but Maxi doesn't notice. His smile is wide, eyes bright: "Opa, read?"

The rest of the day, we are pulled along a conveyor belt of funeral preparations, not really knowing what to do but grabbing onto anything that keeps our hands and minds busy. The last time we all organized like this was Kathrin and Uli's wedding eight years ago. I remember folding programs at this same table with Kathrin, a glass of Crémant in hand. Now I fold funeral programs with her photo smiling up at me. The comparison slices a papercut across my heart.

With one last gentle caress over Kathrin's photo, I finish folding the programs and wedge myself between a firetruck and the sorting bucket onto the floor. Maxi climbs into my lap and snuggles into me. With focused dexterity, he fishes a Cheerio out of his snack cup and sticks it in his mouth. Our eyes meet, and he pauses, the Cheerio on his tongue. Then he changes his mind, pulls it out, and pushes the soggy ring between my lips. "Thank you!" I grin. Shared soggy cereal are a toddler's expression of love. He chews a few more, then looks up.

"Where is Mama?"

Reality crashes down on me, leaving me like a wreck along the sound barrier of the highway. My thoughts weave around the crushed metal, trying to find a way out. There are no words. How do you explain to a two-year-old that his mother isn't coming back? Did Uli even tell him yet?

"Mama?" Maxi insists, eyes scanning the room.
Silence spreads.
Movements cease.

Uli exhales, steps forward, and lifts Maxi into his arms. "Mama is in heaven now," his voice breaking. "We talked about this, remember?" Too abstract for him to grasp, Maxi shrugs his little shoulders, content in the belief that she will be back. With sticky fingers, he stuffs more Cheerios in his mouth and grins at the circle of silent faces.

In the morning, the milky haze of the winter sun slides across my pillow, and I roll toward its cool touch, snuggling deeper into the duvet. I had left the guestroom window ajar overnight, and for a few oblivious moments, I relish the oxygen rich air that fills my lungs. Its breath is heavy with fog. *"Spatzel[16], you up?"* Kathrin's voice echoes from my last visit up the stairs, and without thinking, I reply, "I'm up. Be down in a second." I throw my blanket off and follow my feet to the door. Downstairs, the blinds are drawn, nothing stirs. I pause and frown. The silent apartment holds its breath in shock as reality hits us both at once.

It is the morning of my best friend's funeral.

Minutes later, life stirs against all odds, and Maxi's laughter races up the stairs, giving me permission to go down into the kitchen to make a coffee. "Can you make me one too?" Uli asks, poking his tired head through the door. His PJ shirt looks worn, and the fabric is stretched from the fight with the bandaged arm in its sling. The sling gives me a sideways look.

"Sure. What about Maxi?" "Bottle's done. Can you make him a bread with jam, cut into small bites?" He retreats towards Maxi's voice, "Papa! Paaaapaaaa," and, from halfway down the corridor, he adds, "The coffee capsules are in the cabinet on the right. Jam is in the fridge."

I feel like an intruder in Kathrin's kitchen. I hesitate to open too many drawers or cabinets as if I were disturbing sacred ground. On the counter, a notepad reads DO NOT FORGET, beneath it a list in her handwriting: bread, diapers, sparkling water, grapes. I trace the letters with my finger.

Time accelerates as the hour of the funeral draws closer. Uli and I swap child duties back and forth, dressing and feeding Maxi, so that we can each take turns in the bathroom to get showered and dressed. Neither one of us doing a great job - Uli, handicapped by an ill-tempered sling, and me by the inability to adjust to this new dynamic.

---

16   *Spatzel - German (dialect). Name of endearment, literally translates to "little sparrow."*

In the bathroom, Kathrin's make-up still lines the sink, her jewelry in a little ceramic dish. I see her in the mirror, as she carefully picks out the thick white gold ring and swipes it on her finger, before stretching out her hand to examine the effect the sparkling metal has on her hand. I know those hands so well. The shape of her long, slender fingers, the way her thumb nail is a bit less curved than the rest of her nails, and the tiny freckle next to her nailbed. Her wrist, small and delicate, with the Nominations bracelet I gave her when we were nineteen. I look down on my own wrist, where the same stainless steel link bracelet has been sitting for over 20 years now. Her hands are the only thing of substance I can recall. I see them on Maxi's jacket, as she fixes his collar, on her favorite gray flower teacup in the kitchen, grabbing her keys from the plate in the entrance hall - her hands are everywhere. I can see her face too, but it appears unexpectedly, like a reflection in the mirror or the snippet of a memory with the fleeting quality of a Déjà-vu. But when I try to summon it, her image frays and dissolves before I can get a good look. I am terrified to be losing that much of her so quickly!

In the guestroom, closets line the walls. I slide open the mirrored door, lean into her blouses and jackets, breathing deeply. All I want is to bury myself in them, one more hug. With a sigh, I close the door - and face my reflection.

I'm in the black dress from my mother's funeral. Black stockings. A touch of foundation. Bare feet. I rummage through my suitcase to confirm what I already know: in my hurry to pack, I had forgotten to bring shoes other than the white sneakers I was wearing on the flight.

Without any other options, I turn towards Kathrin's overflowing shoe closet. We always shared shoes, but now I pause and bite my lower lip. The cold air has made my lips chapped, and the skin cracks under the pressure. The pain feels good. In its sudden intensity, it overrides the grief for a moment. The taste of iron stings my tongue.

I pull out a pair of black, knee-high boots - the very pair Kathrin lent me for my mother's funeral. In Dubai, I had no use for boots, least of all high boots, which were one of Kathrin's obsessions. I count at least six pairs of varying colors and leathers piled in the closet in front of me, their shafts bent and wilted against one another, yearning for feet to carry them, to give them life and purpose. I slip the boots on my feet and straighten up to look again at my reflection in the mirror. Walking in her shoes today gives me comfort. They carry me. Literally and figuratively. To finish, I swipe on my hot pink lipstick, pull the sunglasses down from my hair, and study myself in the mirror. My armor is complete.

"What do you think?" I say to the empty room, hoping she hears. "Ok!" I whisper, glancing down at the 'Together 100' bracelet on my wrist. "Let's do this!"

The sun is a pale white disk behind a veil of fog as I step out of the chapel, suspended between small clusters of mourners near the ornate wooden doors. Even the clouds hang low today, occasionally shaking off sprinkles of rain. A cold wind plays with the treetops and rushes down to lift the coattails of the cemetery worker ahead, his black scarf saluting briefly before settling again. I slip my arm into my dad's as we descend the stone steps. Kathrin's shoes hesitate, the heels foreign under my feet. Walking with him through this grief feels wrong - too sharp a reminder of my mother's funeral. Today's grief deserves its own space.

We follow the urn along a damp gravel path lined with trees, sculptures, and mausoleums. Weeping angels peek out from a blanket of moss; imposing black tombstones etched with names and photos of the dead hold flickering lights. In its stillness, the cemetery carries itself with the formality and precision of an imperial park with tree-lined alleys, flower beds tucked in for winter, and the imposing Art Nouveau architecture of the main church and surrounding chapels. Bare branches of ancient trees claw the sky like upside-down roots, while evergreens stand in defiance of winter. I pull my coat higher, wishing for a scarf to block the cold settling into my bones.

At the forest's edge, the small bamboo urn will be sunk under a blanket of earth and leaves. No stone or cross, not even a path, just a tree grave.

My breath forms white clouds in front of my face, a cold reminder that there is still life ... somewhere. From the safety of my sunglasses, I scan the faces of her family and friends and feel detached, as if watching a movie. Her parents are shadows of themselves. Her brother distracts himself by fussing over his seven-year-old son, who is complaining about his itchy scarf. How I miss Andrea and my girls. They are back in Dubai - not because I wanted to shield them from this, but because I need to face it alone. I need to feel this alone. I owe Kathrin my full presence - every shattered piece of me.

The crunch of gravel under the soles of my boots is unnaturally loud in my ears: crunch, thud, crunch, thud. A soft, moldy leaf sticks under my foot, its broken stem trailing. Above us, mistletoe hangs in filigree rounds of silvery green in a stoic, black network of branches. Kathrin loved mistletoe, which must be why we are all carrying tiny bouquets of it tied with a red ribbon. I cannot recall who gave it to me, but there is a little army of mistletoe bouquets holding the hands of every mourner here. They lead us forward to a tree with an inconspicuous hole at its base. No flowers, no candles, no picture propped up on an easel. Nothing but the majestic presence of a family of trees standing guard next to a little hole. How can this be her final resting place?

I can't look at the urn or the tears. Instead, I seize every tiny distraction I can find: I notice every rock and every plant around me, the cold smell of earth and moldy leaves, the crisp air, the gentle fall of a solitary leaf through the branches, swaying in the breeze before settling on the ground in front of me. It is yellow, with brown edges and a fragile-looking web of veins and arteries connecting papery tissues of dried chlorophyll. Soon it will disintegrate and provide nourishment to the trees and plants around it, becoming one with nature once again, in its final moments, providing for the continuation of life, just like …

… the urn.

The cemetery workers lower it into the ground. Their blank professionalism jars against the grief carved into every face. Cold creeps from my bones into my stomach. One by one, the mourners drop mistletoe into the hole, shoulders heaving in silence, arms locking for support. My fingers cling to the small bunch of mistletoe twigs, and I hold it tight to my chest, unwilling to let go. *I am not leaving you here. Not in this cold ground.* I am not sure whether I am speaking to her or myself. Still, I follow my dad and the others away, bouquet and ribbon clenched in my hand.

By evening, the tide of family and friends recedes back to their respective homes. Their voices, shared stories, and even laughter echo in my ears long past Maxi's bedtime, long past the muted goodnight with Uli as we retreat into our separate shadows. I am glad for the extra two days I get to spend here, the one place where I can pretend; pretend she is just running errands; pretend that I can still hear her laughter; pretend our 'Together 100' promise still holds.

CHAPTER 7

DUBAI 2016

I don't know if it was the exhaustion from the funeral or Kathrin's presence still lingering in her apartment, but in Vienna, I dipped into sleep like a warm bath each night. Back in Dubai, the pretense collapses. Her absence sinks its claws into my back, and insomnia stretches the hours as I toss and turn. The glow of the projector clock mocks me, its numbers melting into grimaces that remind me time stands still at night. At 5 am I roll out of bed, unslept hours hanging off me like dead weight. I close the bathroom door before turning on the light, so as not to wake up Andrea, who still has an hour and a half before the new day coaxes him out of bed.

The lights above the mirror take a moment to brighten to their full honest glare, exposing every flaw: every wrinkle, every pore, every inch of soft, listless skin. I've lost more than my best friend; I've lost years. They slipped off my face in the blink of an eye. Maybe this is just me wearing the insides of my soul on the outside, like a mask. A sad, tired-looking mask that feels too real to be a cover-up. This is what happens when the one person who knows you best dies: You age instantly!

Kathrin had been my constant companion through first crushes, heartbreaks, long summers, and winters with *Glühwein*[17] and waffles. Now her memories of me have died with her. When she looked at me, she saw the child, the teenager, the mother. She saw the silly, the serious, the drunk, the adventurous, the heartbroken, the sick, the successful, the scared, the free - an entire time-lapse fused into one person. Without her, that version of me is gone.

What is left?

A woman in her early forties. Blonde hair of her childhood long gone. Instead, she wears her hair short; dark auburn strands stick up on the back of her head from a sleepless night. Blue eyes are a deep, watery gray, desaturated like the rest of her. Her shoulders droop, washcloth in hand, as she stares at the face in front of her, trying to reconcile that reflection with who she thought she was. She clings to a past that has slipped away.

I used to be under the beautiful delusion that most people my age looked a lot older than I did. HA! - I bet everyone else feels the same way! The hours spent in the gym and teaching classes were showing results. I was proud of what I achieved when I looked in the mirror. I never felt a day older than 35, silly and immature at times, and definitely not dressing my age - whatever that is anyway. There used to be a sparkle in my eyes that transformed the fine wrinkles at the corners into nothing by laugh lines -witnesses of the happy times in my life. I even tried to force them as a child.

I was twelve or thirteen years old on the bus home from school. My backpack, heavy with books, my blonde hair cropped into a

---

17 Glühwein - German. Mulled, hot wine, a staple at every Christmas Market.

straight bob, and the rain had curled a few frizzy locks near my temple, which refused to be tucked behind my ears. Across from me sat an older woman, probably late seventies but ancient to me. A scratchy sweater-vest poked from her plastic raincoat; shopping bags clutched like weapons. She radiated a gravity that pulled everything down - deep lines dragging her mouth into shadow, a sour musty smell of age cloaking her. In that moment I swore: Do not let life carve those lines onto your face! For days, I walked around smiling - on the bus, at dinner, brushing my teeth - until my cheeks hurt. I smiled even in bed until sleep pried my jaw open. I wanted laugh lines, not scowls. Of course, it didn't last. My skin was too young to crease.

As I stand in front of the mirror now, I think about the old lady again. Maybe in my youthful ignorance, I was too quick to judge her. My eyes wander over the landscape of my own face, as I discover new lines, new shadows, and valleys that are alien to me. The accident was an earthquake, cracking my soul and leaving my outsides visibly altered. With a sigh, I reach for the eye cream, which holds the promise of stopping time. If only it were that easy.

The following Saturday, I pull my white Tahoe into the unpaved parking lot of a villa near the beach. Sand clouds boil up behind me, and I turn off the engine, waiting until the dust settles, before stepping out. Desert sand, even this far into the city, has the viscosity of water, and I am grateful for my high-top sneakers, which keep the powdery grains off my feet. A luscious canopy of pink bougainvillea hugs the wall surrounding the property, and a harmony of wind-chimes rings beyond. I've never been here before, and for a moment, my hand hovers between the bell and the gate, unsure which one to push first.

I could leave. I don't have to be here. I don't know anyone inside, and the 500 *dirham*[18] I paid to be here is isn't enough to make a departure painful.

But Liv' told me to come. She's the only one who gets close to understanding how I feel. I can't tell if this is grief that I am going through or if I have graduated into a depression; they feel the same. In hindsight, it surprises me that I never once considered a support group or therapist. Instead, I bottle it up.

Arschbackenzusammenkneifmentalität.

Livia knows. She is still working through losing her husband. She sees behind the bright pink funeral lipstick I now hide behind every day. I don't want to be among people. I can't stand my own company, so how can I impose it on anyone else? Even my shoulder critic triggers me now. And I try to avoid triggers. The unpredictable nature of grief means that everything can be a trigger. So, I avoid everything: people, conversations; bars because there is music; the radio for the same reason; but most importantly, I avoid talking to Andrea. How much more grief can my husband witness? I have lost so much of myself that I am scared of losing his patience as well. I do not know if this fear is real or just snatched out of the debris my life has been spiraling into.

Today, my shoulder critic has come along, probably to prove a point. He's been in my ear all day about what a stupid idea this is. Despite the warm temperatures, he wears a brown '80s velvet tracksuit with rainbow stripes along the chest and yellow Converse. I really don't know how he comes up with his outfits.

I press the sun-bleached bell. Nine out of ten doorbells in Dubai are useless; the sun gnaws everything plastic, rubber, or fabric. I tilt

---

18   *Dirham - Arabic. Currency of the UAE, subdivided into 100 fils.*

my head, listening for a chime. "Nobody home," my critic mutters, turning on his heel.

It feels strange to be here, actually doing something. Since returning from Vienna, I've been doing "things" - or so I want people to believe. In truth, nothing gets done. When the kids are at school and Andrea is at the office, my shoulder critic and I sink into a stupor in front of the TV, hours gliding by. When someone's home, I run a hamster wheel, making a big racket and a show of how busy I am without getting anywhere. Too busy for friends, too busy for the gym, too tired to eat dinner with Andrea - because dinner means talking. And I have nothing left to say. Four years of describing loss have exhausted all my words. I feel empty, needy, scared of losing him. My life is careening into a dark spiral.

I look up and down the road and towards the other five or six cars parked nearby. Nobody is coming. No sound from within the walls apart from the windchime, so I ring again.

By now, my grief and insomnia have taken on a life of their own. I'm a raw, open blister with no words, no tools, no belief system to help me. Alcohol and cigarettes only accelerate the fall. Livia had mentioned Sandra to me several times, but I never reacted. I can't meet new people, I feel too tired to explain my pain. If it hadn't been for Livia sending a WhatsApp group message to Sandra and me, I wouldn't be here. I would have found a million excuses. But she nailed me down and signed me up for a guided group meditation with Sandra - some breathwork-thing. Sounds fancy, and I have no idea what it is, but it has the word "work" in it, so I am already exhausted. Yet here I am.

I give up on the doorbell and push the metal gate. It swings open with a desert-worn squeak onto a lush carpet of grass and a paved path curving towards the villa. I pass a bright yellow tasseled umbrella shading a cluster of cushions. A water fountain gurgles among dwarf palms, rose petals bobbing on the surface. My critic jumps off my shoulder. "That's as far as I go - I'll stay here. This is niiiiice!" He pulls a newspaper out of thin air, plops himself in the middle of a cushion, and peers over his yellow-rimmed glasses. "You know this meditation bullshit is not for me." He leans back. "But you do you, hon'." With that, he props up one leg, crosses his ankle over his knee, and unfolds the paper.

The carved wooden doors to the main house stand open. I step into a cool, marble-clad entrance hall with a Balinese vibe: fabric wall hangings, bowls filled with crystals on a low glass table. A woman, dressed in white, floats towards me. "Hello, darling! You must be Alex!" Her voice is airy, tinged with a warm Spanish accent. She pulls me into a brief hug and introduces herself as Sandra. Her eyes are bright and welcoming, her long brown hair tumbles over her shoulder as she turns and motions for me to follow her.

I don't know anything about meditation. Never tried it. Don't understand how it's supposed to help with grief. Livia has tried all sorts of spiritual things. Some I could relate to, others not so much. Meditation is one of those. I don't want to be alone with my thoughts. Distraction is the only thing that keeps them from spinning into an abyss.

Despite the warmth outside, the room is cool and dimly lit. Ten yoga mats form a circle, each with a pillow and a soft blanket. Salt lamps and candles cast an amber light. Incense and the scent of essential oils hang in the air. I choose a mat and sit down on it, taking in my surroundings. I'm early, as Germans often tend to be. My mother used to say, "Five minutes early is on time and on time is late." Punctuality is in my DNA.

I feel shy and out of place, as meditators trickle into the room, greeting Sandra with hugs. I take a sip of water and watch them over the rim of my bottle: a guy in his thirties with a scraggly beard, hair in a knot, harem pants and a green muscle shirt exposing a hairy chest and a long bead necklace; two young women in yoga outfits; an older lady with shaved gray hair and a flowing dress, countless bangles jangling on her delicate wrists. I toy with the idea of leaving, but by now I have people sitting to my left and right and feel too self-conscious to get up.

Sandra takes a cross-legged seat in the center and begins. Her soothing voice weaves unfamiliar terms such as "Holotropic Breathwork" and "altered states of consciousness" into her explanation with such ease that my cluelessness does not make me uncomfortable. The whole experience will last up to three hours.

THREE HOURS! I had no idea!
Shit!

Talk about jumping into the deep end. I don't think I am prepared to go from zero to THREE HOURS in one sitting! But getting up now is out of the question.

Oh well, I guess I will have to give it a try.

"All right, my lovelies." Sandra continues. "This is how it will work: you'll lie down on your mats and get comfortable. We'll start with a few minutes of guided meditation, then turn our attention to the breath. We will breathe very fast in and out - basically hyperventilate for one hour!"

ONE HOUR! I am hyperventilating just thinking about this! How on earth am I supposed to do that? I am going to faint!

"Don't be scared," she adds. "It sounds like a lot, but it passes quickly. Breathing fast changes the carbon dioxide oxygen balance in your bodies, allowing for deep emotional release."

I glance around wide-eyed. Am I the only one freaking out? I hear a faint voice from the garden outside: "Told ya so!" My shoulder critic again. Nervous energy builds up inside of me, seeking release. My fingers fiddle with the "Together-100"-bracelet on my wrist, but as soon as I become aware of it, I drop my hands in my lap. This bracelet is too precious to be a fidget toy.

"After the first hour, we return to a normal breath and I'll guide you into one hour of silent meditation to integrate whatever the breathwork has brought up. In the end, if you feel called, you can share."

I should have looked up breathwork before signing up for this crap. Sandra adds a disclaimer: "Do not be alarmed if people scream or laugh. That's just their way of releasing trauma. Just keep your eyes closed and focus on your own breath. If you struggle, I'll sense it and come to you."

Sense it? Does she sense my panic now? My palms sweat, and I wipe them on my leggings. Before we start, Sandra asks each of us to state our intention in one word. Does "just getting through this" count? I pause and take a deep breath. I'm grateful to be second-to-last, which gives me time to come up with something that rings true. My fellow meditators answer things like "closure," "insight," "enlightenment," "connection to spirit" - all things that are intangible and far removed from my reality. My hands are still sweaty with anxiety, and I am wracking my brain for an answer.

When it's finally my turn, the word "acceptance" falls from my lips and lands in the middle of our circle with a loud thud. Out of nowhere, a torrent of tears is unleashed. Until now, I've been too nervous to even think about Kathrin, but confronted with my real intention, I lose it.

A kind woman across from me points to a box of tissues in the center of our circle. I hadn't noticed it before, but apparently, tissues would be needed during this kind of meditation. Nobody seems uncomfortable with my outburst. Nobody rushes to comfort me, nobody offers platitudes. They just sit, warmth and acceptance radiating from their smiles. Some place their hand on their heart; others hold their palms to their chest as if in prayer. And then it is somebody else's turn.

Shortly after, the meditation starts with soft music. I lie down and cover my eyes with a soft fabric mask that Livia had reminded me to bring. Bodies rustle under blankets, throats clear, deep sighs as everyone settles. Sandra's voice guides us towards a place of deep relaxation. I lose track of time as I drift into what feels like sleep while being awake. Once fully relaxed, she instructs us to accelerate our breath until we're all huffing and puffing in unison. I am not sure how this is meditative, as I am completely in my head. Am I doing this right? Wait, I think I have to go faster. The woman next to me breathes louder. Is that how I have to do it? I cannot match her rhythm, though. My hands and feet tingle, and I have the urge to move and wriggle my body. The sheer act of breathing occupies me so completely that I have no time to think of Kathrin or grief. My mouth goes dry, and I fall out of rhythm a few more times, but somehow it gets easier as time goes on. Does time go on? I am not sure how long I have been doing this now. Five minutes? Ten? Thirty? There is no way to know.

A whimper on my right turns into sobs, then fades. I keep my eyes closed, waiting for some magical moment. I am not sure what I am expecting, but there is nothing. Just the constant in and out of breath and the awareness of the people around me. Am I too much in my own head? Too self-conscious? Am I doing it wrong? A loud scream yanks my eyes open under the eye mask. A man on the other side must be having one hell of a trip. He screams and groans, making my skin crawl.

Oh my God! I hope this is safe. Breathe, Alex. Breathe.

The screams ebb away, and the room is once again filled only with Sandra's soothing voice, gentle music, and the huffing and puffing of our breath. Now I understand why it is called breath"*work*." I'm exhausted.

After what feels like an eternity, Sandra guides us back to normal breathing. Relief floods me. A deep sigh escapes my chest as I stretch my arms and legs. The music takes me on a gentle journey, and finally, I can think about something besides breathing. Too bad this experience has not worked for me. I have not had any enlightening revelations, visions, or otherwise deeper understanding of anything, except for the realization that meditation is not for me. Again, I can hear my shoulder critic's voice from the garden, "Told ya so! Should've spent those 500 dirhams on a massage."

Acceptance clearly wasn't granted to me. At that thought, quiet tears soak my eye mask.

Why did I even hope for relief through this nonsense? What did I expect? Kathrin is gone, and I'll have to figure out how to accept it on my own somehow.

At that moment, I feel Sandra behind me. Her hands hover over my head, her fingertips barely grazing my hair, tickling my scalp with the lightness of a feather. She was right - she knew when I needed her. I don't know what exactly she does, but suddenly a warm wave washes over me. It feels like a day at the beach, like croissants fresh from the oven ... it feels like ... love. My tears stop instantly as I float in an ocean of acceptance.

It's ok. I'm ok. Yes, Kathrin is gone, but it's ok!

The heaviness of these past days spills out of me like sand from an hourglass, and gratitude fills my heart. Sandra has opened the gates to acceptance. It's pure magic. I want to thank her, so with my eyes still covered, I reach up to touch her hand. There is nothing. I wave into the air where I can still *feel* her hands hovering, but ... empty space. Confused, I pull off the mask and glance behind me ... nothing! Sandra is sitting next to someone else, her head bowed in meditation, unaware of what had happened.

I settle back into my mat. What had just happened? I *know* I felt those hands. I could even distinguish every single finger. My mind races, then gradually the music, incense, and quiet breathing lull me back into letting go. My muscles relax, my shoulders sink into the mat, and ... there it is again! Hands hover over my head, an inch or so from my scalp. Occasionally, they brush over strands of hair. I hone in with laser focus. Yes, no mistaking it. Two hands cradle my head, and with them comes the same flood of love and acceptance, washing everything else away. Sadness and grief are drowned out.

But again, when I peel up the mask to check - nothing. The space behind me is empty. Only the inner peace remains.

Sandra moves from person to person, whispering: "Time to come back." One by one, people stir, stretch, and sit up. Everyone looks disheveled but deeply relaxed and at peace. Some begin to share their experiences, relating fantastical stories of visions and revelations, insights and explanations for the sobbing and screaming I had heard. When it's my turn, I hesitate. I sit here a different person than I was two hours ago - at ease, swaddled in warmth and love. When I describe what happened, I am met with knowing smiles. These strangers, who seemed so eccentric an hour ago, now feel like equals. We've traveled the same path. As I leave, Sandra hugs me like an old friend, and I feel kinship and gratitude.

I collect my shoulder critic on the way out. He's sitting on the edge of the fountain, pants rolled up and feet dangling in the water. The velvet jacket is gone, and he's down to a white ribbed undershirt. His feet are cool and wet as he jumps back on my shoulder. "Hmm," he mutters over his glasses. "I wonder how you're gonna explain *that* to Andrea."

For once, I agree with him.

The early evening sun stretches the shadows of the tall palm trees across the street to our house. The moment I open the door, our Retriever-mix Dante runs on bouncy puppy legs towards me, closely followed by the intoxicating smell of sauteed garlic, onions, and tomatoes. Andrea and the kids are having dinner, and my stomach wakes up with a roar. I am starving. My appetite has been nonexistent these past weeks, but the smell of Andrea's cooking revives me until my stomach grumbles loud enough to make the girls giggle. "I don't need to ask if you are hungry," Andrea grins, heading for the kitchen. "Be generous!" I call after him. I kiss the girls' heads and let their chatter wash over me like fresh spring water. Andrea returns with a nest of spaghetti crowned by basil leaves - the fresh scent dances with the umami aroma of the tomatoes and garlic, and my mouth waters.

With a flourish, he holds up the Parmigiano grater. "Say when."
"When." I finally give my husband the first genuine smile in weeks
before digging in. Between bites, I start to tell my story, but Giulia
interrupts after only a few sentences. "Mami, look what I can do!"
She forks a few spaghetti into her mouth, lets them dangle past her
chin, then twists her ears like knobs until the noodles disappear into
her mouth. We all laugh, and Giulia beams with pride. I try to continue, but Gia cuts in: "Why did the guy scream, Mami?"

"Good question, bella! I have no idea."

"Maybe he saw a bee," she shrugs. "I get scared of bees, too."

The thread of my story slips between the spaghetti and I twirl it
onto my fork. I am not surprised - I lost them at the word *meditation*. Andrea just mutters "hmmm," his attention on his second plate
of pasta. My excitement deflates but stabilizes when I realize that
despite the bizarre events, I got what I asked for. I felt the acceptance
then, and it still lingers within. Thinking of Kathrin now does not
throw me into a tailspin. The pain is still immense, but I don't fight
it anymore.

The real surprise comes the next morning. I wake up, realizing
that I've slept like a stone all night! ... and every night since. My
insomnia is gone. I'd forgotten how amazing sleep is, how energized
I feel even without coffee. The grief is still real and sometimes overwhelming, but sleep is what I live for now. Everything in between is
just what I need to get through.

They say, "Time heals all wounds." Well, time needs to pass a little
quicker!

The profound trauma of four losses has left my reality altered.
The solid ground I built my life on feels spongy. Nothing was real,
and everything was real. The line between what I know for a fact
and what I hope for is blurred. All I longed for was certainty. But

everything needed reshuffling - my sense of self, my belief system, my friendships, ... everything.

I pull a bunch of fresh mint from the fridge and wash the fragrant leaves. The kettle clicks off, steam curling from the spout. Mona is arriving shortly, and tingles of nervous excitement prickle through me. Weeks after my return from Vienna, she texted and accepted my invite for tea with "I shall come and see you, *inshallah*." In Arabic culture, time and reliability sit in the hands of Allah. The addition of *inshallah*, "God willing," to any plans keeps the door open to delays and cancellations, and there is not much I can do about it. God willing, Mona will come. *Inshallah* challenges my need for punctuality and forces my German DNA to loosen its tight grip into an Arabic understanding of time.

I pile the mint and a generous heaping of brown sugar into the round-bellied glass teapot and pour the boiling water over it. The tea isn't the real reason for our meeting; rather, it is the sense of an unfinished conversation. Since our brief meeting at the Book Salon, I've been aching for a continuation of our talk. In those short moments when we met, I had felt understood and seen for the first time since the accident. She simply knew. And more importantly, she seemed to connect to Kathrin in a way that was more tangible and vivid than whatever I was left with.

I set the teapot, matching gold-rimmed glasses and a bowl of nuts onto a tray and carry it out of the kitchen. Dante raises his head from his bed next to the couch, and his tail thumps the cushion. I pass Kathrin's photo on the sideboard. The single lamp halos her wedding day smile. I smile back and want to say, "Talk to you in a bit," but swallow it.

Since Kathrin's death, my world has been divided into BEFORE the accident and AFTER the accident. Everything - my life, my memories, my kids' milestones - falls on one side or the other. Every memory of her happened BEFORE. And that realization hurts! Every time!

Except for three. There are three memories of her that I now carry in my heart that are different. They are from AFTER; a lifeline cast down towards me from wherever she is right now: the memory of feeling Kathrin in my car the day I got the phone call, the memory of Mona telling me that she was right there next to me, and then the hands on my head flooding me with acceptance. Those are memories made after. And even though they are not based on physical experiences, they are more real, more vivid to me than the years of fading memories stored in the depth of my brain.

How crazy is that?

I am hoping Mona's visit will spark more "after-memories." Some wild part of me thinks it's the only way to make new memories with Kathrin. That hope ignites the nerves fluttering in my stomach as I open the door to the terrace and step into the silky evening air.

Unlike most villas in our neighborhood, which boast the rather excessive style - or lack thereof - of their Emirati owners, our house was built by a Moroccan architect. Its stark simplicity is stunning with thick walls in a red, sandy finish and open arches inside and out. Depending on the time of day, our home glows in various shades of desert colors. Tonight it rests in the glow of spotlights hidden behind arches and palm trees, creating a geometric mosaic of light and dark set against a velvet sky.

Our *Majlis*[19] room is a separate little building at the back of the garden with a domed ceiling and a large, filigree Moroccan chandelier. Despite its beauty, we rarely use this part of our home, so the lantern now shelters a few large geckos who keep the ants and mosquitos at bay. Built-in stone benches along the walls wear seating

---

19   *In Arab culture, a Majlis is a sitting room used to receive guests, traditionally used by men only, while the women gather in other parts of the house, while socializing amongst their girlfriends.*

cushions in the traditional black, red, and white woven Bedouin fabric, matching the dormant Shishas and Arabic tea lights. I set the tray down, arrange the teapot, glasses, and nuts on a brass table and light the candles. Sweet mint warms the air. I close the door behind me and walk back into the house, turning back just before I reach the door to the living room. Nestled in the garden's dark folds, the Majlis glows with a quiet, mysterious sparkle.

The call to the *Isha* prayer, the second prayer after sunset, still lingers in the air when the sonorous gong of our doorbell rings through the house. I open the gate to a figure haloed in a billowing stream of cream and orange silks. Her big smile and sparkling eyes are the only fixed points as the fabric ebbs and flows like liquid. We melt into a long embrace, sharing the same space in a silence that is unusually comfortable for two people who barely know each other. We drift on a few welcoming phrases along the path to the Majlis, where we settle into the seating cushions, legs tucked under, shoes by the door. I feel immediately at ease, enveloped in a sense of familiarity. Her warm, inviting aura is more palpable than the aroma of the tea spiraling in lazy wisps of steam from the pot. The folds of fabric settle around her like wings. We fall into an easy conversation, mostly about her background, her work, and our common friend Livia. With each breath, my shoulders drop; tension unwinds. The tinted floor-to-ceiling windows of the Majlis cocoon us from everything outside, suspending us in a warm bubble, detached from sadness, grief, and expectation.

I pour two glasses of mint tea and savor the first sweet sip on my lips. Mona slips off a beaded bracelet and idly clicks the rose quartz against her fingers. Without breaking the rhythm of conversation, she places the heavy strand in my palm, the beads cool on my skin. In theory, we are still strangers, yet there is an unspoken connection. My fingers play with the bracelet, picking up where Mona left off.

Hearing about her life, her Pakistani heritage, and her work here in the UAE is fascinating. I'd never considered mediums existing within the boundaries of the Islamic faith, where mediumship is considered *haram*[20]. Even though the UAE is quite tolerant towards other religions - Dubai even hosts several churches and temples - I just never thought that there would be a place for such an unconventional spiritual practice. Had it not been for Livia's rather insistent introduction, I would probably not have initiated a visit with a medium or psychic by myself. Mona explains that her "gift" is not something she can openly talk about, or even practice professionally. She was born with it but only recently learned to accept and practice it. The fact that she is basically an "undercover medium" makes our meeting even more serendipitous. It's funny: in daily life she hides this part, but here she can be fully herself - **even the parts Islam won't hold. I get it. With her, I can be wholly myself too - the BEFORE and AFTER wrapped into one new me.

At last, our conversation slips into a natural break, where silence stretches between us like the soothing warm waters of the Gulf. Her last sentence about her family hangs in the air like a cliffhanger, drifting further away in time and importance as the silence expands. The stillness naturally draws my focus to my breath, which comes in gentle, deep waves. The clicking of the beads slows and subsides. My heart wavers between relaxing and bracing for what is to come. Mona takes my hands into hers. They feel soft and smooth, warm to the touch, henna shadows along her fingers.

"She is ready to talk to you."

Eyes closed, she begins. "She is right next to you, her hand on your heart."

I feel the rough fabric of the seating cushions under my legs and bare feet. Heat blooms from my chest and slams against my skin, sending cold shivers racing outward. The air on my left grows dense;

---

20   *Haram means forbidden by Islamic law*

goosebumps prickle that side. I can feel her - not physically, but unmistakably - deep within.

"She is always with you, she tells me." Mona's voice shifts now that she is relaying these messages. It has a deeper timbre, and there is a smile playing around the edges of her mouth. "It hurts her to see you in so much pain, but you need to remember that she is always here."

So far, this is nothing that I don't already know; nothing I need a medium to tell me. Yes, it feels good to hear those words, to hear a confirmation of my own belief that the soul continues after death and connects us beyond the physical. But anyone could have said that - if it wasn't for the fact that the air in the room has changed. And what Mona says next is something only Kathrin and I know, and is all the validation I need:

"I think she shows me a bracelet." Mona's eyes are still closed.

"It was a gift, wasn't it?"

My heart thumps against my ribcage.

"And something about a promise, and that you should stop worrying about the promise being broken. It isn't."

The bracelet! My fingers find the small silver plaque on its string hidden under my sleeve, a giggle and a sob racing each other up my throat.

"You need to understand," Mona continues, "she's liberated from body's restrictions; her spirit is free to be with the people she loves - anytime, all the time."

Goosebumps roll through me as relief washes over me like a physical sensation. My left shoulder tingles.

Mona's voice shifts again, as if channeling Kathrin's words directly:

"You know air exists, even though you can't see it. That's how I am. You know I'm here, even though you can't touch me or feel my physical presence. I am here." Mona squeezes my hands and continues with more intensity: "You know that already. Remember!"

Strangely, those words bring me back to a knowledge within that I'd lost. I know and feel this message to be true. It is not only a hope, but a genuine knowledge of the fact. I had known this in the past, in a time of my life when I was more "connected" in a spiritual sense, more grounded than I am now.

CHAPTER 8

NEW YORK 1998

The morning my grandmother passed away in November of '98, I woke hours before the alarm clock was supposed to sound, with the unquestionable knowledge that she was gone. The room was dark; Andrea snuggled under a heavy duvet beside me. The last hours before dawn, usually the darkest of the night, glowed with the incessant heartbeat of New York, casting our bedroom in a cool, misty light. The air was still. I had grown used to the constant hum of life outside and barely noticed it unless sirens or loud voices pierced it - even those rarely woke me.

Omi, as I affectionately called her, was a beautiful lady even in old age, who exuded a sense of elegance and style. Perfectly groomed, she valued her looks: the confident clicking of her modest heels, perfect posture, stylish outfits, and a cloud of perfume trailing her like a secret admirer. She wore lipstick that often blurred into the small wrinkles along her lip line, where her skin had relaxed into the golden years of life. Her home smelled of lavender and reheated bread rolls. We had a standing Wednesday after-school date at her house. I did my homework to the tick-tock of antique clocks while she napped. I loved the large antique cabinets in the living room that always smelled of her hidden chocolates and cookies. Later, we had tea or a short walk around the block, her delicate hand resting in the crook of my elbow for support. I miss those walks. Last time I visited, it had rained, and Omi was unsteady on her feet.

I sat up, New York City humming outside the window, took a sip of water from my bottle on the nightstand, and squinted at the fluorescent green hands of Andrea's old-fashioned alarm clock. My eyes are blurry with sleep, and the clock hands do not hold much light after a long night of darkness.

My grandmother had battled cancer during the last years of her life, braving round after round of chemotherapy, and was, miraculously, recovering. But the treatment had left her visibly altered - fragile and wobbly, a baby bird with a shock of white hair. Stoic and not one to fuss, she regained her regal composure and still took pleasure in shopping and coordinating her outfits and accessories.

At eighty-nine, her death did not come as a surprise. Her health had faded over months; she seemed to be loosening her hold on this world. We spoke regularly - I was in New York finishing college and couldn't fly home - but our bond did not waver. We'd been close all my life, and distance never changed that.

And that morning, our bedroom still shrouded in pre-dawn dark, I felt her presence near the door. It wasn't visual - no ghostly figure glowing in the corner. It was like a memory projected into the room. It was internal, but felt external, outside of myself. She emanated a profound sense of love and peace, which caressed my cheek, the way she used to. She stood tall, exuding more strength and vitality than she had in years, smiling at me. Without moving closer, she seemed to envelop me. Then she was gone, and the room felt a shade darker.

Nothing about the experience was frightening; instead, it left behind a soothing feeling, like the visit of a loved one (which it was - not physically, but metaphysically). There was no question in my mind what had happened: she had died! Strangely, that thought did not make me sad, even though she was my favorite grandmother and I'd dreaded her passing for months. Her visit left me at peace. I knew she was ok and not "gone" in the finite sense of the word, the way most of us understand death. Even though this was my first experience with Death since my grandfather's passing decades earlier, I wasn't grieving - my heart filled instead with warmth, love, and gratitude for this wonderful lady and her influence on my life.

I slipped out of bed - Andrea still sleeping - and tiptoed to the living room. I grabbed a blanket, wrapped it around my shoulders with a slight shiver, and turned on the heat. November mornings in New York can be chilly, and the wooden floor was cold under my feet. I moved to the carpet, sank against the couch, and gazed at the dark ceiling with a sigh. There was no thought of sleep at this point.

I picked up a matchbox from the side table and twirled it in my hand as my thoughts turned into a silent, improvised prayer, sending love and thanks to wherever Omi was now. The red-capped wooden soldiers inside the matchbox rattled with every turn in their cardboard housing. I struck one: a hiss and a spark, the match caught fire. First white and blue, then golden, as the flame sprang up and held steady for a moment. A golden aura expanded and pushed back the darkness of the apartment. The light reflected in the TV in front of me made the window sparkle and painted a glow over the brass table next to me. Sulfur scented the air as the clear blue core licked along the wood towards my fingers, leaving the tip glowing red. Blackened wood curled downward. The thinnest whisp of smoke snaked ahead of the flame towards my skin. I fought the urge to blow it out and watched it shrink in on itself until it was only a blue glow, fringed in a golden crown that dropped into darkness before it reached me. Back in a dark, reflectionless room, I dropped what was left into the ashtray and struck another, and this time touched flame to wick. The candle caught, and I let my thoughts drift to Omi as the brass tray shimmered in soft gold. Reflections winked and waved - old friends.

The room warmed as the heater hummed to life. I soaked in the lingering feeling of love and connection, waiting for the phone to ring.

Occasionally, the flame sputtered and spat, then settled into a quiet dance around the wick. Despite the city's endless background noise, I felt bathed in silence and savored the stillness as the blackness receded to grays and blues of early morning.

The phone rang at 7 am sharp. My parents knew that I usually wake up at this time to get ready for class and didn't want to call earlier with bad news.

"Alex?" my mother's strained voice asked. "Is Andrea awake yet?"

"He is about to get up," I replied, knowing she wanted to be sure I wasn't alone.

Before she could speak, I said:

"Mami, I know. I know she is gone."

My mother paused, puzzled, then confirmed what I had known all along. The moment my grandmother slipped away in Germany, surrounded by my aunts and my parents, was the moment she had come to say goodbye to me. For the first time since I realized Omi was gone, my eyes filled - not with grief, but with awe for the gift I had been given.

Losing Omi could have derailed my last months of college - studying, finals, and job applications could have been severely impacted. But strangely, her visit had softened the loss. I thought about her daily, missed our calls and conversations, but my heart stayed full of love and gratitude, freeing me to face the future, rather than cling to the past.

CHAPTER 9

DUBAI 2016

So, yes. I do know that life continues after death. I just have to remember it. Mona's words reawakened this deep knowledge and brought back with stunning clarity the memory of my grandmother's visit. Whatever lies beyond death feels hopeful - not a biblical paradise, but rather a continuation of energy, of souls continuing with a sense of memory and connection to the loved ones left behind.

Mona keeps her eyes closed, listening to something or someone.

"She wants to talk about food." She tilts her head slightly, as if to hear better.

"Remember her through food. Something about cooking together?" her voice is raised in a question.

Kathrin and I always enjoyed cooking together, and many of my handwritten recipes in my cookbook were born from evenings spent together over food and wine - and quite a few of those recipe names start with "Kathrin's famous ..." Meatballs, for example.

"I don't know what this has to do with food," Mona continues, a frown of concentration on her face, "but she mentions potatoes and "marriage" or something like it."

I snort in a giggle I cannot hide. Just last week, I'd cooked one of her favorite dishes, a specialty from our hometown, "*Geheirade*," a simple coalminers' dish of potatoes and dumplings in a creamy bacon sauce. In our dialect, *Geheirade* means "married," the perfect union of potatoes, dumplings, bacon, and cream. The memory warms my heart. I smile through tears, unsure whether they are from sadness or happiness. Mona still holds both of my hands. Silence holds its breath. My nose starts dripping, but I do not dare to break the moment by releasing her hands.

Now that we've established that it is, in fact, Kathrin, I am ready to hear it all; to answer the burning questions:

What happened?
Why were you not wearing a seatbelt? (I am still mad about this one!)
How will I live this life without you?
How am I supposed to get through this?

I study Mona's face as she remains silent - her cheeks are flushed with a rosy pink, the thick dark eyelashes are held by a wave of black liner that wings upwards, lids dusted in brown and beige tones that glitter in the candlelight. Her features are completely relaxed. I realize that suspense made me hold Mona's hands tighter than necessary and release my grip, careful not to let go and inadvertently break the connection I've craved. The silence stretches like oceans, and I freeze in anticipation, every sense alert.

"She has a message for you." Mona's voice finally breaks the stillness.

YES! I lean forward, holding my breath.

"Trust."

I lean in closer, waiting for more. Mona sits still, her head cocked Outside, a seagull screeches, her night routine interrupted. Wings skim the garden and disappear in the distance.

Mona opens her eyes, and our hands drift apart. "That is it."

Wait. What?
Where is the rest?
What about all my questions?
Trust?
What on earth is that supposed to mean?

I look at Mona, confused. But the connection is broken. The magic is gone, and I can feel reality settle over me like a cool mist, as if a window has opened somewhere, letting in cool air. The candles flicker. To say I'm disappointed is an understatement. Why didn't she say more? Why were none of my questions answered?

Trust? Trust what? Trust whom?

My mind reels, and my heart floods with a kaleidoscope of emotions: love, acceptance, happiness, sadness, disappointment, frustration, loneliness, and hope - overlapping, merging and disconnecting at dizzying speed.

The night has settled in around us; stars fight for their place in the sky above the permanent glow of the city. Crickets remind us that it's later than we thought, and Mona gathers her flowing gown and scarf around her as if preparing to float out of here, rather than walk. She smiles, calm and almost ethereal. I can see it takes her a few moments to "come back." I wish I could go wherever she had been. Is it learned or is it a gift, I wonder? A tender stillness carries us towards the front gate. Mona hugs me again. Time folds in on itself;

the next thing I know, I'm sitting in the now-empty Majlis, where the cold smoke from the extinguished candles waves its goodbye to the night. I'm still floating as I gather my thoughts. I choose to focus on the messages that did come through, rather than the questions still knocking on my heart. Yes, not all went according to plan - if such a thing exists when speaking to a medium - but I did get a lot of answers.

And I got "Trust".

Little did I know that this one word had the power to literally change my life.

Before leaving, Mona reiterated that Kathrin will continue to communicate with me. It is only up to me to receive those messages. I'm not sure how exactly that will work, but maybe it is time to *trust*. After all, there have been messages before. Sometimes they're subtle, but occasionally they can be quite blatant. Grief had blinded me these past weeks; that's what grief does; it throws a thick blanket over everything, leaving no space to breathe or center myself. Yet those are exactly the abilities needed to see and hear messages from other - for a lack of a better word - realms. (Even to my ears, that sounds like spiritual gibberish.)

My shoulder-critic giggles. "Where have you been all evening?" I ask. I'm grateful he didn't interrupt, but his sudden appearance now startles me. I don't want him to taint the feeling of peace I am carrying. He is dressed in a beige bathrobe and white bunny slippers with pink, fluffy ears, a towel turban on his head, and a face mask slathered over stubble. "I think you should shave." I point out. He hops onto the armrest of the seating cushions and crosses his legs, exposing far too much of his skinny, hairy legs. I make a face and turn away. He's been surprisingly quiet, but now I can tell he has plenty to say. "Please. Not tonight. Let me just sit with it for a bit."

He glares at me, uncrosses his legs, and jumps to the floor. His nose held high, arms crossed, he stalks out of the Majlis and disappears into the dark. A moment later I hear a tiny splash in the pool. Let him have his night swim. Maybe it will improve his mood.

He doesn't need to speak out loud. I can hear his voice in my head anyway. I get it. To him and anyone with a healthy amount of skepticism, Mediums do cold readings at best, making general statements that fit most people, waiting for a hit to chase. But that isn't what happened tonight. Mona's words were too precise; the bracelet, the promise, the exact food we used to cook. There wasn't much, but the pieces that did come through were so unique, so expressive of us and our friendship, that there was no room for doubt.

Thinking back on all the signs and messages - not only tonight, but over the years: my grandmother's goodbye, my mother's rainbow, Kathrin's appearance in the car, the meditation, and the inexplicable touch of hands last week that brought the much-needed sense of acceptance, and now the words from Mona, make me believe that signs are indeed real.

Andrea is fast asleep as I walk into our bedroom that night. He left my bedside lamp lit, and there is a note on my pillow, written in his handwriting with the squished letters and the tall vertical lines of the t's and h's. "Hope it was everything you needed. Cannot wait to hear about it tomorrow. xo - A." I watch his features, relaxed in sleep - the goatee framing his lips, sun-streaked surfer curls breaking over his forehead, hands tucked under his chin. The warm glow of understanding, acceptance, and love that has lingered since Mona left swells with gratitude for this man next to me, who has been with me through every loss. He has supported me and been patient - even when things grew strange over the past few weeks. Maybe it is time to be a bit more open about the pain I am in. I think he can take it. That night, I go to sleep with a big smile on my face, clasp my hand over Kathrin's bracelet, and whisper "Good night" into the dark room.

The next day, I wake up feeling light and energized. Andrea must have gotten up early; the sheets beside me are already cool. I take a few minutes to snuggle into my blanket, reliving the memories of the night before. The sun needles through the curtains, and dust motes glitter and dance in the air. The smell of espresso is a few steps ahead of Andrea, who balances his phone and two espresso cups into the bedroom and sits on the edge of the mattress next to me. "Grazie, Amore," I murmur and inhale the deep, rich aroma. The crema is thick and dark brown, and the first taste is fruity, dancing along my tongue, then turning spicy with a hint of sweetness when the teaspoon of coconut sugar hits. I lean back with a sigh. I haven't felt this peaceful in a while.

Throughout the day, I retell Mona's visit to Andrea, my dad, and then Livia. Their reactions range from indulgent, skeptical to excited, respectively. I would have loved for my dad and Andrea to be as thrilled as I am, but I refuse to allow their doubt to steal the wonder I carry.

It doesn't last. Like a dream, the memory of feeling Kathrin so close fades over days and weeks. What felt like a certainty evaporates bit by bit, leaving only a faint residue behind, dampened every time the raw grittiness of grief erupts. The wonder of that night has settled itself somewhere deep inside, finding a quiet space to perch and take root. The reality still overwhelms me at times, plunging my fledgling spiritual certainty into a deep well inhabited by murky creatures of mistrust and skepticism. In those moments, what I thought I knew unravels, as fear and doubt walk hand in hand with grief.

Weeks and months blur in a milky haze of indifference. I get up every day because I have to. The sharp stabs of grief dull to a monotonous absence of happiness. Gray days wear a constant listless frown. Now I understand that life becomes meaningful because of the vertices of our existence - the continuous up-and-down of events, with life passing between opposite poles.

I sit on the stairs in front of our house after dinner and watch Dante and our Saluki Venus chase each other through the garden. Venus's graceful, slender body stretches and contracts, gazelle-like, as she sails ahead of Dante's excited bark. Judging from the dismal state she was in when she was found on the streets of Dubai, our vet assumed she'd been a race dog, dumped for lack of performance. Yet here, she runs with such beauty and joy that I cannot take my eyes off her. Watching them from behind the thick glass of indifference is as close to happiness as I can get.

It makes me think about something my dad used to tell me. He'd explained how important it is to figure out the right combination of meds for people with bipolar disorder. The pendulum of their moods needed to be kept slightly leaning towards mania, to make sure they did not lose their zest for life and creativity. Dulling the mood swings too much and life flattens into gray. That's where I am now. Gray. Without purpose or direction. And I don't even have the wrong meds to blame.

Dante breaks off his chase and bounds over to me. His eyes are wide in puppy excitement, and his long pink tongue is flopping. He nuzzles his wet nose into my face. I push him away, laughing. "Ewwwww! Go play with Venus, silly dog!" I wipe my neck.

I cherish these moments. Whenever I can, I slip away to nature - listen to the sound of the waves, watch the dogs run through the garden or over the desert dunes at sunrise, when the air is still crisp.

We have been living in Dubai for more than nine years, and despite it being a city built of sand and dreams, I've grown roots here. Not palm tree roots, which remain superficial, but oak roots, punched deep into the ground. They have weathered storms and flourished - not despite turbulence, but because of it. Every loss, every heartbreak, every obstacle forces them deeper. They did not inch their way over time with a bit of water here and there. No! These roots were jack-hammered into the flowing sands of the Arabian Desert until - despite the hostile terrain and the unforgiving nature - they became the foundation I had built my life on. Kathrin's accident and the loss of my mom, Alireza, and Milly, broke me in more ways than I can count, but I feel held here - by friends, family, dogs, and work. Maybe one day I will look back at this "gray period" of my life with a deeper understanding and appreciation.

The call to prayer floats from the nearby mosque, trickling through the branches of my soul like dew. I don't understand the words, but each drop is a refreshing reminder of the home, my oasis, that I have created here. The heat of the day still radiates off the wall behind me; I lean into it, taking comfort in its embrace, inhaling the heavy scent of frangipani and dry grass. The sun bowed behind the mosque a while ago, and the date palms in our garden reach their fronds black against the inky blue sky, swaying in an evening breeze that brings no relief from the heat. The thick clusters of dates wait in their nets for harvest. I reach under a flowerpot for my cigarette pack. Without ceremony, I crush it in my fist and stuff it into my jeans - time to leave this vice behind. The movement startles a small gecko, who rolls his eyes at me from the mosaic of lights and shadows cast by the arabesque wall sconce before scuttling off. It is in moments like this that the gray gives way and color starts seeping back into my life. First, the evening's desaturated blues and grays, then the stubborn pink of the bougainvillea bush along the wall of our garden. Muted by the night, but there is a promise: one day soon, life will be in technicolor again.

This is my home. Here I am held and loved, and I feel safe, despite the searing heat, the cultural complexity, and the dark shadows lurking in the history and the present of this glorious jewel of a city. In nine years, I have glimpsed both its glory and its shame and have been awed and heartbroken, respectively. I think it is that stark contrast between light and dark, rich and poor, east and west, old and new that made me fall in love with Dubai. Especially on Fridays, when men from all around the neighborhood rush to the mosque, cars clog the street and every inch of space is used for parking. If I had to go somewhere with my car on Friday during prayer time, I would either have to find an alternate route or wait until the streets clear. Prayer overrides traffic rules and common sense. I love the sight of Pakistani workers in their *shalwar kameez*, an outfit made of loose pants, a long overshirt, and a scarf. Emirati men in their Friday best rush to *Jumu'ah,* the most sacred of prayers held every Friday. Kneeling side by side, they're equals in the eyes of Allah, equals for the duration of the prayer. But once it is over, they scatter off to their respective corners of the city, divided by an abyss more profound than physical distance.

As I call the dogs back inside, a hint of Oud incense whispers from our neighbor's house, stopping me in my tracks to inhale deeply. We chose a predominantly Emirati neighborhood over the cookie-cutter expat enclaves; here, oud, spices, and prayers often float in the air. I love the smell of Oud. It is an acquired taste, but I love how it drifts through the Arabic wings of the malls, where tailors, carpet vendors, and abaya stores line the corridors. I used to pinch my nose at the oily, almost tangible smoke unfurling in languid landscapes across polished marble floors. Oud is a scent that assaults your nose. It comes in hard, sharp and spicy, with the arrogance of a young prize-boxer, strutting in the ring; woody notes with something else that demands attention. At first, it's all tannic leather, like a souk hand-bag whose sharp scent takes over your closet, the kind you end up sealing in plastic and forgetting. Oud remains aloof until you give it time. That moment when you dare to smell it a little bit longer, allowing the depth of the scent to make itself known. It opens its ornate door to a secret, forbidden place - sensual and exhilarating. It clings to your clothes like a dream you can't shake. With every pass-ing year, the scent has grown on me - heavy with memories, layered and intricate, the shadow of a thousand nights.

Andrea and two glasses of wine are waiting for me on the terrace as I walk back into the house. The time with the dogs has washed off some of the gray, and I feel lighter. I love those stolen moments when it is just us. I sit, take a sip, and look up at the stars. I am glad Oud hasn't followed me - Andrea isn't a fan. Only now I notice the soft music drifting from the window. He's thought of everything. My heart quickens - did I forget something? My shoulder critic, in a grey suit, his hair slicked back, pushes horn-rimmed glasses higher up on the bridge of his nose and flips through a thick, leather-bound calendar. Anniversary? Nope - months away. He paces along the back of the couch, tearing out pages. Something to celebrate? A new project? I glance at my bare feet poking out from my jeans, which I'm wearing despite the heat, my ribbed tank top clinging to my skin. Should I have dressed up? "Well, that is kinda' obvious!" my critic mumbles under his breath, as he looks me up and down with a raised eyebrow. Before I can spiral, Andrea inhales and says, low:

"I think it's time. We need to move."

Both my shoulder critic and I stare, mouths open. Andrea searches my face as the words land. All I can do is stare at him for a moment, at a complete loss for words. My shoulder critic reappears on cue and whispers urgently, "What did he just say? He didn't mean that! Did he?" It wasn't a question. It was a statement. The kids have been asleep for an hour, and it is obvious that he chose this moment on purpose. We are bathed in silence as the ripples of the shockwave wash over me. The outdoor curtains framing the strong arabesque arches of our terrace undulate in a gentle breeze, as if to say all will be well.

My shoulder critic jumps off my shoulder, shrugs off his jacket, loosens the tie, and shuffles out of his pants and shoes, dropping clothes in a trail to the pool. Dressed only in neon yellow briefs, he meets my eyes, crosses his arms over his scrawny chest, and with a final "Fuck that!" falls backwards into the water, stiff as a board. I hear him splash around for a while, but don't pay much attention to him anymore.

I shouldn't be this shocked. Tonight was not the first time we'd spoken about a move. The possibility of leaving Dubai for California had been flickering on the horizon like a mirage. I was not ready, so I just ignored it. A move would happen - just not now. But Andrea's business called us. In fact, it yelled at us from Los Angeles, where he would have access to a much wider pool of clients, who consider it an obstacle to work with a company based in the Middle East. It makes sense on paper. After nine years, he's itching to go. I'm not. Not now, when friends and work are the scaffolding keeping me upright. I don't want to start over where no one knows me - explaining again why my smile sometimes misses my eyes. Where I would have to choose to hide this part in favor of a bright, shiny new me, incomplete and artificial, or would I dare be honest and show the scars?

The evil-eye charm on my gold bracelet twinkles. The light from the wall sconce reflects in the shiny, bejeweled center. For a moment, I get lost in the rhythmic swinging of the charm, as it sparkles with every turn. Is it winking at me? A reminder that it has my back? It wards off ill intentions, but I doubt it can sway my husband. The dogs rustle in the bushes, panting as they follow an invisible trail. I rest my arm on the glass table; the charm slips from sight with a soft clink.

Until now, every move has felt enticing and full of wonder and possibilities. Now the thought feels threatening. I barely have the energy to get out of bed; how on earth would I manage a move? I'd need strength I don't have. A new place? ... without friends, without routines, or a backup system in place. No nanny to take charge when things got too much.

A place without memories of Kathrin.

I don't know why that matters, but it does. LA would be a new chapter, missing a main character. Here, I have places we shared, moments we lived. There would be no memories of us together, no resonance of her voice in the air. But maybe that is a good thing. Some crave change after a loss, a new house, a new city to escape the painful reminders. I don't know if that's what I want, though. I don't know if I am ready to leave the memories behind.

I exhale with a sigh, place my wine glass back onto the table, and turn my head up at the sky. The stars blur and multiply as they dance above us. I blink. I don't want Andrea to see the tears brimming in my eyes. I know he's right. But that doesn't make it easier. With a deep inhale that is more like a sigh, I turn back to him and whisper, "Alright."

As soon as the decision is made, the long song of goodbye begins, its haunting melody permeating every moment, every breath, every hello and every goodbye, tinging them with melancholy. Just seven months after Kathrin's accident, we started packing our lives into boxes and prepare for our move to the States.

Being busy with the move has forced me out of my gray phase. I don't have time to mope. There is so much to do - people to see, places to say goodbye to. I embark on a pilgrimage along the well-trodden paths of the last nine years.

First, I visit the Old Souk in Deira, one of the old parts of Dubai. I hand a single *dirham* coin to the *abra*[21] captain, an older Pakistani man with gray, wiry hair, a weathered face, and one milky blue eye. His callused hands hold the steering wheel of the wooden boat with the nonchalance of someone who knows what they're doing, humming an unfamiliar tune under his breath. The boat is packed with about fourteen passengers, all squeezed next to each other on the raised wooden center platform. I pick up fragments from various

---

21   *Abra - Arabic. A traditional wooden boat used in the UAE. Literally "to cross"*

languages - Arabic, English, Tagalog, Russian, and something I cannot recognize - Urdu maybe? I grin to myself, aware that just nine years ago I would have had a hard time telling all these languages apart, but now I almost take them for granted. Dubai is an intoxicating melting pot of cultures, customs, colors, and flavors. The traditions of the Emiratis are just an underpinning to this vast and varied landscape of people. LA is a big city - and pretty international, too, I'd guess - but can it hold a candle to Dubai?

We pass rows and rows of large wooden cargo boats tied up along the canal. The snapping of straining ropes and loose tarps fills the air, pierced by the screeching of seagulls bobbing their necks at each other. It is mind-blowing to see these traditional dhows packed almost beyond capacity in such a random, haphazard way that it looks like the vessel might capsize at any moment. Piles of electronic equipment are tied down with heavy ropes. Boxes, stacked in lopsided towers, keep their balance with the help of what looks like old fishing nets draped over the cargo. There is even a car strapped down precariously on top of a large tower of wooden crates. This would not pass a single European safety standard, I muse, and wink at the little Indian girl sitting next to me. She isn't paying attention to the boats but looks up at me with curiosity from under a curtain of thick black lashes. Her dark brown hair falls in gentle waves over the pink fabric of her gold embroidered *shalwar khameez*[22]. Matching hot pink pant legs peek out from the hem, and a thin golden scarf drapes around her small shoulders. She sits completely still; only her little feet in their golden sandals twitch, as if they can't wait to reach the shore and run. I know how she feels. Thankfully, the *abra*-ride is short, and within minutes, we dock on the other side. I watch as she

---

22   *Shalwar kameez - Farsi. A traditional outfit commonly worn in South Asia by men and women, made of loose pants (shalwar), a long tunic or shirt (kameez) and a scarf (dupatta).*

reaches her little arms up to her father, who lifts her into a tight hug and steps onto the weathered wooden planks of the old pier.

Thankful to escape the hot sun, I cross a few busy roads and make my way to the old Deira Souk. The air is thick with humidity, and the hum of aged air conditioners perched on shuttered windowsills mimics the city's buzz. In contrast to the sparkling high-rises, malls, and luxury cars Dubai is famous for, a visit to the old souk is a step back in time. A rusty pickup is parked nearby, three goats bleating in protest as they wait for the driver. Tiny stalls line the streets with overflowing displays of spices, fabrics, and souvenirs. There are Arabic lamps and pottery, silk scarves and perfumes, Oud vendors and *shawarma*[23] stalls with meat roasting on long vertical skewers. I see Kathrin's head bobbing in and out of sight ahead of me, obscured by scarf-clad women and dark-haired men. I hurry to catch up, but as I get closer, the woman turns and the illusion dissolves into a stranger's face. Merchants call out, praising their wares.

"Madame, come look at my fabrics. They are the best you can find!" "*Guten Tag? Deutschland, Deutschland? No? Bonjour, je parle Français.*" When I don't react, they try again: "*Italiano? Ciao bella!*"

I get annoyed by their constant buzzing and shrug them off, letting the scents of spices carry me along the busy streets. Languidly, like the smoke drafting from incense burners, I float over cobblestones smoothed by time and pay homage to the flavors of the Middle East with all my senses, stocking up on spices, dried fruits, and nuts before moving on.

After another short *abra* ride and an even shorter walk through winding roads - past mosques and shops with outdated electronics, household goods, and knick-knacks - I arrive in *Bastakiya*, another historical neighborhood of Dubai. I leave the hubbub behind and dip into the shadow of the narrow lanes, trailing my hands along

---

23   *Shawarma - Middle Eastern dish made of thinly sliced, marinated meat stacked on a vertical rotisserie, then shaved off and eaten in flatbread.*

warm stone walls, losing myself in the maze. Around each corner waits a new discovery: art installations, murals, galleries, and tiny cafés serving Arabic coffee and juices, alongside curiosities like camel milk ice cream. I make my way to the shady courtyard of the XVA Art Hotel, where I stayed not long ago for a little writing retreat. I sigh at the memories, my heart heavy at the thought of leaving this magical place behind.

One thing can be said about Dubai - it boasts the most luxurious hotels in the world, but the XVA is unique in its simplicity, true to old Emirati architecture. It's a place where artists congregate, a maze of narrow corridors, wind towers, courtyards, and hidden seating areas that invite you to linger. I settle under the large tree in the center of the courtyard and order a fresh watermelon juice. The light summer scarf around my shoulders slips to the floor, and I enjoy a brief respite from my habit of modesty. When I wander these more traditional areas, I take care to cover my shoulders and legs, sometimes even my hair. It isn't required, but I see it as a simple gesture of respect.

Above me, a group of Myna birds click their bright yellow beaks and whistle at each other, craning their necks to peer down at the tray that a waiter carries towards me. They've spotted the dates and cookies that accompany my juice, and I keep a keen eye on them; they are fearless food thieves. I take my time, savoring every sip, watching beads of condensation roll down the glass and pool on the gold print of the Hotel's paper coaster. Before it can get too soaked, I pull the coaster from under the glass and drop it in my handbag - another little souvenir to take with me. I leave a few *dirham* bills on the tray and continue my stroll, drinking in the sunset, the sights and sounds of this city I love so much.

How can I leave you behind?

My suitcase at home is filled with tokens of love for this country, this city, my friends, my people - everything and everyone I will leave. Boxes of dates; Arabic coffee with an ornate *dallah,* the traditional coffee pot with its elegant, curved spout and spire-shaped lid; matching tiny golden coffee cups nested in bubble wrap; candle holders with Arabic calligraphy; handbags by my favorite Lebanese designers; bracelets and keychains with a *nazar* - the blue eye that wards off the curse of the evil eye. There are gifts from friends, souvenirs - even cheesy ones: like a bottle opener with a smiling Emirati man in *kandoora*, or a Sheikh-Mohammed bobble-head. I am not discriminating now - anything I can bring to keep the connection alive will serve me well. I think if I could have walked around Los Angeles in an *abaya*, I would have done that too, just to hold on to my Dubai a little longer.

PART 2

KINTSUGI

CHAPTER 10
MANHATTAN BEACH 2017

California greets us, dressed in its finest summer attire: bright blue skies, a gentle breeze, and a distinct absence of sand. This is the one thing I'll definitely not miss about Dubai: everything was dusted in a thin layer of sand. No matter how many times I'd sweep our terrace, within minutes, everything would feel gritty and dry again. And God forbid a sandstorm hit, then the sand would creep all the way inside the house, through every nook and cranny, every door and every window, no matter how many wet towels we snaked along the windowsills. In contrast, arriving in Manhattan Beach feels like jumping into a soothing pool of cool water: no sand, no grit, no humidity, no sweltering temperatures. Tall palm trees are scattered over the rolling landscape of homes, which squeeze tighter together the closer we get to the coveted beach properties. White shiplap homes with sprawling views and tropical gardens have replaced the small surf shacks from the 60s. Jasmine laces the walls and fences along the road, turning heads with their intoxicating scent. A few streets fanning out from the pier have retained their beach town charm with one-story buildings and bars and restaurants spilling their tables and umbrellas onto the sidewalk.

I struggle to unlock the temperamental door to our new home. Excited barking greets me, together with what sounds like a stampede of dogs rushing down the stairs toward me. I have barely enough time to shrug off my handbag and close the door before Dante and Venus jump all over me. After the 17-hour flight from Dubai, they made it quite clear that the new house was theirs and theirs alone. Two months in, we're still waiting for our moving container from Dubai, so we live in a bare house with only three mattresses and a couple of cardboard boxes serving as a dinner table. Thoughtful neighbors have lent us four sets of dishes, cutlery, and glasses, so we can at least stop using disposable plates. After the excess Dubai offers, this simplicity is refreshing and eye-opening. Not having "stuff" feels liberating - almost enough to wish our moving boxes would never arrive. Almost.

I drop the take-out boxes containing our dinner on the empty kitchen counter that still feels like someone else's kitchen. Until I fill the space with the tantalizing scents of my own cooking, it won't really feel like home. I guess we do need at least some of our things to make this place feel like ours. The four lonely forks and knives rattle in their drawer as I pull it open to start setting the table on the cardboard-box "table." As I close the drawer, I notice the edge of a small card sticking out from behind the kitchen cabinet. A quick tug reveals a dusty business card for a Reiki practitioner, probably left by the previous tenants. With a shrug, I toss it in the trash.

The dogs trot into the kitchen, lured by the smell of food. I had been worried about how they would settle in this new environment, so different from what they knew. They might not miss our mornings in the desert, but I sure do. I loved getting up while it was still dark, driving the sleepy roads for 15 minutes until we were in the wide-open expanse of the desert. The air was still damp with the last breath of the night before the sun rose in a spectacular display of pink, orange, and gold. Sometimes there would be cotton candy fog lingering around the few *Ghaf trees*[24] lining the road, and camels would saunter by with heavy feet. The ever-changing slopes and valleys of the desert would push Dante and Venus' endurance, as they galloped and stretched their limbs at breakneck speed. At the end, two panting dogs would collapse at my feet, wriggling themselves into the cool, damp sand.

"A tavooooolaaaaaaa![25]*"* I call my kids to the table with the high-pitched, exaggerated intonation and stretched vowels my mother-in-law used when she called my husband and his sister to dinner when they were small. The dogs settle down close enough to catch any scraps falling off the plates. I did not have to worry about them. They seem very well settled already and spend hours sitting on the balcony in the sun. With eyes closed, their wet noses up in the air, nostrils flaring, they take in the damp ocean breeze that lifts from the beaches in the morning and carries with it the aroma of the eucalyptus trees down the road. Afternoons smell of warm lavender and roses, thick grass, punctuated by the chatter of chubby squirrels that tease them from a safe distance up in the trees. Evenings are heavy with the perfume of jasmine, extinguished only by the thick ocean fog that creeps up from the beaches at night. I wonder what they are making of it all. They seem happy and content living in the moment, while I am still in limbo. My heart is swimming in nostalgia, yearning for the comfort of the well-known, while my mind is ready to explore and make this new place our own.

---

24   *Ghaf tree - Arabic. National tree of the UAE, an evergreen tree whose roots can reach up to 30 meters depth.*

25   *A tavooooolaaaaaaa! - Italian. Shouted version of "a tavola," calling everyone to the table to eat.*

After years in this bubble of Dubai - its glitz and glamour, its lifestyle, and its sense of safety - had lulled us into a sense of normalcy. But it was not normal to live in a place where the sight of Ferraris, Bugattis, and Lamborghinis was commonplace. It was not normal to leave my handbag on the table in the restaurant while I went to the bathroom, safe in the knowledge it would still be there when I returned. It was not normal for all children to attend private school, because public schools were run in Arabic only. Private schools are not "normal," yet for our kids, they were. And that scared me. As much as I hated leaving Dubai, I knew it was vital for them to step out of the bubble.

But once in LA, seeing the homeless hunkered down in tents along the roads and under bridges, the shocking amount of trash along the highways, and the overall impression of grime made me realize what a big change we are in for.

But that is Los Angeles. Instead of living right in the hustle and bustle of the big city, we are making our new home in Manhattan Beach, just outside of LA - a quaint little beach town with small schools where everyone knows each other, where Santa Claus, with the help of the fire department, visits each street on his sleigh during Christmastime, and hands out candy canes. Manhattan Beach has the charm of a small town with the convenience of living near one of the West Coast's biggest hubs. Little did I know that this quaint town is very much a bubble of its own.

Days flow into weeks and into months. Adjusting to a new place makes time blur at the edges, and I only survive with the help of my calendar, which gives my day a structure and purpose. I am sitting in my car, drumming my fingers on the steering wheel. "C'mon now," I mutter under my breath, looking back at the open front door of our house. The minutes tick by, and anxiety niggles under my skin. The girls always take their sweet time in the morning. My car is parked in the driveway, and I give a quick wave to some of Giulia's new classmates riding their bikes past our house. They give me a blank look. I don't think they recognized me - what do I expect? We've only been here a few months. Now I am actually glad Giulia is not in the car yet. She would've hidden in embarrassment. Kids are funny that way.

Finally, she comes running out of the house, backpack over her shoulder, one shoe on her foot, the other dangling from her hand, her lunchbox tucked under the other arm. With a sigh, she plops into her seat and slips her foot into the other shoe. The car door is still wide open, waiting for Gia. "Why is your sister taking so long?" I snap at Giulia as if it were her fault. She just shrugs. I can feel my patience slipping. Every morning, the same spiel. My anxiety about being late makes my German DNA coil in frustration. I exhale with intention, feeling my body grow heavy in the seat as I force myself to be calm. With a sigh, I pull down the car's sun visor, study my reflection, apply a layer of lip gloss, and toss the half-empty tube into the cupholder next to me, where it joins a few loose coins and a hair scrunchie.

Another glance at the empty doorframe.

The clicking of my fingernails fills the air as Gia stumbles out of the house. Her blonde curls bounce in a wild halo around her face, and she shrugs an apology at me as she takes a bite of a half-eaten granola bar, crumbs snowing all over the seat. I roll my eyes, but choose my battles wisely. This one isn't worth it. She barely has time to close the door before I pull out of the driveway and head down the hill towards school.

It is a 5-minute drive to the girls' elementary school, close enough to walk, but they rarely wake up early enough. My shoulder critic lies on top of the rearview mirror. "I wouldn't walk either!" he chimes. "Going there is fine. But the way back? That steep hill? Nahhhh!" He's probably right. The walk to school is all downhill with a full view of the coastline, but the way back is not as much fun. By the time school is out, the sun has burned through the fog and beats

147

down with little shade. The heavy weight of the backpacks forces the girls' eyes to the ground, making the incline feel steeper, as they trudge on one step after another.

Still, driving such a short distance irks me. "I think you two should walk home today. It's good for you!" My shoulder critic clamps his ears as the girls erupt in protests. "I'll make a deal," I raise my voice to be heard. "Every day that you're late getting into the car in the morning, you walk home from school." More protests. "Consider it a little incentive not to dawdle." I wink at my shoulder critic, and he leans back across the mirror, grinning. He's wearing mesh-paneled yoga leggings, a muscle shirt, and a pink trucker hat. Oversized sunglasses hide his eyes, and layered gold chains dangle from his neck all the way to the mirror, where they clink against the glass. I frown at his outfit.

Today, we make it just in time. Their elementary school is a collection of light-blue wooden buildings connected by open-air corridors and courtyards. A large grassy field with a playground and basketball courts hosts recess and PE classes. The mild California weather means that most of the school life outside of the classrooms is taking place out in the open. The car idles while the girls grab their things and scurry towards their classrooms, a quick "Bye, Mom" tossed over their shoulders. The door thuds shut, and I relax as the demands of motherhood soften for a few hours. I'd be at peace if it weren't for my critic, who has jumped onto the ledge of the passenger door and crossed his legs with a flourish. He puckers his lips into an exaggerated duck face and raises his eyebrows over the rim of his glasses as he looks out the window. I follow his gaze and watch a few mothers rush their kids toward school as the bell rings. Quick kisses, hurried goodbyes, and off they go. The moms stop by the school gate for a quick chat, and I study them. Cropped leggings, casual tops, and trucker hats with shiny gold print, gold bracelets, diamonds sparkling against curated California tans. I glance back at my critic and grin - his outfit tracks.

Before we moved here, I had made a list of "pros," containing all the things to look forward to. One of them was that I was looking forward to living in a country again, where I would not have to worry about not recognizing people.

I loved the sight of people in traditional Arab clothing: men in their white *kandooraas* and colored headscarves, but especially the women in their black *abayas*. There is something so elegant about them. Contrary to Western headlines, being covered is not imposed on women; it's a choice shaped by culture as much as religion. Oftentimes, *abayas* are tailored to flatter, the soft, fluid fabric caressing their bodies while still allowing for modesty and floor-length coverage. Bejeweled sleeves add a bit of unexpected sparkle. Red-soled high heels flash beneath black hems, matching the designer handbags casually slung over their shoulders. *Abayas*, despite their modesty, could be quite a fashion statement. But sometimes they would make it harder for an outsider to recognize people, especially when worn with a *shayla*, the traditional headscarf that covers the hair and sometimes the neck as well.

The moms step away from the gate and settle into conversation. I squint to make out their features under the rim of their trucker hats, still learning to match names to faces. Before Dubai, I had always taken people's faces for granted. Recognizing someone by their features, smile, eyes, hairstyle, or body shape felt normal to me. In Dubai though, I had learned to identify people by new landmarks.

I had been friends with another school mom, Noor, an Emirati lady with beautiful twin daughters in Gia's class. She always wore the traditional straight-cut *abaya*, but instead of wearing it with a *shayla*, she wore a more modest black *niqab*[26] that covered her face, leaving only a thin opening for her eyes. Her religious and cultural background was more conservative, as she often wore black gloves

---

26   *Niqab - Arabic. Meaning "to veil." It is a face veil worn by some Muslim women.*

as well, effectively shielding all of herself from view. She was very open and welcoming, and her eyes always twinkled with a smile. She had a sister who, at first glance, looked identical - same height, same head-to-toe covering. They alternated school pick-ups, and it took me a while to even realize that they were two different women. Over time I learned to tell them apart, finding new landmarks to orient myself on: body language, the way they walked, the tilt of a head, microgestures - because their eyes and even their voices were similar. I messed up more than once, much to their amusement and my embarrassment.

One day, I accompanied Gia to their house for a playdate. We were welcomed by a Filipina maid in a simple uniform and ushered to the *majlis* room. Six women sat on chairs or floor cushions, Arabic coffee scenting the air. Six smiling faces turned toward me, and I halted, disoriented. Since there were no men present, everyone was uncovered, wearing bright, flowy dresses, their hair hanging long and shining down their backs. I looked around in confusion. Without the usual black head-to-toe covering, I couldn't recognize my friend or her sister. I had never seen them in "normal" clothing, and the silhouettes and mannerisms I'd spent so long learning were all gone, replaced by bright colors and beautiful, unfamiliar faces.

Who should I greet first? The women noticed my stunned expression and giggled, which only sharpened my insecurity. One of them approached me with a welcoming smile, a *dallah* of Arabic coffee, and a plate of dates. I thought I recognized Noor - but nope. It was her sister. The room erupted in laughter, and I joined in with relief. The sister introduced me to everyone and, grinning, reintroduced me to Noor. We laughed and hugged. "Come, come, sit!" Noor pulled me beside her on a floor cushion. I folded my legs with the grace of a newborn calf, not used to sitting on the floor. Once I settled, I accepted the small, engraved coffee cup with a grateful smile.

I smile at the memory, craving the spicy flavor of Arabic coffee. My shoulder critic pulls a tiny pair of binoculars out of nowhere and watches the group of moms approach. I still can't make out their faces - I think I recognize the taller one's sunglasses until I notice two of them are wearing the same pair. I sigh.

I thought moving to LA meant I wouldn't have to deal with that anymore - that I'd recognize people quickly without awkward doubt. But as the moms walk down the street, I realize that Manhattan Beach has more in common with Dubai than I expected. Instead of *abayas,* the traditional clothing of the native Manhattan Beach mom consists of trucker hats, athleisure, oversized sunglasses, gold jewelry, and designer handbags. Long, perfectly dyed blonde hair; toned bodies with curated curves; age-blurring lips; immaculate skin.

The group passes my car together, and one mom waves. "Do you know them?" my shoulder critic asks. I wave back with a smile, drop the car into gear, and pull onto the street. "I think, kinda, maybe ...," my voice trails. "Honestly? I have no idea." Here's hoping for a few weeks of bad weather so the sunglasses stay home, and I finally get a fighting chance to know who's who.

CHAPTER 11
MANHATTAN BEACH 2017

Christmas is just around the corner, and the weather has cooled, not quite cold enough for my breath to become visible, but enough to make me wear my padded jacket. The sky is milky white today, teetering between patches of light blue and angry bunches of grays along the horizon. I lock my bike near the Farmer's Market and catch a glimpse of my tousled hair in the window of a car next to the bike stand. With one determined rake of my fingers, I ruffle the short strands into a rebellious pixie. I grin as I catch my shoulder critic doing the same. He looks back at me, and we laugh. We're twinning today: black skinny jeans, black and white Air Jordan 1 high-tops, a black short jacket with the contrasting white fluffy lining in the hoodie, and a silver belt slung low. After a year in California, I've still not given in to the athleisure look.

We stroll along the market. Year-round, the tables heave with fresh organic produce, eggs, bread, and flowers, but towards the cooler months, the variety thins. I pick a few heads of broccoli and cauliflower and then go over to the flower stand to pick up something for the ceramic vase in the kitchen. "Hey, how are you?" I greet the older man behind the counter. He is wearing a green apron and a broad smile. "Could I have two bunches of Eucalyptus, please?" I lean over the bucket and inhale their fresh aroma. "Sure. Let me wrap these up for you." He flicks water off the stems and swaddles them newspaper. "How about these? You know, 'tis the season and all." He grins and points at an army of mistletoe bouquets, tied with thin red ribbons.

The world around me still rotates as I am fixed in time. Movements and people blur; sounds dim to a distant hum. The air chills, and I'm no longer at the Farmer's Market - I hear gravel crunch underfoot along the endless path stretching into the distance of my memory at the cemetery in Vienna. My heartbeat slows to heavy, painful contractions as a thin shell of grief solidifies over me.

Grief is about to remind me of another lesson: has its own calendar. It doesn't care about the human construct of time and the myth that "time heals all wounds." Here I am, - fine one minute - strolling the market, joking with my shoulder critic - and the next I'm flattened under feelings I thought I had dealt with already.

I'd been doing okay these past months. Fall was great in Manhattan Beach: deep blue skies tempted us with sunshine and cooler temperatures. We lived outside - biking, exploring and lazy lunches. After 6 months we started to settle. I finally knew most of the moms in the girls' classes, even behind their trucker hats and sunglasses. The kids made new friends. My heart filled with quiet appreciation when I dug my feet into the sand, watching dolphins arc through pewter waves, a fresh ocean breeze giving my hair the perfect messy beach look. I wouldn't say I was happy, but I was content, which is a HUGE improvement over my state of mind in Dubai just six months ago.

I stare at the mistletoe and watch my arm extend inch by inch towards the red ribbon, lured by an inaudible siren's call. My index finger traces the satin loop of the bow as memories shake loose from the silvery branches. Bouquet after bouquet falls into that small dark hole that already holds Kathrin's ashes. The smell of cold, damp earth rises to meet me, and I shrug deeper into my jacket.

I thought I was doing so well. Maybe it is simply the fact that the honeymoon phase of our move is over. The frantic months of relocating are done and the reality of a new place without the trusted support of my mother or best friend is finally hitting me. Until now, I was surrounded by a whirlwind of activities and responsibilities, leaving little room to tend to the landscape of my innermost thoughts and emotions. And now that there is a certain routine in my life, grief walks in uninvited.

The hum of voices around me solidifies to scraps of words. The green apron leans in and draws my eyes up towards the face of the flower vendor, a question in his eyes. I shake my head, not sure what he asked. He shrugs, picks up a mistletoe bouquet and hands it to me. "On the house." The bouquet holds my hand like it did in the cemetery. Next to me a woman orders a bunch of flowers in a buttery California drawl. Cars drive past, and seagulls heckle each other from nearby lampposts. I feel the mistletoe lift me out of the scene. I am not part of it anymore. I float somewhere in the empty spaces and watch from the outside. Awareness becomes its own creature, separate from the body. It looks this way and that, tilting its head until it crawls back inside, into the missing part of myself, the gap left behind by loss. And once it finds this empty spot within, it does a few turns, tucks its tail and curls up inside. It runs its tongue along the broken, ragged edges to feel the searing pain of loss and loneliness again.

Without my doing, my awareness is acting on instinct. It needs to sit in grief. It needs to feel that empty space. There is wisdom there. There is only one way through: I need to lift it up onto a pedestal, put it under a spotlight and study it. Running won't work; avoiding only postpones the inevitable. I have to face the reality that once again grief is the centerpiece, the focal point. And today, grief is mistletoe-shaped. Just like a sculpture wrought by the hand of a master, with branches of filigree silver, it demands my full attention. The back of my throat aches with unshed tears. My shoulder critic whispers, "You need to pay him." I watch my hand pull out my credit card.

What am I going to do with this pain?

He rings up my transaction and hands me the eucalyptus. "You need to nail it above the door," he grins. Confused, I look at him, and to illustrate, he lifts another mistletoe over his head and smooches a kiss into thin air. My face smiles at him, and I turn, the eucalyptus sticking out of the shopping bag, while the mistletoe tugs me down the street toward the pier that stretches over a gray ocean crowned by whitecaps.

I know that grief and I need to spend time together; only then will it allow me to move on. I study every branch, leaf, and berry, marry the feel of it in my hand now with how it pressed to my chest when I walked behind the urn. I lift it to my nose and smell Vienna in winter. The wind slips inside my jacket. I pull the zipper up to my neck and keep walking until grief and I reach the end of the pier. Ahead, the horizon is an endless seam where heavy clouds and gray ocean merge. I pull grief close to my chest once more, feel it in my bones, then reach back and throw the mistletoe into the dark water. The red ribbon flutters, kisses the surface, bobs, and rides current. The clouds on the horizon crack open, and a thin drop of light spills downwards until it hits the ocean and shatters into million sparkles.

I know that grief and I will meet again. It'll be waiting on a pedestal in an illuminated case, just around the corner in another room of my life. While wandering the halls, I will end up right in front of it again. Running away never helps. I have to face it, honor it, until I can find a glimmer of beauty within. Something sparkling at the edge of darkness. A tiny drop of light, of hope. Each visit hurts a little less than the last. Next time there will be a red velvet rope on brass stanchions, giving me space as I circle. It still hurts, but the rope allows me to know that there is a space, a physical distance. Before, grief was an interactive art installation that I was fully immersed in, where the pain was within and without, all-consuming. Now it is a sculpture in front of me that I can look at but that I am not physically a part of. I can walk away again.

I WILL walk away. I'll move into other rooms of my life and enjoy all they have to offer until I turn a corner and find the grief sculpture once more - maybe just for a glance, or maybe an extended visit. But that is all that it is: a visit.

CHAPTER 12
MANHATTAN BEACH 2017

It is early on a Saturday morning, that I walk towards a tiny yoga studio in downtown LA. My shoulder critic has been yapping through the whole 45-minute drive - life in the "suburbs" means everywhere worth going is at least 45 minutes away. I duck into a grungy-looking bodega for some nuts and iced tea. My hand hovers between a bag of chips and a chocolate bar. "What are you doing?" my shoulder critic interrupts. "You are not hung-over, you are going to a class. At least pick something that does not scream "Depressed midlife crisis!" Fine. I grab a plastic cup of melon and strawberries; a plastic fork taped to the side.

A rental scooter skims my ankle. "Watch it, dude!" my critic barks, shaking a tiny fist. He's gone full hipster today: groomed beard, tight washed jeans, suede boots, checkered shirt with suspenders, beanie, tattoo sleeve. Of course.

The yoga studio is just around the corner. The wooden floor creaks under my feet as I open the frosted glass door and look around the small entrance. Windowsills are lined with crystals, incense drifts from a brass holder, and hushed voices float through a gauzy curtain, separating the entrance from the main room. "Hello?" I try. Summoned by my words, a petite blonde in a purple scarf wrapped around her head pops up from behind a tiny reception desk, bells jingling on her anklets. "Welcome, welcome! We are about to start. Grab a mat." I slip off my shoes and take a seat on a yoga mat in the far corner of the room. The sprite-like woman, who had welcomed me, sits in the center, her legs crossed underneath, as she passes out a bunch of spiral-bound notebooks.

"Welcome to Reiki 1." Her voice lowers to a soothing purr. "What a blessing to have you all in class."

My shoulder critic leans forward from my shoulder to catch my eye and raises his eyebrows in annoyance. "Reiki?" he mouths at me. "WTF!"

I ignore him and focus on the teacher again: "Let's start with a little introduction."

I suppress a sigh. At this rate, we will be here all day. Oh no, wait. We WILL be here all day. The course is scheduled until 5 pm. Finally, the sigh does escape my lips, as I wonder once again why I even signed up for this. "Yeah! Why have you!! What a waste of time. I hope you did not have to pay for this!" I glare at my critic. "Of course you did!" He rolls his eyes and flops dramatically on a cushion behind me.

One by one, people speak. They all seem very confident and excited. Some of the participants seem a bit "out there," if you know what I mean. There are a lot of flowing fabrics, vegan snacks, herbal teas, incense infused clothing that look like they had not seen the inside of a washing machine in a while. There are bare feet and jingling anklets, piercings and dreadlocks wrapped in makeshift turbans. There is a guy covered in tattoos, the holes in his jeans held together by a few overburdened strands of fabric. His arms are cuffed in rows and rows of crystal bracelets and leather straps and his sinewy arms hold his hands in a constant prayer position in front of his chest.

What am I doing here? What am I going to say?

I scan the Indian wall hangings and jars of crystals as if the answer is hidden there. My shoulder critic crosses his arms, pouting. Then, hands on hips: "PLEASE," he stretches the word "Do tell why we're here! I'd love to know why I am wasting my time."

I tune him out and replay the breadcrumbs that lead me here. Since we landed in LA, Reiki kept popping up everywhere - a business card in our rental, flyers, ads in magazines. I would notice signs for Reiki healer practices along the streets. Friends would mention it to me out of the blue. I would see it on Facebook and Instagram. I wasn't interested but the repetition felt like a nudge. Supposedly it's Japanese energy-healing modality working with chakras. That's about all I knew at this point.

Having old-school physicians as parents I was raised to side-eye anything "alternative," whether that was Homeopathy, Acupuncture or Ayurveda. Energy work sat at the far edge of the map. But since Kathrin's death I've become more aware of "the other side" of things, things we cannot see or even explain, things beyond the scientific foundation that my world was built upon. And didn't Kathrin tell me to "*trust*"?

Okay. Let's say I do. I trust that the repetition means something. But what? Book a session - or learn it myself? Start smaller, I thought. Book a session. I googled practitioners. Wow. Reiki shares a room with crystal healing, psychics, mediums, astrology, sound baths, chakra balancing, "Holy Fire," "Angel Reiki." "Immerse yourself in the uplifting divine light of Angel Reiki." I read.

No, no, no. Nope.
I am not doing that!

I was turned off by the whole esoteric vibe. I can handle this stuff in homeopathic doses: a couple of signs here and there, a breathwork session with inexplicable results, a visit with a medium are all good and well, but does that mean I have to embrace it all, sight unseen?

That would be a hard NO!

Still, if Reiki keeps popping up - and if I'm going to honor Kathrin's message - then how can I turn away now? One thing was clear: unless someone I trust recommended a practitioner, I wasn't handing my body to God-knows-who with crystals, incense, angels, or Holy Fire. Trust is great, but blind trust isn't. But there was another path, one that suits a control freak like me: learn it myself and see first-hand what it's all about.

That's why I am here!

But I can't cram all of that into a chirpy intro, so when it's my turn I say, "Hi, I'm Alexandra. I'm not sure why I'm here, but I'm curious."

"Hmmm." My shoulder critic pushes his lower lip out like a pouting toddler, his arms folded stubborn against his chest, but his face has softened. Glad that the attention has moved away from me, I take a nervous sip of iced tea and worry the label into a tiny square while the others introduce themselves - relaxed, excited, already fluent in this world. I wish I could shrink into the corner and just watch. Maybe I should have done a bit more research before surrendering to trust.

Over the next six hours, we meditate, skim Reiki history, and learn to "feel the energy," practicing first on ourselves and then on each other.

It does nothing for my imposter syndrome. While my classmates seem to be blown away by the amount of energy they feel coursing through their hands and bodies, I am mostly trying to stay under the radar and not make it too obvious that the only thing I can feel is a slight tingle in my left foot, which has fallen asleep from sitting in a cross-legged position too long. Maybe it is all just a bunch of BS, this energy healing thing. I felt nothing. Nada. No tingle, no energy, no hot or cold sensations, just the flush of being out of place. Luckily my shoulder critic snoring in a tissue box on the shelf. I don't need his commentary layered on top of my humiliation.

During breaks, most of my classmates flock together to talk shop: angels and astrology, tarot cards - the whole spiritual buffet. To be fair, I do believe in reincarnation, souls and after-death communication. Even "everything is energy" makes sense to me. But manipulating this energy to heal is something that the jury is still out on, pending the completion of this course. But consulting angel cards before decisions or communicating with aliens from an ancestral galaxy far, far away (pun intended) is a bit of a stretch for me.

Nose-ring-girl pipes up above the hubbub of voices, relaying what happened during our last meditation. "It was Metatron. I could see him clear as day. He stood in the center of our circle. Supporting every one of us. And …"

Her voice is drowned out by the appreciative murmur of her audience. Metatron? Who is Metatron? Sounds like a Transformer.

What do you mean Metatron "showed up" in your meditation?

That's kinda cool, I guess. I mean, why not?

All I saw in my meditation was the back of my eyelids.

In my mind, a rusty blue sedan unfolds into a towering robot over our mats. Her tone doesn't match the movie in my head, so I sneak a quick Google search behind my Reiki manual: apparently, Metatron is an archangel.

Archangels. Really?

I mean, I know nothing about angels. But I do know that meditation can have strange effects on people. I witnessed it firsthand back in Dubai when I felt those invisible hands and the sudden flood of acceptance … but angels? Hmmm … I think for now I'll just ignore what I don't understand and focus on Reiki.

Class resumes, and our blonde, turbaned Reiki Master explains that Reiki is not something you have to have a special gift or talent for. "You don't have to believe in it for it to work," she purrs, eyes sweeping the room.

Is she talking to me?

"Everybody can learn it. It's already inside you." I feel her eyes linger on me a fraction longer. Maybe I am the famous exception to the rule.

Something shifted on day two. Reiki 1, which is all about self-healing, had been pretty unremarkable for me. But after the Level 2 attunement, which lets you work on others, the ground under my skepticism moved.

Before our hands-on practice, we settle for a guided meditation. The room is bright, and sunshine filters through the fire escape ladder outside. A saxophone player is practicing somewhere in the neighborhood, and wisps of languid blues ride on the breeze through the open window. I've come to enjoy this part. My mind slows down and expands; sometimes it goes blank, as if asleep, other times colors bloom behind my lids, with colors morphing from purple to gold or silver. Trippy, actually, and all substance-free, mind you. My shoulder critic, in a lab coat for no obvious reason other than to annoy me, mutters that it's all rooted in some sort of neurological phenomenon.

Of course he does.

As we settle onto our respective mats, we are taken on a guided meditation by our Reiki Master. I melt into the floor, carried by her soft voice and the gentle background music. My hands are resting on my knees, and my eyes are closed. My breath rises and falls and my sight drops to the back of my consciousness. Tiny lights rush down a tunnel toward me, then fade to velvet dark. I can't feel the cushion. Only breathing anchors me - feather-light, effortless.

And then I float.

It feels as ordinary as stepping out of a pool: one moment inside the water, the next above it - unconfined. I'm hovering a foot over my body, awareness bright and clean. I "see" without eyes. The music and incense don't reach me. The room looks far away, as if through the wrong end of binoculars, yet my own body is crisp: blonde roots under auburn, the stubborn cowlick at my crown, my gray hoodie slipped off one shoulder, the black tank strap exposed. My face looks foreign the way it would to anyone who isn't me - I've only ever seen reflections, never the real angle.

The moment widens. I relax into it.
Then my brain notices.
Holy crap - what is happening?

My body jolts; consciousness drops back into place like an elevator reaching the lobby. I open my eyes, heart sprinting. No one seems to have noticed. My shoulder is empty; my critic is on the shelf, playing hacky sack with an amethyst.

I glance at my Reiki Master, and she catches my eye with a twinkle. "Now that was interesting," she smiles. "I could feel your energy lift out for a moment."

Hearing her say that lands like proof. *My energy had lifted out.* It feels surreal that a sentence like that even makes sense. And from that moment on, everything shifts. Maybe there is more to this whole Reiki thing than I could have foreseen.

CHAPTER 13
MANHATTAN BEACH 2017

A few nights later, a scream cracks through the air in our home. It is dark outside, and the warm glow of the fireplace dances in the windows. Andrea and I jolt upright. "Gia!" Dante is already thundering down the stairs. We fly after him, two at a time, and follow the sobs to her room. The nightlight glows as we reach her bed. Dante is pressed to her side, tail thumping the nightstand. Loose curls plaster Gia's sweaty forehead; her eyes are open, fixed on the empty space beside her bed, body heaving.

"*Amore!*" I slip past Andrea, invoking a mother's first-right-to-soothe, and climb onto the mattress, wrapping my arms around her. She doesn't blink, doesn't turn. The tears flow and drip onto her duvet. Ragged breaths make her body shake, and she continues to wail. "Gia, *Amore*! It was just a dream." Andrea crouches low, his voice like velvet brushing matted strands of hair out of her face. She stares straight through him. "This will take a while," I whisper to Andrea.

Night terrors - she used to have them often. Even at eleven, they ambush us. She looks awake but isn't - words don't reach her. Lullabies make it worse. Hugs turn into thrashing. All we can do is sit and wait. Andrea settles down at the end of the bed. Dante walks over to him and puts his head on his lap, worried eyes flicking between them. I ease my arms away and place one hand over Gia's head, the other in front of her heart. "Let me try Reiki," I whisper, mostly to myself. I close my eyes, slow my breath, and follow the steps I learned last weekend.

An unfamiliar tingle runs through my hands, and Heat builds in my palms. A tingle pricks my fingers. I lift my hands a few inches, thinking I'm catching her body heat. And then - it's over. The sobbing stops. Her breath steadies. She sighs, curls onto her side, and drops into sleep.

I open my eyes and find my husband staring at me, stunned. "Wow!" I mouth at him in the dim light. I breathe a kiss on Gia's now cool forehead, and we tiptoe out into the hallway. "I know! I cannot believe it!" Andrea whispers. The floorboards under our feet creak, and another small voice rises from the room next to Gia's:

"Mama? I can't sleep."

"Round two," I grin, slipping into Giulia's room with my new superpower.

A few minutes later, I'm back on the couch, glowing. "It worked like a charm. One minute and she was out!" Andrea shakes his head, and I giggle. "Man, if I'd only known about Reiki when they were babies …"

He turns back to the TV, but my mind is racing. This was the first time I've seen and felt Reiki work. I spread my hands open and look at my palms and fingers. They look and feel exactly the same as always, but that tingle - that was new. Maybe I judged too quickly. The weird "lifting up" during meditation was just the beginning.

Now this. I think I have to rethink a lot of things. I'm not ready to sign up for Starseeds, Galactics, or angels, but the flat no of my inner skeptic has softened into a live-and-let-live. After what I have experienced so far, ... who knows what is real and what's not.

Andrea mutes the TV. "Ok! Explain. I don't get this whole Reiki thing. But ..." his voice drops away. "How did you just do that with Gia?" I scoot closer, tuck my legs under me, and kiss his cheek. "Alright. Think of it like this: everything's energy. Even Quantum physics proves that what appears solid to us is mostly electrons vibrating at various frequencies. Only the tiniest percentage within each atom is actual "solid" matter." I knock on the side table to emphasize the point. Andrea likes "sciency stuff," and Quantum physics is something he can relate to. "We also feel energy without calling it that." I am reaching a territory he is not very familiar with. "Take a crowded room, for example. When you enter, even before you hear voices or make out individual faces, you get a "feel" for the vibe. You can feel whether the atmosphere is good, tense, or simply uncomfortable. That's energy." Andrea raises his eyebrows in doubt and leans back into the couch, arms crossed.

"Now, Reiki works with that energy field - just in and around the body," I go on, "It's supposed to relax the system, help it rebalance, sometimes nudge healing along." I skip the emotional/spiritual bits for now, doling out Reiki lessons in homeopathic doses. "I just followed the steps and... her nervous system downshifted."

"Hmm." My husband's furrowed brows tell me that even that simplified explanation stresses his comfort level. "Ok," he sighs and unmutes the TV. I bite back a smile. I know he needs time to digest this, honestly, so do I.

CHAPTER 14
MANHATTAN BEACH 2018

Addyson lies on the massage table, blonde hair fanned over the edge, candlelight flickering across it. I use Gia's downstairs room as my makeshift Reiki space when she's at school. The room smells of sage and lavender and is filled with the deep resonance of meditation music. Today I picked a track that takes the mind on a journey through a rainforest with birds singing to the playful gurgling of water, ethereal chimes, and a deep sonorous hum in the background.

Since Gia's night terror, energy work has become part of our lives. I started with daily self-Reiki; now the girls ask for it most nights and fall asleep without a fight. I practiced on friends for free, then eased into paying clients.

Addy's under a thin blanket, her eyes are covered with a soft eye mask, and her breath is slow and even. The persistent spring fog is pushing its nose against the window; the room is cool. I'm not as focused today as I would like to be. I glance at the clock - another few minutes to go. Most sessions leave my hands hot and tingly, and sometimes I can even "feel" my client's symptoms, not as pain, but as mirrored sensations within my own body. A backache might reveal itself as a soft thud in my own spine, a toothache like a string pulled in my jaw, or a sore knee feels like sand rubbing against carti-lage. Today, though there is nothing. No heat, no pull - nothing that calls my attention. She came in for insomnia. For over a year now, she's tried everything from melatonin, acupuncture, meditation, to weed, and nothing has eased that grating weight of sleeplessness. She gets a few hours every night with the help of pills and a couple of glasses of wine, but that is not sustainable.

Doubt creeps in. Is Reiki doing anything? Does it work when the issue isn't strictly physical in nature? I look at her chest as it rises and falls in slow rhythmic breaths. Her features under the mask are softened with deep relaxation. I wonder if she is asleep. If nothing else, at least that. I close my eyes and follow the hum of the music, reminding myself: don't force it. Reiki goes where it's needed.

I drift to the side of the table. My hands float a few inches above Addy's hip. I wince as I step on something sharp, and I bend down to pick up one of Gia's hair clips. That wasn't the sensation I was waiting for. I give up. Today's session is a bust. As I straighten, I feel a soft tickle inside my upper abdomen, just under my rib cage. I pause and listen to my body. The tickling sensation returns. This time it starts under my ribcage on the right, just above my waist, and arches up towards the sternum. It feels like tiny legs are crawling over ... over what? Is that my liver? It hits me.

I know what's wrong!

In German, when "a louse crawls over your liver," you're angry. The realization pops like a bubble. A ridiculous image - still, the message lands. Now I just have to say it out loud.

I take a few deep breaths to end the session and wake Addy with a soft touch on her shoulder. "Addyson, we're done," I whisper. "There is a glass of water on the shelf behind you. Relax, take your time, have a few sips of water, and I will be back in a few minutes."

When I return, she's sitting on the edge of the table, legs dangling off the side. "Ahhhhh," she sighs with deep contentment. "That felt amazing." "I am glad. Did anything come up during the session? Thoughts, emotions?" She tilts her head. "No. It was just super relaxing. I think I even fell asleep for a moment." "Well," I start, "I think I might have found your sleep issue." Addy perks up, her eyebrows lifting.

We've known each other for about six months now. Her son goes to the same school as my girls. But we have only chatted during pickups and drop-offs so far, and our relationship has not moved past the acquaintance level just yet, so tread carefully.

"I might be off here, but … are you angry at someone?" Addy stares at me, and I try to read her expression in the dim light. Addy's posture changes, as tension sucks her body closer around her spine and her mouth pulls into a thin line. Bottled feelings set her jaw, and her voice is strained as she replies "Yeah, you could say that." A short, bitter breath. "How could you tell?" "I felt your liver during Reiki," I say, skipping the liver-louse story. "That's where we often store anger. You might want to address it - Somehow." I add.

She stands and grabs her bag. "There is nothing I can do. I have not spoken to my father in years. Too much water under the bridge." My heart sinks. One session can't untangle all that. But at least now we know what we're really working with.

Before school pickup I head to the beach to clear my head, still thinking about Addyson. Fog has lifted into low clouds, and a busy wind rushes over the waves, whipping up white caps and throwing foam in the faces of determined neoprene-clad surfers. I flip up the collar of my jacket and lean against the wind as my Ugg boots leave striped tracks on the wet sand. Tall-legged Willets rush in formation towards the shallow water, where the ocean is pulling back from the shore, leaving sand crabs vulnerable to the long, skinny beaks of the birds.

I wonder how Addy is doing right now. It wasn't Reiki that shook her; it was the insight that came with it. Physical ailments might be easier to address than emotional ones. At least now she knows the cause. Whether or not she'll address the issue is up to her. Could I've done more, I wonder?

Something black and glossy bobs on a wave towards me, and the ocean lays it like a gift onto the sand at my feet: a length of driftwood, gnarled like an old hand. It is light, polished to a sheen, the broken edges buffed by time and waves. I rub a thumb over the fracture where it must have broken off once, and wonder: storm or gravity? Did it miss the tree, or is it content as itself? What was once torn is now made beautiful.

It makes me think of Addyson. Arguments and hurtful words cleave internal scars and canyons. Shiny surfaces distract from the pain beneath. I hope she will be able to look underneath the surface and find a way to sit with her anger, look at it, and recognize it for what it is: something that has broken her in the past. But the state of brokenness does not define her. I believe that recognizing the broken parts is the first step to healing them. Her scars become not a mask but a thing of beauty. Like kintsugi. That is how the Japanese mend their broken ceramics, with lacquer and gold, so the fissures are not disguised but honored. The vessel returns brighter for what it has survived.

I turn the driftwood in my hands. In the elbow of the gnarled wood is a small patch pockmarked with holes and indentations, glazed with green algae. A movement catches my eye. A tiny white claw waves from a miniature crevasse. It opens and pinches, waves, and pulls back into the hole. There it is - life, the tiny drop of hope.

I remember when I had scars that I hid under the shiny surface of a fresh marriage - invisible scars from trauma that I carried for years.

I had become an expert at polishing away the ugliness. Nobody knew. Not even my husband. I hid the one thing that filled every hour and breath - until one touch changed everything. Maybe that was my first Reiki session, long before I knew the word. A shiver of deep understanding washes over me.

Another wave reaches, asking for its treasure back. I give in and throw the driftwood - hope and all - into the mouth of the oncoming wave. It bobs, winks one more time before disappearing from sight.

I feel lighter, almost giddy. I tossed my doubts together with the wood into the ocean because something shifted today. Reiki spoke in a new, almost secret language - and it braided it to the past.

A plump wave rises and crashes headfirst into the shallow water next to me.

"There is still so much I have to teach you."

That phrase echoes from a memory stored deep in the folds of the past. I pause and listen as the next wave stands up behind the first, white caps flying in the wind. It leans forward to whisper in my ear, tips from the top, and crashes louder than the first.

"There is still so much I have to teach you."

With it, memories unfold from what seems like a lifetime ago. Connections grow like moss through time, bridging years with a simple touch and the flow of energy. I can still hear his voice in my ear. My first Reiki teacher before I knew what Reiki was. Before I knew much of anything, really.

"There is still so much I have to teach you."

CHAPTER 15

BERLIN 2004

Just months after our wedding, we left New York for Berlin, packing hopes and dreams, and too many boxes, and watched JFK fall away beneath our airplane wing. The move hurt. Leaving New York felt as if there was a physical connection that had to be forcefully ripped out of my body. I tried to ease the separation with a ritual of "lasts": the last sushi at our favorite spot, the last farmers' market, one more book in Union Square, one more slow wander through Barnes and Noble, one more dinner with friends. Nothing satisfied the craving of burning every second into my memory. The city that felt unapproachable and cold had become mine. I'd moved here for my senior year at Parsons, and the first years had been rough - graduation, then the first job in the fashion industry straight out of The Devil Wears Prada. The corporate world was cutthroat, all elbow jabs and back doors. I had learned the hard way that you had to be tough; otherwise, the city would eat you up and spit you out. There was no room for gentle hearts, which led me to the conclusion that maybe there was no room for me here. I refused to toughen up or lie to get ahead. It was not meant for me.

Then 9/11 changed everything. It brought the city to a momentary standstill, yet the resilience, the heart, the compassion shown in the days and weeks after were unlike anything I had ever witnessed. Neighbors checked on each other, strangers helped, and new friendships and bonds formed to heal the wounds inflicted by this horrific tragedy. The days I spent with the guys riding the truck to Ground Zero welded us together - they felt like brothers. That unconditional respect and trust, that feeling of belonging, made me a New Yorker.

Had it been solely up to me, I wouldn't have chosen Berlin. Being born and raised in Germany, I should have welcomed the idea of moving "home." But I had made my peace with leaving. Everything about it seems stifling to me: the language felt sharp, the mentality, so narrow-minded and righteous; the politics, well, let's not even get into the politics. Even the food, heavy on potatoes and meat, could not tempt me.

But Andrea was about to start a company with his best friend, and Berlin offered everything a young creative agency needed: affordable rent, a highly creative environment, a booming economy, and something intangible, raw, and fresh. Plus, our parents and many of our old friends were a train ride away. It was still a seven-and-a-half hour drive to my parents' house, but being back in the same time zone meant we could Skype and call without having to do math - a luxury.

"Ein Caffe Latte, ein Cappuccino und zwei Croissants! Lasst's Euch schmecken![27]" Our tall, bearded waiter sets down thick-rimmed mugs and a basket of croissants. He slides me a latte crowned with a perfect foam heart (with a wink); Andrea gets a palm-frond leaf, no wink. I blush, quite aware of the sparkle in our waiter's eye. Andrea

---

27   *One Caffe Latte, one Cappuccino, and two croissants! Enjoy!*

raises an eyebrow, and I kiss him on the cheek, brushing off his mock jealousy with a grin. As I pull my chair in, a red condom wrapper under the table catches my eye. Ugh. I nudge it away with my shoe. It wedges between cobblestones, the torn edge sticking up like a rude little flag.

We're outside the red-brick roastery of Kaffee Einstein, tucked behind the building along the Spree, where small boats glide by. It's oddly serene this close to one of the neighborhood's busiest roads. Cool August air, the smell of roasting beans, classic music drifting from a speaker hidden in a potted cedar - all of it turns these sneaky pre-work dates into a tiny vacation, lasting as long as it takes us to savor our coffees.

Andrea tilts his face towards the sun, eyes closed, utterly content. I watch my husband: the way his wavy brown hair reveals a few sun-kissed streaks, a souvenir from our honeymoon. His wedding band gleamed the way only a new ring can - free from scratches, untouched by the wear and tear of years and the ups and downs of marriage yet to come. We are still in our honeymoon phase, three months after our New York wedding, building our new life together here in Berlin. After a handful of viewings, we settled for a spacious two-bedroom in Moabit.

Moabit is an area of Berlin that had been on the wrong side of the tracks for many years. A large immigrant population offered diversity, which was not necessarily a good thing in the eyes of many Berliners. Subway stations and parks were dotted with junkies and alcoholics; the neighborhood was just now starting to shake off its bad reputation. Not even the slow wheels of German bureaucracy could stop the gentrification. Instead of being torn down, the old buildings, stooping under the weight of graffiti and prejudice, were bought up and renovated, bringing them back to their former

Gründerzeit[28] glory with a hint of pre-war beauty. Shisha bars and kebab stands held their ground, standing shoulder to shoulder with shiny supermarkets and new restaurants.

Building by building, the neighborhood brightened, the shadows of poverty and despair pushed back a few more street corners so that higher-paying renters could walk their dogs in relative safety, without having to suffer the soul-crushing sights of what unemployment and hopelessness did to human beings. But because of those lingering shadows, and because Moabit was still lacking the "it" factor, we were able to find a reasonably priced apartment in one of those older buildings that still carried the bones of the old Berlin. The front house featured an oversized doorway leading past the mailboxes towards the backyard, which was shadowed by a canopy of three ancient trees. A side wing rose on the left, while a rear building completed the layout. Together, they housed a total of 30 apartments.

The former coal cellar had become an overstuffed bicycle room - the highlight of the house tour, our realtor claimed. She marched us down uneven stone steps, worn hollow by generations of feet, probably dating back to pre-war Berlin when the city was proud and vibrant and heated by coal. The air down here was cool and stale, with a distinct scent of humidity and memories stashed behind padlocked wooden doors to individual cellars. The nervous flashes of a lonely fluorescent light bulb illuminated the walls of the long, narrow corridor. As Andrea and I passed the lightbulb, our shadows grew large and threw grotesque shapes on the wall, merging occasionally with the realtor's shadow bopping ahead of us, jumping to the ceiling and back down. I had to shake the feeling that the figures moving along the wall were remnants of Berlin's dark past.

---

28   *Gründerzeit - German. "Founders period." Refers to a specific time period, (1850-1914), marked by a lavish architectural style. Think tall ceilings, grand staircases, parquet floor and decorative plaster molding.*

We reached a poorly lit, damp room, stuffed with a silent gathering of at least 15 bikes of all ages and in various stages of repair, several rows deep, and even hanging from hooks along the wall. The realtor rapped the door's hefty locks with pride. "Isn't it a bit of a hassle carrying your bike down the stairs every day?" I asked on the way back up. "It beats getting it stolen," she said, mildly offended, as if that were obvious.

Back at Kaffee Einstein, I sip of my latte, lean back in my chair, and notice a wheel-less frame padlocked to the far railing, the chain a ribbon of rust. The number of bikes stolen in Berlin is staggering; if a thief can't break the lock, he'll take whatever comes loose and leave a skeleton behind. Despite the threat of theft, Berliners ride their bicycles with a certain grim determination. They tackle the unforgiving cobblestones and potholes and brave the cold and often miserable weather: raincoat-covered figures, huddled over their handlebars, leaning against the wind as if they are entangled in a fistfight, headlamps skittering over wet asphalt. And God help you if you're in their way - especially in those "quiet" tree-lined residential streets, seemingly quaint and peaceful, but turn treacherous the second a cyclist appears. I cannot count the number of times I was left with my heart pounding out of my chest because some kamikaze rider zooms past me, yelling profanities at my sheer audacity for being in his way. This, in turn, forces me to slam my brakes, my adrenaline and anger rising in equal measures. Needless to say, I never got a bike.

Andrea still has his eyes closed, enjoying the moment. The sun warms the brick wall behind us, throwing red reflections onto the river. The ducks have gathered where the branches of a nearby willow tree kiss the surface of the water, chattering up at us for a crumb or two. With as much stealth as I can muster, I lean over to bite off the crunchy tip of Andrea's croissant, my chair wobbling on the uneven cobblestones underneath - I'm busted. Before I can react, he steals mine in retaliation, and a few crumbs rain down to the excited ducks, as he evens the score. The croissant battle makes our table wobble. My coffee spills over the rim, bleeding onto the paper coaster underneath. I lift the coffee cup, take a sip, and cover up the drowned coaster with a fresh, pristine paper napkin. I do not want anything spoiling the perfection of this morning.

Berlin is stunning - and raw. To tourists, the city seems beautiful and exciting, filled with stunning architecture, museums, bars, and coffee shops. Living here, I got a glimpse behind the façade: War has left scars still visible to this day, humming with the aftershocks of guilt and disbelief, even more shocking when contrasted by the sparkling jewels of modern buildings or the stunning resurrection of pre-war architecture throughout the city. The division of East and West still hangs in the air despite continuous efforts to level the playing field. Add the influx of immigrants and refugees facing social-economic struggles on one side and the creative, vibrant money-movers of Berlin Mitte, where business, fashion, art, and music string the wires between the opposites of Berlin until it reaches a precarious tension.

Our apartment is my little refuge from the not-so-friendly surroundings. Lofty ceilings and old hardwood floors, lovingly restored, made it easy to turn the space into a home. We even have a small balcony with herbs and flowers bursting out of their pots, around a tiny blue table - my outdoor oasis after years of being confined to a shoebox-sized apartment in New York.

I love snuggling with Andrea in the morning, the window of our bedroom wide open, crisp air caressing our skin, while the sun throws sparkling patterns of shadow and light on the floor, filtered through the majestic branches of the ash tree in the courtyard. Watching tiny specks of dust dance in the beams of light makes me want to stop time. It fills my heart so completely I could burst - and still, a thin melancholy threads the light. Joy pairs so easily with a fear of loss. As my love overflows, I pull Andrea into a tight embrace, squeezing him with all my might to make him understand the crushing intensity of my happiness. Right now, he is my everything: my soul mate, my lover, my best friend ... my life raft.

CHAPTER 16

BERLIN 2005

As our first summer in Berlin comes to an end, things change; the temperature drops, the days become shorter and darker. But it's a darkness that stems from something different than just a lack of light - it feels dark. A mantle has settled on the city and on my soul. Maybe this is what Berlin winters are like. With a shove of my hip, I close the oven door, placing the hot dish on the stove to cool down. Our small kitchen with its orange accent wall glows with *Gemütlichkeit*[29]. The candles are lit, the table is set for two, and the whole apartment is infused with the comforting scent of my famous lasagna - the tomato sauce, heavy with minced meat, bubbles over the edges of the mozzarella. I can't wait to serve it, with the cheese

---

29   *Gemütlichkeit - German. A term which is very much a part of German tradition, yet at the same time so contradictory to the otherwise grumpy demeanor of most Germans. It means coziness and warmth.*

pulling glossy strands, that stretch then snap onto the plate. I plop back into my chair in front of the empty plate and take a sip of steaming tea. The warmth from the wall heater behind me makes my back feel sticky and itchy under my knitted sweater. Despite the warmth, I clutch my mug; cold fingers seeking out every inch of hot surface for relief from this cold feeling of dread that I cannot shake. I play with a loose thread on the edge of the olive-green placemat, wrapping it around my index finger, pulling tighter with every turn until it snaps and I rub it together into a tangled ball. Our Yorkie, Tina, sits by the door, whining at her leash on the hallway hook.

"Later, Tina. Go to bed!" I reprimand her and look at the clock.

8:05 pm

I straighten the fork and knife next to my empty plate and arrange the wine glass just so. My shoulder critic appears in my periphery. He'd slipped back into my life a few months ago. I am not sure how long he was gone. A year? Maybe longer? During our wedding preparations, the honeymoon, and the first months in Berlin, things were so busy that I had not even noticed his absence. And now he's as if he never left. He is wearing dirty overalls, a khaki turtleneck with elbow patches, thick knit socks - no shoes, his big toe peeking through a hole. His hands are burrowed deep into the pockets as he paces back and forth on my shoulder, grumbling into a new, scraggly beard. He glances at the clock, too.

8:06 pm

With the colder temperatures and the icy January winds blowing west from Russia, the face of the city that had been so charming during the short summer suddenly gives me chills. The blue skies give way to low, dark clouds. At first, I relish the opportunity for "*Gemütlichkeit*,"- that German coziness: lingering for hours after a meal without the hovering presence of a waiter rushing you away from your table to make space for new customers. The warm lights from restaurants and cafes invite you to linger while boutiques and shops turn up the heat just a notch to lure customers away from the cold winds outside. As if to rally against the forces of nature, people socialize more - huddled in tight clusters around the heating lamps at the Christmas market, hot mugs of *Glühwein* held close to their faces, where the steam would do on the outside what the alcohol does on the inside.

In early December, I was invited to an Advent afternoon at my friend's house. Traditionally, the *Adventszeit*[30], the four weeks leading up to Christmas, is filled with cookies, candles, *Glühwein*, tea, vanilla, and cinnamon. We spent hours together - a small group of six girls, laughing, drinking, and baking, Christmas music in the background. Pre-kids, pre-responsibilities of adulthood, even though we were all in our late twenties already. We were trying to recapture a bit of the Christmas magic we all experienced as children. Yet somehow, I could not relax into the spirit. A nagging restlessness urged me home. I forgot I still had to walk a few blocks through the pelting rain to my car.

Every time I leave my friend's home and the heavy front door closes behind me with a clunk of metallic finality, the stale, cold air of the dark stairwell has the sinister ability to yank me straight out of my happiness. The lights in front of her apartment and down the stairs are broken more often than not, the tiled walls assaulting me with the echo of my steps. Hand on the wooden banister, I felt for each tread in the darkness. The stench of urine tells me that I am close to the ground floor, where dark corners offer invisibility for drunk passers-by, too inebriated to make it home before nature

---

30   *Adventszeit - German. The time of advent, the four weeks leading up to Christmas.*

calls. I lean all my weight against the large front door, push out into the cold air, and find that the rain has stopped. Thank God!

The memory makes me feel anxious. I had not visited my friend since. The echo of my heels clicking in the dark of her hallway triggered a primal fear, even if I walked those steps with friends. Their laughter turned to a cackling crescendo thrown back from the tiles set to the urgent staccato of heels. HAHAHA! Click, click, click, click. HAHAHA! There was no logic behind it, nothing to explain the cold dread dripping down my spine. But it was real enough to find excuses every time she invited me over.

Sorry, I can't.
No, I am busy.
Next time, I promise.

The guilt of lying was the engine that drove a wedge in our friendship. She stopped asking after a while. I stopped reaching out. And now the guilt of not calling settled on top of the guilt of lying. A guilt-sandwich that I had no energy to chew.

I get up. The Biedermeier chair I reupholstered in orange and yellow fabric to match our kitchen, scratches over the wooden floor in protest. The silence in the apartment is choking me, and I stare into the moonless courtyard feeling claustrophobic as the absence of sound closes in.

"Turn on some music! I cannot hear myself think in this silence!" my shoulder critic prompts, leaning toward the radio. I turn the knob and notch by notch the volume of classical music rises, pooling at my feet first before swirling up into the air all around me. I take a deep breath of music, flavored by the scent of lasagna, and feel my heartbeat slow down. Classical music was a new thing, too. I'm a pop or 90s girl. But *Klassic Radio* feels safe. Mozart and Bach swaddle me in childhood memories: Sunday mornings, my mother preparing breakfast, the fridge door opening and closing, the sound of plates being put on the counter. The smell of my father's Earl Grey tea, the chirping of the kitchen timer when the eggs were done. The crunch of the first bite of a *Brötchen*[31] fresh out of the oven ... but today the galloping energy of Beethoven's Symphony #5 stokes the glowing embers of my anxiety. The sounds of my memories are whipped into a frenzy, rushing along the silent walls of our kitchen. Everything speeds up: thoughts, heartbeat, and breath. I jerk my head to break the spell, then turn the radio off before my heart starts to race out of control.

Transfixed by silence, all I hear is the occasional drop of water plummeting out of the faucet. Upstairs, chairs scrape, footsteps pass before everything is silent again. I glance at my shoulder critic without turning my head. He perches on my shoulder, head cocked to listen, hoping for anything to disrupt the absence of sound. He looks gaunt despite the warm glow of the kitchen light, and I wonder if he is unwell. But I do not have the energy to worry about the personification of my own emotions, so I look away. Another longing glance into the empty courtyard where the big door remains stubbornly shut.

8:10 pm

It isn't only the weather that's weighing me down. I start to notice things that barely registered before: the bullet holes in the facades of the old pre-1940s buildings, screaming Berlin's past at every passerby. Brass plaques set into cobblestones mark the houses where victims of the Holocaust lived. And once you notice one, you see them everywhere! I can imagine their feet walking along the same street I was on. In my mind, it is always children. Little hands clutching their mothers' as they rush along at night, staying close to the walls, looking back over their shoulders. Scared. Hurried. Persecuted. I

---

31 *Brötchen - German. Bread rolls*

can feel their fear. I hear their labored breathing. Until their image dissolves into smoke.

Where I had felt safe just months ago, walking my neighborhood in the evenings, I am now easily spooked, finding threats in every shadow. Walking my dog becomes a *Spießrutenlauf*[32], darting from safe spot to safe spot - from our heavy front gate past the illuminated windows of the pharmacy to the flower shop on the corner. When things get bad, I usually stop here for a short respite, picking up a few fresh flowers for the kitchen table. I love chatting with the gay couple who runs the flower shop. They have a wonderful way of dispersing the internal and external shadows with some light banter and the occasional glass of Crémant. I can't stay hidden here forever. Tina is all too eager to relieve herself and mark her territory. So, off I go across the street, taking advantage of the brightly lit supermarket entrance, never venturing near the broken streetlight, where the shadows thicken. When I finally make it home, I rip my winter coat off, my body covered in a cold sweat.

What is wrong with me?

Tina settles on the carpet, shooting me a reproachful look. "I know, my love. I am sorry." I bend down, scratching the spot behind her left ear until her hind leg twitches. I couldn't do it today. I just could not. Andrea should be home soon, though. I'll tell him I'm not feeling well. I couldn't walk Tina, because …. a headache. No. I used that last time. Upset stomach? No. No one makes a lasagna from scratch with a stomach bug.

8:13 pm

---

32   *Spießrutenlauf, German, translates to running the gauntlet*

Tina's last walk was at 4 pm, just before dark. She can wait a bit longer.

"Check your phone! Go! Check it now! Maybe you missed a message," my shoulder critic urges. But the screen is blank. No message. I'm sure Andrea's coming home any moment. I mean, he did say he might be late. There was a "might" in the sentence, though. "Might" is leaving the door open for the hope that he'll be here soon. But maybe not. He's been so slammed since the company launch. Starting a new business is crazy, and I was not expecting anything else. He is passionate and dedicated to his craft. I admire him for that. Tonight, though, I wish he were a little less focused on work. I step towards the window and look out into the dark courtyard.

Maybe I could take Tina down for a minute - just a quick pee. The wind has picked up. The branches whip against the wall of the building. A dark figure, a scarf covering half the face, and a hoodie pulled up, hurries from the bike cellar towards the side entrance. "No! Sorry, Tina." I scoff. "I am not going out."

The last time I was afraid of the dark, I was about six years old. "Alex, go grab me another roll of kitchen towels from downstairs," my mother said. "And don't forget to turn off the light after!" She had no idea that turning off the light was the hard part. The cellar was the dark center of our home, the place where the deep hum of the water heater mixed with the rhythmic beating and sloshing of the washing machine. Void of natural light, this was where pipes with strange dials and valves stuck out of walls, where light was never strong enough to reach corners or cabinets where my mom kept our pantry items. I cracked the heavy metal door and stretched my small hand through to find the light switch. Spiders lived on that wall near the switch. I have never seen them, but I saw a tattle-tale spiderweb once. The fluorescent bulb clicked on, flickered a few times, deciding whether to muster the energy to actually turn on. With a push, I let the door fly open. I waited a few seconds, allowing the light to seep as far as it would reach before stepping onto the tiled floor of the cellar. Five steps and I was under the light bulb - the only safe spot in the room. I looked down - I was wearing jeans shorts, and a bright red t-shirt - my dad always likes bright colors on me. My bare feet were firmly planted a few hand-widths to the left and right of the floor drain. The rusty drain cover was the one thing that challenged the safety of the brightest spot in the room. Spiders lived under there too, obviously. The washer turned one lazy circle, gurgling sounds rushed down a drain. Towels and a few t-shirts hung on the clothesline above, and I wove my head around the fluttering cotton to see both halves of the room.

Without moving my feet, I stretched my arm, my whole body, towards the paper towels, until my fingertips brushed the soft surface. Not daring to leave the safety of my position, I scratched and pulled with my fingertips until the paper roll toppled over. I grabbed it and dashed out, slamming the door shut. A huff escaped my lips as I realized I'd forgotten to turn off the light.

But now it feels different. I'm not six anymore. I'm nearly 30 and married, yet winter comes on, and this fear grips me every time I leave the house alone. In the beginning, it was only the dark. And if Andrea came home before dinner, I'd ask him to walk Tina. But that made me feel guilty. He worked all day at the office while I worked from home with a relaxed schedule and less pressure. And how was I supposed to explain a sudden fear of the dark when I didn't even understand it myself? It was childish and irrational.

I hadn't joined a gym in Berlin yet. Honestly, it was low on my priority list. I got enough exercise during the day when I took Tina to the nearby Tiergarten, the Berlin version of Central Park. We'd walk, jog, and run together. I would throw her ball over and over. I loved watching her sprint on those little legs, full of energy and determination. Sometimes, instead of the ball, she'd drag a branch three times her size and drop it at my feet with a proud expression on her face. But in the last couple of weeks, anxieties invaded this happy place too. Just this morning, I went to our favorite meadow, determined to work up a good sweat before heading home. I pulled the tennis ball from my pocket and hurled it until it disappeared into a bush; within seconds, Tina was out of sight. The meadow - busy during the summer, was now empty except for the odd jogger or dog walker. The people-less expanse sent shivers down my spine, and my eyes darted from tree to tree. Even the crunch of leaves underfoot felt like a threat - sharp, loud, and rhythmic, chasing me with every step I took. I walked faster, fighting the urge to look back for the dark figure that must be following me. "Tina!" I called. - Nothing. No dog, no bark - nothing. I kept my own breath shallow, straining for a rustle, a bark - anything - while my heartbeat drowned out the world. Finally, Tina burst out of the bushes, the tennis ball in her mouth, legs flying. With a quick glance over my shoulder, I bend down, clip her leash to her collar, and rush home. In my haste, I don't even notice that Tina dropped the ball.

8:21 pm - ping, ping.

A double ring announces a message. "Sorry, Amore, I won't be home for another couple of hours. Don't wait up. Miss you."

With a thump, hope drops into the pit of my stomach, and the light in the kitchen dims a few shades. I shouldn't be disappointed. I knew he'd probably be late again. "What were you thinking? That the smell of your lasagna would lure him home? Ridiculous!" my shoulder critic scowls and flips his legs over towards my shoulder blades, turning his back to me, arms crossed in a pout. "You'd better not push him away with your clinginess. You're being such a pain in the ass. And why? Because you are scared of the dark? Pah!" he spits the last word with such disdain that I recoil. He's right. I feel ridiculous. Laughable. I'm a grown woman hiding in her apartment, hiding from the dark, hiding from my friends, from my husband. I don't even recognize myself anymore. What happened?

I don't know what I'm so scared of. Nothing suggests I'm - in any real way - in danger, but that doesn't ease the anxiety. If anything, knowing that my fears are irrational makes me feel insecure and weak, like I am losing touch with reality. And weakness is not something I can admit to. My mother raised me to be anything but weak. Weakness is a flaw; it diminishes you, makes you less... and I refuse to be less. Less than what? Who am I when I'm reduced to a shivering mess by an irrational fear? I only feel whole when my husband's around. I can't be dependent like that- some woman with nothing to live for but her beloved. RIDICULOUS! Haven't I learned anything? I am independent. I don't need anybody's help. I can do this. *Arschbackenzusammenkneifmentalität!* It shouldn't be that hard. I've done things alone all my life.

But telling myself to "suck it up" is just a quick fix, a temporary bandage that lasts as long as my current train of thought. A dismissive grunt from my shoulder critic is all it takes to make my fake bravado crumble. I put a tinfoil cover over the lasagna and walk to the bathroom to get ready for bed. Might as well call it an early night.

Before I turn off my bedside lamp, I send Andrea a quick text.

> I am off to sleep, Amore. Don't work too late. Lasagna is waiting for you in the kitchen if u re still hungry. Before I forget ... Could u take Tina down for a quick pee when u get home? She refused to go out just now. Must be scared of the dark, silly dog. xoxo

Once again, I was fast asleep by the time he came home. Andrea worked a lot during those first years in Berlin. As much as I missed him, I was almost relieved that he didn't witness what was going on with me. Starting a new business takes every ounce of determination and support; it means long hours in the office, pulling the occasional all-nighter, and always pushing towards deadlines. I tried my hardest to make sure that he wouldn't know that anything was amiss. I didn't want to add to his stress - he had enough to worry about as it was. Most evenings, I was already asleep when he came home, and if he managed to take time off on weekends, we spent it together as usual, uninterrupted by my fears. His presence calmed and reassured me, and I was back to my normal self. In fact, the weekends together made me forget my anxieties, and I cherished our time more than ever. If I could just pretend that everything was okay for a little while longer, maybe those weird fears would dissipate, and life could go back to normal. I felt guilty for keeping things from him. But what would I say anyway? Every time I thought about how to approach the subject, my shoulder critic shut me down. "You sound ridiculous," he would say. Or "Pathetic!" That was his favorite word. The one that cut the deepest.

I was pathetic.
So, I said nothing.
And then the nightmares started.

At first, there was nothing tangible, nothing I'd remember later. I'd jolt awake in the middle of the night, heart hammering, sheets drenched in sweat. It was not so much a visual dream - more emotions and feelings than images. As the dreams continued, they grew more visual, more frequent, more terrifying. One night, I woke to find myself choking. There was dust in my nose, crusted on my eyes, clogging my ears. Every time I breathed, I inhaled fine particles, and my throat clenched tight, causing a coughing fit. In panic, I grasped blindly for Andrea's arm in bed next to me, but all I could feel was rubble. Shards of glass cut my hands, and I yelled in blind pain. I smelled the destruction around me and the crushing weight of something huge and heavy on my chest, pinning me down. "*Amore!*" I croaked, choking as the words scratched their way up my dried throat. Thirst! I was so thirsty! The dust dried me from the inside out. Tears ran down my face and vanished in a desert on my skin, leaving dried riverbeds. Panic gripped me, and I screamed.

With the shriek still ringing in my ears, I woke, sobbing. Andrea held me by the shoulders, shaking me. "Wake up! It was just a dream. Wake up! I am here!" he hushed me, cradling me in his arms, and I dissolved into a sobbing mess, clinging to him for dear life. My sobs still strangled me, and I couldn't speak, couldn't explain. Not trying to push me for an explanation, he leans back into the cushions, pulling me with him, and I snuggle into his arm, allowing my breath to slow until I fall asleep.

The next morning, we overslept, and when we finally woke, there was no time to talk before Andrea rushed off to work. And what is there to talk about anyway? It was just a dream … one of many. Sometimes, I'm falling from great heights or standing at the edge of a huge cliff, being pulled towards certain death by an invisible, relentless grip. My nights are filled with increasing emotional terrors, ending in a crescendo so terrifying that I am afraid to go to sleep.

So, I didn't.

Many nights, I waited until Andrea's breathing slowed, his body melting in deep relaxation into the mattress. My eyes widened against the smothering darkness around me, and I flinched at every creek and moan of the sleeping old house cupping me in the palm of its hand. I snuck out of bed, sliding out between the sheets without disturbing the folds of the fabric draped over Andrea's sleeping body. I spent the night on the couch, under my grandma's blanket, my dog fast asleep by my side and a mug of steaming chamomile tea next to me - or a joint, or both. Weed numbed the fear. I read or watched TV until I finally gave up and slipped back into bed, trying not to wake Andrea. There I lay, staring up at the shadows on the ceiling until finally drifting off just as the first hints of sunlight trickled through the curtains. Despite the lack of sleep, I usually woke a short time after with a sudden burst of energy. We had breakfast together, and I made plans for the day, not mentioning anything about my disrupted sleep. I usually had a long list of things I wanted to accomplish, determined to get stuff done. But as soon as the door clicked behind Andrea on his way to the office, my steam-train resolve slowed for its first stop. If I just lay down for a few minutes, closed my eyes, I could catch up on some much-needed sleep, and then the rest of the day would be even more productive.

How sweet the lies we tell ourselves?

CHAPTER 17

Highlighter poised and ready, I pick up the top page from a stack on my desk and blow off a layer of dust. My desk is clinging to the far corner of my small office in the spare bedroom. I keep the curtains closed most of the time, hiding the shameful mess my workspace has become. But today I pull the curtains wide open, letting sunshine - and a little hope - flood the page. I'm wearing my usual sweatpants that have molded themselves over the long winter, carrying the shape of my knees and hips in stretched-out bulges. I've perfected the art of hiding my troubles with fake smiles, curtains, and sweatpants. I'm always afraid that something will make the mask slip, that Andrea will catch a glimpse of the ugliness of my current reality. Hopefully, my issues are like the butter in the fridge that I ask him to grab for me. Unless it hits him over the head, he won't notice.

As winter tilts into spring and the first sunny days offer a much-needed respite from the daunting darkness of the past months, I mask my panic with daily short bursts of "productivity": spring-cleaning the house, planting fresh flowers and herbs on the balcony, starting little projects here and there - anything - to give Andrea and me the illusion that I am happy and busy every day. I am convinced whatever is going on with me must be related to the darkness and long nights of winter. It can only be a matter of weeks now until I snap out of it. My eyes zig-zag off the page in my hand, and I watch the white undulations of the curtains, the secrecy of the shadows, the bare trees in our courtyard. I long for the telltale signs of spring. I've printed hundreds of pages of research to make myself feel like I'm doing work, finishing my book, which is stalled on page 50. Most of those pages just sit around collecting dust; I rarely read them. But today I'll do it - at least a handful of pages. I pull the cap off the highlighter. It is dented and rough at the end, bearing teeth marks of absent-minded stress relief. I trace the tip along the lines on the paper, my thoughts trailing right off the page. My thumb flicks the cap's pocket clip a few times, until it snaps, sails through the air, and clatters against the wall somewhere behind my dark computer screen. I don't even move to look for it.

I'm angry with myself for falling into this hole. I question everything - myself first and foremost. What good am I? Every simple task is an insurmountable obstacle: writing, doing housework, or - God forbid - the laundry. Everything requires a Herculean effort and, instead of filling me with a sense of accomplishment, only spotlights my inability to function. I read the first paragraph; my eyes fixed on one line that stands out. The highlighter makes a dry scratching sound as I pull it along the words. A faint yellow streak appears, then dies - the words sink back into the rest of the text. I try to resuscitate the pen, shake it, and breathe onto the dried-out nib, then dab it again. Nothing. I stab harder - again and again, until the felt tip disappears into its plastic casing. Done. Dead. The text blurs in front of my eyes. I wish I could blur and fade into the background, too. Soon, my façade will crumble, and I'll be exposed as the fraud that I am. Not good enough for anything, really. Who am I to even attempt to write a book? In a sudden flame of anger, I crumple the paper and fling it toward the overflowing paper bin under my desk. It arcs and lands on the floor, joining a sad gathering of paper balls - all witnesses of my failed attempts to be a writer.

I live for the moment the door opens and Andrea comes home. Our time together is my anchor, my time machine back to a version of me who knows how to feel happiness. We laugh and tease each other, we cuddle, and we cook together. Sometimes I catch my reflection in the window or the oven door and see a smiling illusion of myself that I hardly recognize.

Yet even his presence starts to weigh on me, pinning me down like the weight on my chest I dreamt about. The number of lies and excuses I've used over these months has stacked up and is closing in, building a wall around me that becomes denser and more foreboding every day; a massive, solid stone wall with moss growing along the bottom, built to last through the ages.

Spring comes and goes, and with it my hope for relief. I need to do something. But what? I wish I could talk to Kathrin. But talking would mean confronting the issue, admitting the guilt and the lies, and that would open Pandora's Box - I'm just too scared, too tired to endure it.

In the end, it only takes four words.

Four little words to break through my solid wall of lies and shame. "What is wrong, honey?" my dad asks, taking my hand as we sit on the couch. A thin sliver of a crack strikes down along my wall, rushing along the mortar lines. His voice is different - deeper, lined with a velvet layer of concern and a subtle tremor of trepidation. It is early summer, and my parents are in Berlin for a long weekend. We spend hours shopping and exploring the city. In a few days, Andrea and I are leaving for our first proper vacation since moving here. My mother helps me pick out a few cute outfits for the beach, complaining that my hips are too bony. "You've gotten too skinny," she worries. Having my parents around is a wonderful distraction and calms my frazzled soul. Throughout the weekend, I feel my dad's eyes on me. I can feel his concern and know he can see straight through me. He is a psychiatrist after all - but not only that - he has an uncanny ability to see beyond my pretense. Keeping up my façade was easy on the phone, but here, in front of him, my wall crumbles.

This is it - the moment of truth.

I sit on the couch, my legs crossed, and my foot jittering all on its own. Instead of my uniform of sweatpants and an old T-shirt, which I'd been wearing pretty much every day since all of this started, I dressed up for my parents: jeans, brown wedges, and an off-the-shoulder top. I even picked out some earrings. I feel uncomfortable in my costume. It doesn't fit right. I don't fit right. I don't fit here, into my life, into my marriage, into my own body. Everything feels off-kilter.

And now what? Which way do I go? What do I say? My mother has retreated to the balcony, a cigarette between her pink-manicured fingers. She is too absorbed in her Sudoku to pay much attention to us. The air in our courtyard is still, and I watch lazy banners of smoke shimmy upward from her cigarette before vanishing into the branches above. The crack in the wall widens, my heart speeds up, my palms grow sweaty. Without meeting my dad's eyes, I pull off the little fuzzballs that have collected on my grandmother's blanket - mangled threads felted together by nights alone on the couch. My shoulder critic is curled up in a ball, his eyes squeezed shut so tight his wrinkles fan out to his hairline. His hair looks unwashed, felted into dreadlocks, much like the fuzzballs of the blanket. He rocks his scrawny little body, hands cupped over his ears, and stammers, "Don't do it, don't do it, don't ..." I think he is losing his marbles. I

can almost envision them: tiny glass globes with colored swirls rolling out of the depth of his matted hair. They clatter onto the floor,
roll under the leather ottoman, and disappear beneath the bookcase
on the far wall. For a moment, I lose myself in the worry of how to
collect them all. My mom could trip when she comes back in from
the balcony. All those marbles everywhere.

Ha! Who is losing their marbles now, I wonder?

My dad's silent expectation pulls me back into the moment. My
hands shake, and I break down, sobs wracking my chest. I don't even
know where to start. The wall collapses and everything floods out:
the months of fear and anxiety, the dark, the nightmares, the feeling
of not being worthy, the guilt, the shame ... all of it. "I'm sorry. I'm
so sorry! It's all my fault. I should have told you!" When I'm done,
time stands still - silence pools around me as time figures out what
to do next. I keep my eyes downcast, not daring to look at my dad.

Before the silence expands into an ocean, he pulls me in and holds
me so gently as if I might crumble, once again his little girl, the
one who scraped her knee falling off her scooter, or the one crying
over her first broken heart. There is no disappointment or anger, no
judgment, just unconditional love. My tears drop onto his red and
blue checkered shirt, and he digs a neatly folded handkerchief out of
his jeans and dabs my face. A deep warmth spreads out in my chest,
filling the space that had been so cold and afraid. The heart, that I'd
tucked somewhere between my ribcage, expands. "I got you," my
father whispers. "I got you. This isn't your fault." For a moment, I'm
okay, relieved, even as I feel broken into a thousand pieces scattered
across my living room. The burden of guilt lifts. I know that something has changed. I take the first hesitant step towards hope. My
shoulder critic hauls himself upright, his eyes are red from crying,
sniffling so loud I can barely hear my own tears, wiping his nose on
his khaki knit sweater. "You need to confront this," my dad continues, holding me at arm's length to get a better look at my face. "I

think you have PTSD. Post-Traumatic Stress Disorder. Maybe from
the time you spent at Ground Zero?"

Shit!

Both my shoulder critic and I look at him in disbelief, and the
rest of his explanation turns into a distorted wah-wah-wah as my
brain reels, processing. In a snap, everything clicks! PTSD! It all
makes sense - the fear, the anxieties, the nightmares. Oh my God!
The nightmares should have tipped me off weeks ago. It all boiled
down to this: The feeling of being trapped under rubble, the dust,
even the acrid smell. Why didn't I put two and two together? The
isolation from my friends and family, the emptiness, loss of appetite,
hopelessness, the depression - They were all part of it. 9/11 had left
a scar on my soul that is only now surfacing. I wasn't going crazy
after all. Oh, man. How could I have missed it? My shoulder critic
perks up at this with an "I told you so," but I know he is as shocked
as I am. Drop the act. I hold him as my father holds me, our sobs
combine into a lullaby until, finally, we just breathe.

My dad is silent for a few minutes, giving me the space to process.

I feel like an idiot! I had been so arrogant! I remember hearing
that some of the guys from my truck at Ground Zero went to speak
to counselors or therapists in the months after 9/11. I was so naive
to think that I had it all under control! *"Nah, I am good! I don't need
that,"* I would shrug off their concern for my well-being. I really
thought that having my dad as a psychiatrist and the art of self-re-
flection and a modicum of self-analysis were enough. I thought I was
ok. Yeah! Look at me now! I am a mess sitting on a huge pile of lies.

But there is also an immediate feeling of relief. I read somewhere
that if you can give your demons a name, they lose their power over
you. Energy buzzes hot over my skin as hope floods through my
body. Despite the early afternoon hour, the sun has disappeared
beyond the roofline of the courtyard, and my mother pulls on

her jacket before lighting another cigarette. She hasn't noticed the breakthrough I just had. After a while, my dad clears his throat. "Remember, this is not your fault! And you cannot do this alone. You need help. Professional help. You need to find a therapist or a psychiatrist." I look up, not quite understanding. "But YOU are a psychiatrist. Isn't that enough?" His eyes are tender as he shakes his head. "You need someone here. Someone who is objective, neutral." My shoulder critic springs to attention like an over-eager student trying to get his teacher's attention. He's wearing the same sweater he has been wearing for months now, and it looks dirty. I think it smells rather funky. As if reading my mind, he glances at me with irritation, raises one arm, and sniffs his armpit. Without a further attempt to catch my father's eye, he turns around and sulks.

I know that this conversation is just a baby step. Nothing has really been solved yet, but my dad has thrown me a lifeline. And not only that: he has given the demon that consumes me a name: PTSD! Now I can fight. I can be myself again, breathe again. And just in time - in a few days, Andrea and I are off to the Seychelles. What better way to celebrate my freedom from the prison I had confined myself in?

I couldn't be happier!

... had it not been for the cautionary warning from my dad: *Just knowing what causes the problem does not make it vanish.* But I'm just too relieved to heed his warning. For the first time in forever, happiness bubbles up from my stomach, fizzy and reckless. I feel like running around, fueled by an abundance of relief and freedom. Finally, free of the ghosts.

Still, I promise my dad I'll take care of myself, open up to Andrea, and seek professional help. A therapist (not my shoulder critic) would be able to support and guide me - an unbiased, objective support I apparently needed. "I will," I promise him. "Just as soon as I get back from vacation." Why start now only to pause for two weeks? I don't admit it to my dad, but I have zero intention of going to therapy. Riding this adrenaline high of finally opening up to someone, I'm now convinced that I can beat this by myself.

My optimism is short-lived, though: the nightmares return the same night. My demon has me by the throat again. No matter if I can call him by his name now, he is not impressed.

- Crap!

CHAPTER 18

BERLIN 2006

I push my head back into the seat as the plane takes off, ignoring the itchy headrest cover - a dull tension headache pulses from my clenched teeth into the back of my skull. The air is filled with the low murmur of passengers and the metallic rattle of the service carts in their cubbies. My hands clamp the cool armrest as lift-off pushes me deeper into the seat. I close my eyes, then snap them open a millisecond later. I don't want to see the plane take off, but I can't close my eyes either. The darkness behind closed eyelids conjures flashes of a crystal-blue sky, a lone plane above the New York skyline, and a fireball. The images strobe across my eyelids at dizzying speed, making me nauseous. This is the first flight I've been on since PTSD hijacked my life. My heart pounds against my ribcage, and I can feel my T-shirt sticking to my skin as sweat trickles down my spine.

"What should we watch?" Andrea nudges my elbow as he leans forward in his chair, tapping the screen in front of him.

Since talking with my dad, I've tried to open up to Andrea, but without much success. I have no idea how to even approach the subject. How do you explain the gravity of something that you've been so good at concealing?

How about:

> "Amore, you remember how excited I would get when you came home from work these past months? Well, that was literally my only happiness since the rest of the time I was drowning in a bottomless pit of my own personal hell."

Well, that's a bit dramatic - probably something my shoulder critic would say. How about:

> "Amore, you know, every time I asked you to walk the dog at night. Well, it wasn't that I was too tired. I was just absolutely terrified of the dark. I know it isn't rational. I know it makes no sense. But it literally made me want to throw up."

Ehm, yeah - not so much.

How would he feel if he found out now that I'd lied to him? Lied by omission. I tried handing out the truth in homeopathic doses. Occasionally, I'd mention a nightmare, my insomnia, or my lack of energy over the past weeks. I figured that if I could just reveal each issue bit by bit, they would all form a whole picture over time. He would get it without me having to explain it. "Yeah, right, as if that would ever happen. Have you met your husband? He is a man! They have problems reading between the lines. Either you spell it out or just shut up!" My shoulder critic, in a dark blue silk PJ with fuchsia Hawaiian print and hot pink slippers, is dressed for our tropical vacation. He sits on my shoulder, legs stretched out as he leans on the headrest behind me. With one last glance at me, he pulls a hot

pink sleeping mask with "Diva" written in blue cursive letters over his eyes, curls himself away from me, and goes to sleep.

Maybe that's not the worst advice. I imagine what it would be like to get a handle on the situation before I would ever have to fess up. And then, why mention it in the first place? He would be so upset with me. I can just hear him say, "I told you so!" He had always been against my going down to Ground Zero. He had been scared for me and worried about how it would affect me. And I hate to admit it, but he was right. Damn, was he right. For now, I run on borrowed time, cross my fingers, and just hope for the best. Maybe during our vacation, I will find a good moment to tell him.

Maybe ....
Maybe not.

"Just don't!" I hear a sleepy murmur from my shoulder. But I have to, don't I? I cannot continue like this. The edge of a Band-Aid I had wrapped around a little cut on my index finger has peeled off and is now sticking to everything I touch. The sticky part is already black and grimy-looking. With one swift motion, I rip it off and stuff it in the seat pocket in front of me. I have to stop covering things up. I cover my weight loss with baggy clothes, the shadows under my eyes with makeup, and my fears with lies.

"I am ok. I'd rather read." I answer my husband with a smile and hide behind my book for the rest of the flight.

I must have dozed off at some point because I woke with a start when I felt the airplane descend for landing. Once again, my heart starts racing as fear grips me. Engine failure, the plane is overshooting the runway, turbulence, birds flying into the turbines, the pilot is having a heart attack ... there are literally a million reasons why we would not make it off this plane alive! I push myself back into the seat again, bracing for the impact, every muscle in my body tense in anticipation. My shoulder critic has changed since the talk with my dad. He seems like a different person. Upbeat and chipper. Always looking around as if the world hid its best surprises just around the corner. Even now, he's standing bright-eyed and bushy-tailed on my shoulder, bouncing on his tippy toes to catch a glimpse of what the night is hiding from us outside. His silk PJs must be in that tiny Louis Vuitton suitcase near his feet (excuse me, how bougie is he!?), because he is now in white shorts and a loud Hawaiian shirt with pristine white sneakers.

I peek out the window just to discover that everything is still pitch-black outside. Our nighttime flight is landing just before sunrise, which is a shame, really. Landing at night leaves me somewhat disoriented. I had been looking forward to seeing the island from above, expecting lush green vegetation and shimmering white sandy beaches. But all I can see is my own reflection in the glass as the airplane approaches the blinking lights of the runway.

"Ladies and Gentlemen, welcome to Mahé airport. Please remain seated until the seatbelt sign has been turned off." The sweetest words ever spoken. A mountain lifts from my shoulders, and I clap in excitement, applauding the pilot for a great landing and myself for surviving. Andrea gives me a puzzled look. I am the only person clapping, and with an embarrassed grin, I drop my hands to my lap. My shoulder critic rolls his eyes and jumps up on the seat in front of me to see if people are leaving the plane already. The sudden release of tension has flooded my body with adrenaline, and I have a hard time sitting still.

Not seeing much of our surroundings heightens my other senses. As we descend the mobile staircase to the tarmac, the humid, tropical air greets us with a potpourri of scents: warm asphalt and jet fuel mixed with the earthy fragrance of moss, a heady note of frangipani, and an undertone of something spicy that I cannot identify. It smells of adventure and excitement; the ideal place for someone trying to escape her demons.

A bored-looking local in a neon-yellow reflective vest waves us toward the low terminal building ahead. Mahé Airport is quiet at this hour; most counters are closed, and the empty, echoing halls make us lower our voices, afraid to wake the airport from its well-deserved slumber. The lights are dimmed in most areas, and the empty corridors and deserted waiting areas are oblivious to the small group of tourists who tiptoe toward the exit.

Thankfully, the immigration counter is staffed. After a perfunctory glance at our passports, the guard waves us through, and we make our way to the baggage claim. The rhythmic rumble and squeak of the conveyor belt is the only sound interrupting the quiet of the early morning hours. We don't have to wait long before we make our way to the front of the airport, luggage in hand, scanning the empty streets until we find the line of cabs with the drivers asleep in their seats. As the tourists trickle out of the airport, the drivers wake from their slumber and wave us over, smiling and moving with practiced efficiency, as if to make up for being caught asleep on the job. Our driver, a young Seychellois with a missing tooth and a cheerful demeanor, chatters without taking a breath as we pull away. Tired from the flight, disoriented but excited about our new surroundings, I strain to understand what he is saying. Even though my French is decent, Seychellois Creole is something else entirely, so I just nod politely as he looks at us in the rearview mirror. "*Un œuf*.[33]" He insists, adjusting to speak clearer. "*Voudriez-vous un oeuf*[34]?" as he hands us a Tupperware container with hard-boiled eggs. Well, at least I assume they are hard-boiled. He wouldn't give us raw eggs ... would he? Not really knowing how to react, I grab a small, brown-shelled egg and hand the container back to the front. Bizarre. Andrea and I exchange a conspiratorial smile as we both struggle to contain a giggle, and I slip the egg into my handbag.

---

33 *Un œuf - French. "An egg"*

34 *Voudriez-vous un oeuf? - French, "Would you like an egg?"*

By now, details of our surroundings start to appear as darkness pulls the curtains on the soft blue-gray of dawn. To our left, a jungle-clad mountain rises out of the gloom, and a chorus of birds exults in unfamiliar melodies, greeting the new day. The road takes us right to the edge of the water, the waves lapping the shore. Even the ocean seems slow to wake.

My head is still filled with the post-flight cotton-ball feeling, and watching the scenery fly by has me transfixed - until a loud honk jolts me out of my reverie. *"Bouge-toi, connard!*[35]" our driver shouts and leans out the window, overtaking another car in a hair-raising maneuver. The traffic is in full swing despite the early hour. Old, dented buses barrel past, honking and overtaking at breakneck speeds, missing us by inches. Our driver remains unimpressed by the high-speed elephant race and just waves at the passing driver - or did he flip him off? I'm not sure, my hands are already in front of my eyes to block out his questionable driving skills. Better not to look at the road. "Ahhhm *c'est rien, madame.*[36]" The driver grins at me in the rearview mirror, his missing tooth exposed, amused by my fears.

After a short drive, we reach our hotel, where a room with crisp white sheets, a faint scent of lemongrass, and a gorgeous view is waiting for us. "According to this," I squint at a printout of the local bus schedule, "the bus leaves in thirty-five minutes for Victoria. C'mon! We can relax later." "Yeah ... NO!" My shoulder critic jumps off my shoulder and saunters toward the open balcony door and the sun chairs. As he walks, he pulls off his shirt and drops it unceremoniously on the floor, followed by one sneaker and, a few steps later, the second. With one hop, he's on the sun chair, stretches out, and I hear a long, satisfied sigh. I guess he's staying at the hotel. As inviting as the lush grounds and sparkling ocean look, I can't wait to head out and explore. Andrea isn't too thrilled to be rushed after such a

---

35   *Bouge-toi, connard! - French. "Move, idiot!"*

36   *C'est rien, madame. - French. "This is nothing, madame"*

long flight, but he knows how much I love local markets. A quick shower, change of clothes, and less than half an hour later, we're on our way to Victoria, one of the smallest capitals in the world. We climb onto a small open-air bus - more like a large van - without windowpanes, which offers not only an unencumbered view of our surroundings, but also lets the warm island wind tussle our hair, giving us an immediate casual-vacation-look. A pandemonium of parakeets executes a precise flyover maneuver, skimming the tree-tops and landing in a large palm tree next to the road, screeching over one another. "Oh my God! Parrots!! Did you see that?" I pull Andrea's arm in excitement. Coming from a rather gray and dark Berlin, where pigeons and crows roam the skies, the colorful birds are messengers of paradise. My eyes are glued to the brightly colored homes, built in Creole-style, peeking out between the lush vege-tation. Their large verandas and pointed roofs look charming and exotic, bearing clear witness to the colonial influence of the past. Closer to town, the traditional buildings give way to newer con-crete-and-glass facades catering to the increased tourism over the last decades. Victoria is a busy little town, even this early in the day. The bus driver, a burly man in his fifties, picks up on the undeniable fact that we are tourists and gestures towards the center of a small round-about. "*C'est le Lorloz,*[37]" he mutters, pointing to a very English-looking clocktower in the center. I leaf through my Lonely Planet Guide to the Seychelles. "Here it is!" I show Andrea the picture and point to the roundabout. "Lorloz is the Creole name for it." It looks like a miniature version of Big Ben, its formal colonial elegance in sharp contrast to the laid-back island life bustling all around it.

My first excursion at any new destination is always to the local market. There is no better way to immerse myself in a culture than by exploring what people eat and where they buy it. A lively riot of colors welcomes us as we enter the open market building. The

---

37   *C'est le Lorloz, - French. "This is the Lorloz,"*

turquoise-colored roofs and red pillars are almost eclipsed by a sea of umbrellas, offering much-needed shade and a respite from the heat for the fruits and vegetables piled on precarious-looking tables underneath. Despite the early hour, the market already teems with people, cats, and dogs. I step closer to a dented metal table heaped with fish. Their scales glisten, eyes crystal clear, as if they'd jumped out of the water minutes ago. A boy of about six shovels ice over the fresh catch, which melts in briny rivulets down the sides of the table, gathering in large puddles. A small white heron stilts among the dead fish on display, utterly ignored by shopkeepers and buyers alike. His pupils are framed by white circles that stare unblinking as it stands, poised on one leg, waiting for the entrails the fishmonger's wife slices free with astonishing dexterity. The bird is white, the feathers near his chest stained red from blood and fish gore. Pirating the tables must be a fruitful endeavor. Its legs are long, light gray, and scaly. The black claws of its tucked leg are curled inwards, as it stands like a statue, unflinching, as a fat fly orbits around its head. With a shiver, I turn away and hurry down the open aisle toward the fresh produce.

Everything here is bursting with color. For someone who just arrived from Berlin, where the dominant palette in fashion and architecture is black, this colorful spectacle is more than refreshing. The Seychellois combine every color, fabric, and pattern with fearless joy, creating their very own fashion statements - the results are astonishing.

"Let's try that!" Before Andrea can object, I hand 50 rupees to a lady behind a cart stacked with strange confections, and she hands me a bag of bright orange pinwheel-looking creations. They gleam with syrup; unlike anything I've ever tried before. Too excited to wait, I take a bite. The pungent sweetness has a soapy, floral undertone, and the fried pastry itself is soggy on the outside and crunchy on the inside. Ugh ... not my thing at all. I turn away from my husband, hiding under the brim of my straw hat, and discreetly spit the bite back into the bag, then slide it into the next trash can, scraping sticky syrup from my tongue with my teeth. The taste won't budge. Yuck. I should've just bought a mango.

The fruits on display steal the show: heaps of juicy reds, crisp yellows, dragon-fruit pinks, and zesty oranges, offset by lively greens of leafy vegetables in between. Half the fruits are completely foreign to me, so we buy a selection, despite the cloying sweetness of my previous mishap that still lingers on my palate. I can't wait to explore the new flavors and textures, but I make sure to add some fragrant mangoes - just in case the other fruits are duds.

CHAPTER 19

This is my happy place! Strolling along the streets of a new city, hand in hand with Andrea, taking in the sights and sounds - what more could I ask for? Everything is so bright, so intense, bursting with color. High on life, I pull him along as I skip down the road, looking for the next discovery. And just around the corner from the market, on Albert Street, a brightly colored building catches my eye. I've never seen anything like it! Built in traditional Creole style, the three-story house sparkles in bright blue, turquoise, red, and yellow. Yellow arches frame purple doors and shutters on the ground floor, while the second floor is blue with yellow shutters and window frames. It almost looks like a Creole Pippi Longstocking house - a chaos of colors, mismatched but cheerful. I peer through the open door, drawn by racks of fabrics, sarongs, beach bags, and souvenirs.

"Entrez! Bienvenue![38] *"* a male voice calls from within the depths of the store. The shop is bathed in shadows. Most of the shutters are closed, but the lack of a working A/C means there is not much of a difference in temperature between the inside and outside. The air is stacked in a curious array of scents, depending on which area of the shop I explore: coconut and vanilla from scented candles, the sharp smell of leather goods, the grassy straw hats and bags, as well as a pinch of dust of wares long forgotten on shelves high up on the wall.

Andrea wanders off to the left to browse a rack of postcards, the old metal display squeaking in lament as he turns it. As I let my hands trail along the various fabrics, my eyes fall on an elderly man, half-concealed behind a large desk in the back of the shop. The desk is piled high with books, papers, fabric samples, and random boxes, reminiscent of Mr. Coreander's bookstore in the NeverEnding Story. He looks up.

Obviously, I'd never been here or laid eyes on the man in front of me, but a sudden, unmistakable sense of recognition hits me like lightning. Electricity crackles over my skin, and I feel a magnetic pull forward. A smile spreads over his face as he sets his pen down, pushes his chair back, and shuffles around the desk, threading through a maze of boxes and bales of fabric without taking his eyes off me. Everything around me falls away as tunnel vision homes in on the man in front of me. He must be in his seventies, dressed in simple khaki pants and a light-colored, short-sleeved shirt. He has a halo of thin gray hair framing the sides of his head. Around his neck, he wears a leather cord with a small, ornate silver rod, topped with amethysts on both ends. *"Mon amie*[39]*,"* he exclaims, arms outstretched as he comes toward me.

He opens his arms wide, and we embrace like old friends. He smells of cloves and spices. My heart races and I am filled with an

---

38   *Entrez! Bienvenue! - French. "Come in! Welcome!"*

39   *Mon amie - French, "My friend,"*

overwhelming sense of happiness, wonder, and relief at having found him. My feelings, yet not MY feelings. They bubble up within me, I can feel them, yet as if someone else is experiencing them. I know it sounds strange, but there's no other way to say it. We have found each other! It seems as if we have known each other for centuries, yet we just met. As we break our embrace, he holds me at arm's length, studying every detail of my face. He cups my cheek in one hand. His skin is warm and dry. His eyes mirror the same feelings of wonder and joy, and he pulls me close again, laughing as he squeezes me tight. As we finally pull apart, we both start talking at once, pause, laugh, then do it again. When we are finally able to communicate, we are both asking the same questions: *"Comment as-tu été? Où étais-tu? Dis moi tout!* How have you been? Where have you been? Tell me everything!"* ... and all of it in French, which somehow feels most natural. I do speak French, having lived in Paris for university, but that was years ago, and I am out of practice, far from fluent; yet to my astonishment, the words fly out of me without hesitation.

After some time - minutes maybe, but it could have easily been an hour as well, since I have lost any sense of time and space - the tunnel vision widens, and I become aware of my surroundings again. The first thing I notice is Andrea, standing a few meters away, staring at us with a look of utter incredulity. "Ahem," he clears his throat. I beam at him, walk over, grab him by the hand, and pull him along with me to make the introductions. For a second, I am baffled, as I realize I don't even know the name of the gentleman standing in front of me. "This is my husband, Andrea," I say as I recover. The old man takes hold of Andrea's hand with both of his, smiling at him as he easily switches to an accented English, "I am Kanti, you are very welcome at my shop."

Kanti! His name is Kanti!

With that, he turns back to me, hooks his arm into mine, and walks me over to his desk. Andrea follows, too stunned to react. I sit down in an old, dusty chair across from Kanti and take a moment to study him as he exchanges pleasantries with Andrea, who stands behind me, hand on my shoulder - casual, yet protective. Kanti's face is round with gentle features, but the most captivating thing about him is his eyes. Depending on how they catch the light, they appear brown, gray, or even blue, with the uncanny ability to look straight into your soul.

Kanti turns his gaze back to me, and once again his eyes sparkle with affection. The light of the old lamp perched atop of a stack of files, casts a golden aura over the desk, gathering us at its circumference, hugged by the store's shadows. We fall into an effortless conversation, recapping the major events of our lives. He wants to know everything: where I live, how my parents are doing, where I grew up. It feels urgent, as if we are trying to catch up on things he should have known already, squeezing the span of my whole life into the finite moment of now.

And then, when it's his turn to answer my questions, Kanti turns and pulls a large leather binder out from the shadows behind him. It is on top of a wooden cabinet with glass doors straining under the weight of countless books, file folders, and chachkas. Near the lamp on his desk is a small turtle figurine, carved from shells, glued to a flat rock, bearing the word *Seychelles*. He pushes the turtle out of the way and places the binder between us. The brown leather is worn, and the seam on one corner is frayed. As he opens it, the scent of old paper wafts out, revealing a thick stack of yellowed documents, newspaper articles, and photos. Page by page, he takes us through his life. Born Kantilal Jivan Shah, I'm surprised to learn he's eighty-three. His youthful spirit makes him seem so much younger. With each page he turns, he tells a new story. There is a selection of official Seychellois stamps of his own design, which he keeps protected under a clear plastic cover. There are faded photos of Kanti with various celebrities, as well as countless newspaper clippings with articles about him and his life. There is even a photo of Kanti next to the actor Omar Sharif. He tells us about the collection of seashells he once presented to Queen Elizabeth while serving as an official representative of the Seychelles during her visit. Ian Fleming, whom he met years ago, even based a character in a James Bond novel on him.

I turn back to Kanti. Time loses meaning as we talk without taking a breath. Once in a while, there are murmurs of people somewhere beyond our circle of light, but they fade away the instant I notice them. Even Andrea's presence drifts in and out. I think he said he'd take a walk, but I can't pull my attention away long enough to register what he said or where he went. One moment, he is gone, then he is back. I have no idea how long we've been sitting here. We talk about the most varied subjects, from his passion for cooking and his garden, where he spends hours tending to his vegetables and his medicinal herbs and spices, which he uses for traditional Creole tinctures and salves. Humble and captivating, he is a true Renaissance man, through and through.

He pauses and looks at me. Silence settles, drawing a slow and deliberate breath. As if making up his mind, Kanti leans across the desk, past his desk lamp, and beckons for me to put my hand in his. I scoot closer until both Kanti and I are fully ensconced within the circle of light. The pale green metallic lampshade is dented on one side, the paint worn and scratched around the rim, revealing the silver metal underneath. The soft light wraps itself around my shoulders like a cloak, drawing me into its spell and deepening the shadows all around me. Even Andrea's presence behind me recedes into the darkness. The dry skin of Kanti's weathered hands feels warm and reassuring against mine.

As he pushes his glasses up the bridge of his nose, he adjusts the lamp on his desk, turns my palm towards the light, and studies my hand carefully. Specks of dust dance through the air above my hand, awakened by the sudden movement of the lampshade. He traces a few lines with his index finger as if contemplating how to interpret what he sees. I lean forward to have a look as well. What does he see? Palm reading is just one of those things I have always been very skeptical of. I don't know much about it, but I can't imagine that the wear and tear on my hands could give away anything of substance. Yet, in this situation, at this dark, messy desk in a little shop in Victoria, Seychelles, in front of a man I had never met, but feel so connected to, even this gesture feels natural. Had my perception of "normal" shifted? If I could just take a step back for a second and look at things, this whole situation would be absurd. I don't know this man, yet I do. I know deep inside it will take me some time to digest and sort out what this chance encounter means.

Kanti exhales deeply and looks at me for several moments. The light blue ring around his iris shimmers, and I meet his gaze without shying away. The moment stretches, confused about whether to continue along the normal path of time or shift into a different reality. I cannot feel my heartbeat or even my breath - everything is suspended in a warm, quiet nook beyond reality. If someone had told me that we are floating in a bubble in space, I would not have been surprised. I feel detached from my everyday life. Kanti purses his lips, contemplating what to say.

Looking at the man in front of me, I am touched once again by the genuine connection I feel. Not just a connection, but a sense of love, a deep-rooted, all-encompassing, unconditional love, and trust. Like the love for a parent, of a parent, or a best friend - a soul connection in the truest sense. Sitting here, looking into his brown eyes, with the mysterious ring of blue, I realize I'm feeling exactly that: a soul connection! But more than that: it is a recognition - a recognition of souls.

Before I can follow that thought any further down the rabbit hole, Kanti smiles at me and simply says, *"Je sais - I know."* What exactly he knows, I am not sure, but he places his other hand on top of mine, hovering about an inch or so above my open palm, and just smiles at me. It is a wise smile, a gentle, caring expression that carries meaning beyond my understanding. I am still studying his face - the deep lines, the age spot on his left cheekbone, and how his temperamental salt-and-pepper eyebrows frame those soulful eyes that are as mysterious as the man himself.

Kanti's hand that is cradling mine suddenly closes; a shock of cold bites my palm, as if ice cubes were placed in my hand. So cold, I'd have pulled my hand away if not for his firm grip. Yet he hasn't moved at all - his hand hovering over mine, posture unchanged. My palm is empty. Everything is happening so fast, yet at the same time in slow motion. Time is playing tricks on me. The sensation is intense, as the cold travels up through my hand and into my arm. The darkness around me intensifies and swallows up everything: the tables with bolts of fabric, the displays with shell necklaces and sarongs, the postcards Andrea was looking at earlier, even my husband himself; it all falls away. The edges of my existence are defined by the cone of light cast down on Kanti and me from the desk lamp, plunging the rest into complete darkness. As the cold reaches my shoulder, I cease to exist.

This is the most difficult feeling to explain, but that is what it feels like. My conscious, thinking self withdraws into a corner of my mind that would be inaccessible under normal circumstances. I'm hiding, getting out of the way of what is happening. Like a child hiding behind her mother's legs, peering at a stranger, I now observe everything from a safe distance.

Where there had been complete silence before, my heart now thunders in my ears. My breath catches as an earthquake rips through my body, rushing down my arm with intense heat, where seconds ago I had been freezing cold. Deep sobs rack my body, and hot tears run down my face. I cry like I have never cried before. From where I am hiding within myself, I just observe and marvel at the intensity of what is going on. After some time, it stops. The heat disperses, and I reconnect with my body, blinking tears away. I glance up at Kanti.

He has not moved at all; his hands still hold mine, and he still smiles gently at me, which suggests that what had seemed like hours to me must have been only moments.

In this short instance, everything has changed!

I sit up, roll my shoulders, and reorient myself. I feel light as air, as if a mountain has been lifted off my shoulders. A mountain, I didn't even know I carried. Not only do I feel lighter, but taller, newer somehow. With a newfound lifeforce within that radiates outwards from every pore on my body. The shadows around us, which had been so dense before, containing Kanti and me within a protective bubble of light, now recede, revealing the shop around us. I hear the traffic on the street outside, a few customers behind me somewhere, talking to a young lady behind a counter. A car is honking nearby.

I breathe in, aware of every sensation traveling through my body. My ribcage lifts, my chest rises. I exhale. My chest falls, my shoulders relax, and I have to focus on Kanti, not to be swept away by the pure joy of the ebb and flow of air traveling through my body. Breathing feels newborn - a glorious feeling to breathe so free and deeply. An intense sense of fulfillment and happiness expands deep inside of me. I have felt happiness before, obviously, but never have I felt as content and settled as I do right now. My eyes widen at the profound change within, and I just stare at Kanti, a huge smile on my face. He releases my hand, passes me a tissue, and says with a wink, "You'll be fine now." Whatever that means, I know deep inside that everything will indeed be alright; that whatever he had done had a radical effect on me. What exactly that would be would take me a few weeks to figure out, but I know this chance encounter had just changed my life.

As if waking up from a trance, I glance up. The world around me sparkles with incredible clarity and saturation. Even the most mundane things now hold a secret only I am privy to. My eyes move around and land on my husband, who still (or again) stands behind me, his hand on my shoulder. Despite my tear-streaked face and runny nose, I giggle at the look he gives me. My heart goes out to him, filled with an overwhelming love for this gorgeous man who stood so patiently beside me. I can see he has no idea what had just transpired, yet he trusts me enough to let it play out. With my new-found clarity and understanding, I see my husband in a completely new light. For a moment, the veil lifts, and I see beyond the surface. I see not only the man that I fell in love with and married, but the soul that resides within; the deeper layer of connection that bridges every divide we ever had, any difference or argument.

"Are you okay?" Andrea leans in, squinting at me. Kanti leans back, arms crossed, that serene smile dancing around his lips. I don't even know what to do with myself. I'm overwhelmed with a flood of emotions. I feel high; dopamine rushes through my veins, as if I'm on a mind-altering drug expanding my consciousness. Is that what LSD or ayahuasca feel like? So much has happened so fast. My understanding of the universe has shifted. I can't grasp it all yet; honestly, I don't understand any of it. But what I do know is that something undeniable has shaken the foundations of what I believed. There are so many insights to sort, analyze, and catalog. I want to laugh, run, jump, and scream with the pure joy of being alive. Instead, I take Andrea's hand and squeeze.

Kanti stands. His wooden chair scrapes across the floor, anchoring me in the here and now. I pull my thoughts from the whirlwind they have been dancing in and focus on him; gratitude pricks my eyes and wobbles my chin. I have no words. Nothing is sufficient to express all that's in my heart: love, kinship, gratitude, relief, joy, disbelief, awe. We hold each other's gaze for a long time.

"Come, stay at my house. There's still so much I have to teach you."

CHAPTER 20
SEYCHELLES 2006

An hour later, I plop onto the hotel bed. I'm wrapped in a towel, water droplets, and a fresh scent of lemongrass cling to my skin from the shower. I'm spent, so exhausted I can barely keep my eyes open. The afternoon sun pours into the room, and the soothing sound of waves tempts me to sleep. My body feels heavy, warm, and content rather than leaden. Even my mind is too tired to process the last few hours.

Andrea's voice drifts in, muffled and distant. ".... yes, the dressing on the side is fine. Could we also have a bottle of wine?" He's ordering room service. He's right - I think I should eat - but I'm just so tired. I let my hand dangle over the side of the bed, where I tossed my handbag earlier. Without looking, I grope around for the fruit we picked up at the market. My fingers close around something smooth and round: the taxi driver's egg. It's brown, freckled with dark brown spots. Its shell is not smooth all around but has a rougher texture at the bottom. It's crazy how everything changed in such a short time, yet this egg is exactly the way it was this morning. Except now it feels like it was given to someone else - someone who looked and sounded like me but isn't the person holding the egg now.

"There is still so much I have to teach you."

Kanti's words resonate within me. They were not just a polite sentiment. They were a genuine invitation. Every fiber in my body had screamed for me to say "Yes," to accept the offer, to cancel our hotel reservations, to scrap our plans, and go stay with him. He was right: there was so much he still had to teach me! I felt like a once-in-a-lifetime opportunity. He was a fountain of physical and spiritual knowledge. I wanted to know it all! But I also felt my husband's presence nearby and the need to be with him, to connect with him on the vacation we had planned for so long. With a heavy heart, I declined the invitation. He smiled, understood without explanation, and patted my cheek like my grandmother used to.

"It's not the time. You're good now."

I hugged him tight before leaving the store; the chances of seeing each other again were slim to none. But it didn't matter. Knowing our connection ran deep - beyond this single lifetime - was enough, even if I didn't yet have words for it.

With a smile, I fall asleep long before the room service arrives.

Sniff, sniff.

I crack one eye. The first light of the day filters through the closed curtains. My shoulder critic leans over me, in lime green swim shorts and a dark blue polo shirt still creased from the suitcase. Concern furrows his forehead; his bushy eyebrows inch towards each other like fat caterpillars. There is a sunburn casting a pink hue over his face and arms. He lifts a strand of my hair, sniffs it, and mumbles, "Something's off. Something feels different." He startles when I open my eyes fully. Unapologetic, he steps onto my chest, his arms akimbo, his chin jutting in defiance. "What's wrong with you?" he demands. "You're different. I can almost smell it. What …" With one big sweep, I yank the blanket back, and my shoulder critic tumbles into the heap of duvets.

I grin and cross the room to the curtains in three quick steps, pull them open, and inhale the fresh air, sunrise, and the sparkling ocean in front of me. I slept like a baby and feel a rush of adrenaline coursing through my arms and legs. I'm not a runner by any means, but right now I want to run. Sunlight tickles my husband awake, and I throw myself onto the bed, laughing and kissing him wherever I can reach through his mock-protest.

Half an hour later, the elevator pings and releases us into the lobby. I hook my arm into Andrea's as we stroll toward the restaurant and into a new reality. Nothing feels the same. Everything's more vibrant, louder, more joyful - bursting with energy. I put my sunglasses on, trying to temper the intensity with which life hits my senses and look around with a new appreciation. Everyone seems different; full of history, love, happiness, sadness, possibility, all contained within each person. Hotel guests we pass along the corridor, the cleaning lady with the cart full of towels, and the gardeners working along the path - their faces, eyes, and movements speak of the lives they've lived, the connections they've made, the places that shaped them. And each is connected to the other, to me, to Andrea, by their sheer presence within the same reality, the exact moment in time. And each is connected - to one another, to me, to Andrea - by sharing this moment. Our lives are interlaced: the kids sprinting towards the buffet, the family that blocks the check-in desk in front of us, the waiter swerving to avoid a collision with the children - all one web where past and future collapse into a single thing: now. Now's all that matters. Unaware, Andrea leans toward the check-in desk: "A table for two, please. Room 213."

Ten days later, we drag our suitcases up one flight to our Berlin apartment. Andrea's skin glows a deep golden tan, his hair sun-kissed, a bounce in his step. My skin finally shows off a hint of a reddish bronze after a week of "No, I'm not sunburnt - this is how I tan." We left Mahé for the neighboring island of Praslin the day after meeting Kanti. The vacation trickled by with lazy days at the pool, jungle hikes, secluded beaches, massages, and sunset drinks under a sky teeming with stars. Despite all the luxuries, I'm excited to be home. Berlin greets us in its finest. Instead of winter's gray skies, everything shimmers bright blue. Birds sing in the courtyard, the sun filters through layers of fresh green, and a light breeze carries the *Berliner Luft*[40] - the fresh air Berlin is famous for. The old song by the same name pops into my head, and I hum it the last few steps up the stairs.

"...*das ist die Berliner Luft, Luft, Luft*
So mit ihrem holden Duft, Duft, Duft
Da, dada, dada, dada da daaaa"

I don't remember the rest of the song.

The air in our apartment lies stale and lazy over the refurbished floors, barely moving as we walk in. I laugh and squeeze past him, rushing to the kitchen to open the door to the balcony. Andrea opens the bedroom and the living room windows, and *die Berliner Luft* chases out the musty vacation air. A new leaf has been turned.

---

40   *Berliner Luft - German, Berlin air*

As every proper Italian does immediately upon returning home, Andrea busies himself with making us an espresso. He takes out the aluminum stovetop Moka pot and fills the bottom with water. Espresso takes priority over unpacking or showering, preceded only by a quick washing of hands and a kiss for his wife. Our coffee maker, basic as it may be, has acquired a beautiful patina of past coffees. I learned quickly never to use soap when cleaning it - it's the patina that gives the coffee depth and the taste of real Italian espresso.

I wipe down the balcony chairs and sit, waiting for the gurgling of the Moka and the click of its aluminum lid. I close my eyes, anticipating the scent of coffee drifting out to me. Church bells ring through the neighborhood. It's five o'clock.

I feel different. Meeting Kanti changed me. It shifted how I see the world - from a spiritual perspective, not in a religious sense, but something that transcends the boundaries of a specific faith.

Faith and spirituality never played a big role in my life. On the contrary, I bristle at organized religion. I see religion as the one thing that divides humankind. Instead of creating a universal sense of love, respect, and appreciation for one another, organized religion creates an "us versus them" mentality. It is a polarity of "We, who believe," and "they, who don't." Without much appetite for the historical and political tangle, I usually relegate religion and spirituality to the back of my mind.

This disillusionment with religion started in my childhood. My parents raised me with a general belief in God and Jesus. We attended church for the major holidays, such as Christmas and Easter, and we prayed before meals and before bed. Those rituals were celebrated out of a family tradition, rather than an internal urge towards a structured belief system.

Growing up in our small rural community, my parents encouraged me to join my friends at the Protestant Children's Mass on Sunday, followed by activities at the community center, where we put on plays, made arts and crafts, sang, and made music. Every Sunday would be a struggle to get out of bed. "Alex, c'mon, don't dawdle in the shower. The carpool is arriving in ten minutes, and you still need to eat!" My mother wore her pink fluffy bathrobe, her blonde hair matted in the back as she spread a thin layer of butter on a slice of bread for me. I hugged her goodbye and inhaled her scent of lotion and love before taking a bite of the bread on my way out. My mother looked like she was ready to go for another quick snuggle in bed as soon as the door closed behind me. So unfair. Why did I have to go to church?

I scooted into the backseat of my classmate's mom's car. The uphol-stery of the seat felt scratchy even through my clothes. I squeezed next to three other kids in the back row. I was the last pick-up on the way, so I always ended up sitting next to a boy who was two grades above me and at least a head taller. He smirked as I squished myself hard against the door, making sure my legs would not touch his. I was easily grossed out by the physical proximity of boys, and being forced to sit so close gave me the heebie-jeebies. Unless it was Marco; he had been my crush since kindergarten. And considering I was only eight, that had been most of my life until now. I would not have minded sitting that close to him during church carpool. But unfortunately, that never happened. He was Catholic.

I had resigned myself to the fact that this feeling of discomfort, which started in the car, would last for the next ninety minutes. All the way through the mass, perched on hard wooden benches in this large, sparse church, I wished to be somewhere else. The tall stained-glass windows hid the enticing blue sky beyond, and the breeze in the birch tree called me to roam around outside. Instead, I had to pray, listen, and sing.

I looked down the pew at the faces of my friends. I loved hanging out with them, but here in church, I felt like the odd one out. I could not relate to their fervor for the priest's every word or to their glowing faces as they recited the Lord's Prayer. It made me self-conscious, a thousand thoughts racing through my head:

"Why don't I feel what they feel? Does that mean I don't believe in God? Of course, I do - so why do I feel so out of place? Will the priest notice? He is looking at me! Oh my God! Why is he looking at me? Does he know?"

My hands were cold and sweaty as we stood for prayer, fidgeting with my shirt button. I breathed a deep sigh of relief when service was over and I could run along with my friends - chatting and giggling - on our way to the community center next door for cake and juice.

Andrea steps onto the balcony, balancing two red espresso cups on a little tray. He sugars my coffee just the way I like it and adds a small plate of Italian cookies. Before sitting down, he smiles, bends down, and kisses me. He can still give me butterflies. With a sigh of contentment, he sits across from me and soaks up the serenity of our little balcony paradise. The petunias in our planter have survived our absence and are thriving in brilliant hues of purple and pink.

"Have I ever told you about how I used to pray to God when I was a kid?" I ask. "That's random," he replies, raising his eyebrows at me. "What made you think of that now?"

"Meeting Kanti. I have been thinking a lot about faith and what I believe in." I pause. "When I was little, I believed in God and knew the overall concept of religion. I'd read the Bible - not all of it, but the parts I found interesting, like Jesus's life and the story of Joseph. The one sold into slavery and later became the second most powerful man next to the Pharaoh. It's so weird, but that story really fascinated me. I even drew it a few times - the well they threw him in, with morbid details like rats and mud and even a few bones scattered across the floor. There was just something about his story of betrayal, suffering, and coming out on the other side that grabbed me. Anyway ..." I sip my coffee and watch the breeze carry a leaf past the balcony. "Even as a child, I knew religion was personal, and my communication with God was private."

I put my cup down and take a cookie. Instead of eating it right away, I look at it, my thoughts back in a time when my blonde hair hung in a thick braid down to my lower back.

"You know," I start, "religion wasn't really my thing. But I talked to God often in the privacy of my dark bedroom, after my parents kissed me goodnight. I had a direct connection to Him, and we talked about my day and the things that were on my mind." I smile more to myself than to my husband. "I imagined a little door in my ceiling. When I opened it, I could see straight into the stars. I'd be right there in the middle of the universe, and God could hear me. He even answered. It was a very personal relationship."

Andrea watches me as I pull myself back from my memories.

"Hmm. I don't think I ever told anyone about that little door," I muse. "I was never a big fan of churches, though. The God there felt different from the one I talked to at night."

Andrea gets up and puts our empty espresso cups back on the tray.

"Well, I am glad I was able to marry you in church then, despite your reservations." He says over his shoulder as he carries the tray back into the kitchen.

"I wonder what Father Zinnamon would have said if he'd seen me cross my fingers behind my back during the Lord's Prayer," I tease him. "You did WHAT?!" he bursts out laughing. "Really? Let's hope Nonna did not see that!" He disappears behind the sheer curtain. "I'm joking," I giggle.

A few minutes later, I hear him turn on the shower. After our long flight, I'm craving a shower too, but for now, my thoughts and I hang out together on the balcony. Our apartment faces the inner courtyard of the building, and apart from the majestic trees and their whispering leaves in shades of green, there's only a rectangle of the afternoon sky above. It smells of summer, and the laughter of our neighbor's kids echoes off the courtyard walls.

I think my belief system is a braid of what I was taught, what I rebelled against, and what feels true now. If I reduce it down to the most important pillars of my faith, it would be belief in God and whatever happens after death. I did believe in God, or at least in some form of God-like presence. Not the wise old man with a beard sitting on a throne in the heavens, surrounded by a choir of singing angels with glowing halos around their heads. For me, God was without a physical body - omnipresent and all-knowing.

Once during children's mass, the priest said, "God is within you." What did that even mean? God is inside of me? Is he inside my body somewhere? Like a part of my cell structure? I stretched my little hand out and looked at each finger, wriggling them, searching for God. I looked at my lanky legs, the scabby knees I did not like, a bright red Band-Aid on the left - always scraped and bruised from outdoor adventures. He couldn't be in there, could he? Or was he the tiny voice in my head that yelled when I was about to do something stupid? No, wait, that was my shoulder critic, even though back then, he was not much of a critic yet. He was more of a friend; someone I would hang out with when I was all by myself. If God was within me, did he know I was struggling with all that religious stuff, or did kids get leeway in that regard?

As the sermon continued, my thoughts wandered. Our priest loved reading from the Bible, especially during children's mass. It felt like story time. But I didn't take the Bible - most of it, anyway - literally. To me, it wasn't a direct message from God, but rather a collection of stories written by men, edited through the centuries. The priest used them as an illustration of fundamental moral concepts. In that, they shaped society as we know it. Humans- just like children - fare best when confined to a strict moral code.

"*Thou shalt not kill. Thou shalt not commit adultery. Thou shalt not steal,*" the priest's voice boomed from the pulpit.

235

For children, parents create a sense of safety by enforcing consistent rules. To me, the Bible served the same purpose: stories that teach moral concepts, allowing people to coexist in harmony within agreed-upon rules. And just like parents doling out consequences to their pint-sized rulebreakers, religion held the threat of damnation and hellfire over its disciples.

CHAPTER 21

BERLIN 2006

I get up, stretch, and follow Andrea inside. Instead of procrastinating on the suitcases, I throw myself into the mountain of laundry. I sort the clothes into black, white, and color piles and throw the first load into the washing machine before Andrea's even out of the shower. Doing laundry had been such a slog this past year. I'd gather, sort, then stall - minutes turning to hours, sometimes days. Often, I shoved the dirty clothes into the nook in front of the washer and closed the door on the mess. Today I want order. I'm facing my life and getting stuff done. I welcome the monotony of chores. It allows my mind to wander.

My problem with religion is the threat of hell and punishment. I can't reconcile a loving God with eternal torture for believing "wrong." We have free will for a reason. Hell makes no sense to me. Not then, not now. Neither did confession. Protestant churches do not offer confession, so as a child, I only heard about it from my

237

Catholic school friends: you whisper your "sins" in a dark cubby to a familiar voice behind a curtain, then say a few prayers and - clean slate? In my small town, everyone knew the priest, and he knew every child by name - so why the secrecy? And what exactly are a child's "sins"? Stealing candy? Saying a bad word? It all felt performative and nonsensical to me.

I pull the first load of clothes from the dryer. We never had one when I was growing up. My mother refused. "Bad for the clothes," she'd argue. Our clothes were washed and hung on clotheslines either in the dark washroom downstairs or, weather permitting, in the garden. She also refused to use a softener, with the result that our towels, after drying on the line, were so stiff you could stand them upright. "Rough towels absorb better," was her justification. There is a satisfying sense of rebellion in the warm, soft tumble of the dryer, and my towels absorb just fine. My mom also taught me how to iron. She ironed everything - she was very meticulous that way. The iron had exact marching order with which to swish over the fabric, the edges and seams lining up like soldiers, stacked T-shirts arranged corner to corner with military precision. Everything had to be ironed, except towels, underwear, and socks. She even ironed jeans, bed sheets, t-shirts, and even sweaters. For years, my dad's jeans held their ironed front crease in a stubborn salute against common fashion trends, impersonating slacks. Forcing our laundry into a stranglehold of precise pleats and creases was a way for my mother to relax. I think having a closet full of immaculate, wrinkle-free clothing was the hallmark of a well-kept household in her eyes.

In design school, I refused to iron. That was the point - rebellion. We smoked pot, wore outrageous clothes, watched obscure black-and-white French films with nudity and foul language, and drank wine out of baby bottles. In those days, I did not even own an iron and cherished the fact that I just shook the wrinkles out of my clothes in mutiny before throwing them into the closet. To this day, ironing feels like one of my very adult habits. And I'll admit: there is nothing nicer than sliding into freshly ironed sheets… Heaven.

And speaking of "heaven," that was a concept I could get behind as a kid: a place where you're happy all the time, pain does not exist, and you're reunited with everyone you love, even pets. I grew up believing that people are born, live life, die, and then spend eternity in heaven. It was a concept I never challenged or even thought about much over the years, until it faded into the recesses of my mind. For now, I find my heaven in ironed sheets that smelled of softener and an imagined nod of approval from my mother.

I pull one of Andrea's shirts onto the ironing board and follow my mother's steps with German precision: collar, cuffs, sleeves, front, and back. Years and distance have softened her military precision to simple guidance. I remember her hands guiding mine as she showed me how to smooth down the fabric, her gold signet ring catching the light. "That's the part that gives the shirt its shape. It needs to be perfect," she said as she smoothed out the seams. The meditative monotony of movements etched into muscle memory links me to her, to my grandmother, who taught her, and the line of women who came before them.

"What? You are already ironing? What's gotten into you? I just showered, shaved, and got dressed, and you are all Martha-Stewarting around the house!" Andrea pulls me into a hug, and we fall onto the bed laughing, forgetting about the laundry for a moment. "Don't!" I mock-complain, "I am still gross from the flight."

Thirty minutes and a shower later, I am back at the ironing board, letting the soft fabric of Andrea's Hawaiian shirt slip through my fingers. This is so different from the starched shirts my dad used to wear when I was a kid. My dad's collars could cut bread. I never learned to starch, and I am glad for it. Do people still do that nowadays? I hated the feeling of starched collars on my neck - especially my church blouse.

I didn't like going to church. Holy Communion was the worst. Those days, our priest pulled out his ceremonial robes and stepped in front of his congregation, his well-worn orthopedic shoes peeking out beneath the beige robe. I stared at those shoes as they came closer and closer, counting the tiles as he moved along the row of his sheep, mouths open to receive the host. I scratched my neck, where the collar of my "good Sunday blouse," the starched one, chafed my skin, and kept my eye on the shoes, counting how many tiles until he reached me.

Three tiles.

"What if I don't open my mouth?" The thought of rebellion crossed my mind as I looked up at the stark marble altar block in front of me, its geometric shape crème colored, just like the floor and the steps leading up to it. There is something cold about it, inaccessible. It felt out of sync with the image of God I had in my mind. God to me was everything but cold. Faith should not be practiced in a place that is inhospitable and angular.

Two tiles.

"I could just turn around and leave. But no - Everyone would stare at me!" It wasn't the wafer that I found revolting. It was the fact that the priest touched it and placed it directly on my tongue. And God knows the rinsing of his hands in the little bowl of water before the Communion was just not enough to make it any less yucky. There is not even soap involved. I saw it. He had been either in front of the altar, on the pulpit, where he rested his hands on the wooden railing, or held on to the Bible he was reading from. Oh, and not to mention the hundreds of hands he was shaking at the entrance of the church before mass started. A little bit of water in a tiny bowl is supposed to wash all that away?

One tile.

And then there was the chalice. The "blood of Christ." Children don't want to drink blood, metaphor or not. I knew it was grape juice. And I don't even like grapes. Could they switch it to apple or orange juice, maybe? And exactly how many mouths had touched that rim? The white cloth was already stained with grape juice and germs. I rolled my shoulder to escape the noose-like collar of my blouse. "Don't fidget!" my blouse chided me in my mother's voice. And why did it have to be starched? Fabric should be fluid and soft, gentle and comforting, not holding its shape, like my mother's towels, with a stiff upper lip.

I squeezed my eyes shut as the host was placed on my tongue. *Don't think about it! Don't think about it!* The dry wafer glued itself to my palate, and I wiggled my tongue to unstick it. I pretended to take a sip from the chalice, my lips barely touching the metal, but the priest tilted the cup so much that some of the juice flowed onto my chin, where I wiped it away quickly, leaving a faint red stain on my sleeve. "Great. That'll leave a mark," I hurried back to my pew, swallowing hard, the collar burning a ring around my neck.

I was confirmed at the age of fourteen, and this joyous occasion marked not only my official entry into the congregation as a full member but also the last time I attended church. With the blessings of God and my parents, weekends were mine once again.

The dryer beeps. I pull the last load of clean laundry into the light-blue laundry basket. Despite the long flight, I'm buzzing with energy. Andrea ran to the store and to pick up Tina from our neighbor. The apartment is quiet: the last light of the afternoon floods the living room. I hear kids playing in the courtyard and the clatter of someone's pots. I never realized how idyllic our apartment was. I pause, inhaling an intoxicating feeling of gratitude. The apartment, the building, the courtyard, the city - all the same, yet somehow new. Where before I felt fear and isolation, I am now fully present. I see both light and shadows. I thump the basket onto the tiled floor. One colored load left to fold and iron, and then I'm done. I pull out a pink sarong and flatten it onto the ironing board, fingertips grazing its beaded tassels. It was a gift from Kanti before we said our goodbyes. Small blue turtles swim its edge, just like the turtle carving on his desk.

After meeting Kanti, the notion of having only one life to live was obliterated. From one moment to the next, I'd thrown one of my most fundamental concepts of existence out the window. I knew we'd met in a former life. It was not so much a thought as a conviction, a crystal clear, unshakable fact. The intensity of the recognition, the deep knowledge and understanding of each other, this feeling of unconditional love and pure happiness at seeing him "again"- all of it was undeniable and felt like the most natural thing in the world. What baffles me in hindsight is how normal it felt. Pre-Kanti me would've called it crazy. My shoulder critic would have chimed in. But he had stayed at the hotel that day, and by the time I returned, it was too late. I had connected to a deeper truth that was just irreversible and real.

But knowing something in your bones and understanding it with your brain are two completely different things. I choose to put a pin in that thought for the moment. No use driving myself crazy with further theological and philosophical explorations. No need to dismantle bliss with overthinking.

I iron the sarong on low, making sure not to damage the delicate fabric. The beads whisper as I line up the edges. "There is still so much I have to teach you." What did Kanti mean? I fold the sarong and the memory into a neat square. I cannot keep it with my bikinis,

I decide. For now, I wrap it in tissue and tuck it in the back of my jewelry drawer for safekeeping.

"There is still so much I have to teach you."

I had no idea it would take years - until that day at the beach in California - for me to understand what he meant.

CHAPTER 22

The hot summer days stretch out, exhale deeply, and lie back into long nights of warm twilight, where jazz music drifts from the park and the usual buzz from the city settles into a lazy hum. Within a few days, we are back to our normal routines. Andrea is working long hours, but I often swing by the office to bring him a picnic dinner or sneak a quick kiss before meeting friends for drinks. Tonight, though, we decide to stay in and catch up on some one-on-one time. We've just finished our dinner - nothing fancy, just take-out from the Greek restaurant downstairs. We clear the table and sit back down to finish off the bottle of wine. The evening is a perfect dinner guest; warm and welcoming, it relaxes into a whispering of a breeze around us. The air is heavy with the scent of fragrant flowers and moist soil from the pots I watered just this afternoon. The sun, like a petulant child, refuses to set, light lingering until well past 10 pm.

"Ahhhh, this was long overdue!" Andrea sighs and stretches his arms overhead, leaning back until the upholstery of the balcony chair groans in protest. His eyes glow with a deep sense of contentment. I can relate. It's the same sensation I feel every morning when I wake up refreshed and bursting with energy, when I stretch, catlike, under the covers, savoring the lazy minutes before bouncing out of bed to make coffee. It didn't take long for me to realize the true change my life has undergone since my encounter with Kanti:

All my PTSD symptoms were gone!

No more nightmares, no more anxiety or depression - no gnawing doubt about my worth - all gone. Berlin is no longer dark and scary. There is light and joy, there are friends and laughter, there are connections, and most importantly, it feels like home. I leave the house by myself without a fear in the world. Life is good. On vacation, I barely noticed the silence where nightmares used to be - I chalked it up to being away with my husband. But at that single crazy moment, when Kanti's hand was hovering over mine, the floodgates had opened. I had cried from that deep part within my soul, scarred by all the things I had seen and felt on 9/11, and the images finally loosened their grip. The difference since coming back is startling to say the least.

My dad would say that recovering from PTSD is a lengthy process that involves psychotherapy and, in some cases, medication, but what I had experienced was something instantaneous - something modern medicine can't explain.

"So ...." My voice trails off as I swirl the last sip of white wine in my glass. The condensation on the crystal shimmers in the candlelight as I put it to my nose to inhale the crisp aroma of apple and fresh-cut grass. Aware that I am using my fake wine connoisseur move to hide my face and avoid an unavoidable conversation, I put the glass back on the table. A few fireflies dance in the bushes near the mailboxes. "There is something I need to talk to you about." Andrea looks up at me, a question in his eyes. "That sounds ominous." He creases his forehead, and his look turns to concern. "No, it is nothing bad. It is just …" For over a year, I had constructed a stage set for our life in Berlin, on which I had played the character of the happy wife. The storyline was a tangle of lies and pretense. Andrea, as himself, was unaware of the effort it took me to maintain the illusion. But now, I was more than ready to get it all out.

"I am not really sure where to start."

Where DO I start?

The words roll out one by one, hesitant at first: our first months in Berlin, the change once fall hit … This is not so difficult after all. Telling the story from my newfound perspective is like recounting a movie I had seen. It is not about me. It is about a person I left behind - someone from my past. The story gathers momentum as I talk about the loneliness, fear, the anxiety and guilt of keeping a secret. Not walking Tina at night, then not even in the afternoon. I talk about the isolation, the façade I had built, and how I finally opened up to my dad. Andrea is silent through it all. His arms are folded over his chest. Only now, when I mention my dad, I detect a shift in his posture. A quick flash of disappointment washes over his face before his calm composure returns. I get it. I should have spoken to him first. Then my dad. Andrea's eyes hold mine as I pick up the story in the Seychelles.

He already knows about the "soul recognition," the intense connection, and my sudden understanding of reincarnation. We had spoken about this pretty much daily during the trip. The part that changed my life, though, and that I am now trying to put into words, was whatever transpired when Kanti held his hand over mine.

That whole encounter had been mysterious to my husband as well, but hearing it in sequence is quite an eye-opener for both of us. This is the first time I put into words what had actually happened. Truth has never sounded more bizarre. He suddenly understands my rather strange behavior over the past months, and all the pieces fall into place. I can see Andrea's mind working as his glance wanders along the dark courtyard and the illuminated windows of our neighbors.

A lifetime passes without a word, and instead of bristling against the silence, I lean into it, relaxed, my mind and my heart completely open. The old me would have been teetering on the edge of my seat, searching his eyes, his features, his posture for a clue on how he would react. I would have expected my shoulder critic to be pacing, pulling his hair in nervous expectation. Yet here I am in complete and utter stillness. Calm and whole. Had we had this talk just a month ago, it would have been a cry for help. Now it is the realization of a wonder, a sharing of deep pain, and the marvel of healing.

My shoulder critic is wandering amongst the planter boxes on the balcony. He is barefoot, wearing a long, flowy dress that reminds me of the one my mother used to wear when I was a kid. The loose fabric catches the evening air, billowing around his legs. He smells the flowers, trailing his hands along the leaves before hopping over to the next planter and out of sight behind a tall sunflower.

Andrea gets up to fetch us a new bottle of wine from the fridge while I relight a few candles on the table that the breeze snuffed out. Night settles around us, and the warm candlelight softens my husband's features as he steps back onto the balcony and pulls me into a long embrace. We stand like this, arms wrapped around each other, swaying ever so slightly to our joined heartbeats, before sitting down again. Andrea pulls his chair closer to mine, so our knees touch. He refills my glass. "Go on," he encourages me. I think he knows we have a long night ahead of us.

I am ready.

Talking feels like a rebirth. It's a profound upheaval of patterns so ingrained within that I notice them now, as I shed them.

All my problems, my fears, my PTSD stemmed from one major source: silence. I am not sure where the silence originated. Was it something that grew like moss over my childhood years as an only child with only my parents to talk to, or did it develop later in life, under the right conditions? In this specific case, the issue was rooted in everything I experienced on 9/11 and the days that followed. But it wasn't just the things I saw things that scarred my soul and stayed with me forever. It was that I didn't talk about them. I never told anyone what I saw or how it made me feel. Not even to myself. A diary might have helped, to make my peace with everything on paper at least. Instead, boxed it up and pushed it to the very deepest and darkest recesses of my brain, shut the door, and then - to be sure - cemented it shut for good.

I did not want to burden anyone with my memories.

Least of all my husband.

Andrea would have been worried sick had he known the reality of Ground Zero. It's one thing seeing it on TV all day long, yet quite another being there, feeling its weight, tasting the burning smoke, not knowing what is burning. Rubble, buildings, gas, flesh? He might even have stopped me from going, which was the main reason I remained silent. So, when I returned home from another long day in the rubble of lower Manhattan, I preferred to just have a hot bath and distract my mind with a movie and a joint or two. He did not ask, and I did not volunteer any details.

I clearly remember the drive down to Lower Manhattan.

The September sun was still unseasonably hot against our faces, even this early in the morning. Another scorcher, the kind that turned lower Manhattan into an unbearable mix of heat, dust, smoke, and pain that hurt on a soul level. "Want some gum? Helps with the smell." One of my truck-mates offered me a pack of chewing gum and nodded at me with the hint of a smile. I unwrap the powder-coated green strip, fold it, and start chewing. A strong taste of mint floods my senses. We were perched on the back of the truck, the wind blowing in our faces, carrying with it the smells of the burning rubble. Now it smelled of mint. I was wearing the same jeans every day. The dust was deeply caked into the fabric, and the color had aged from dark denim to stonewashed grey. I doubted that I would ever wear them again. They were marked with more than just dirt. The collective trauma was interwoven with the fabric, seeped so deep that no washing could ever dislodge it. My truck mates were silent on the drive down, bracing for what was to come. The anticipation of the alarm sirens, the threat of collapsing buildings, and walking past makeshift morgues with bags that held nothing but parts and pieces wears you down. We were all deep in our own thoughts, figuring out our individual coping mechanisms. The sky was a sparkling blue, yet, depending on how the wind blew, there was a haze of smoke in the air. Lower Manhattan was cordoned off by military roadblocks, and only authorized vehicles and Search and Rescue personnel were allowed through. The entry point to the evacuated area was always crowded with people. During the first two days, there were friends and families of missing people, clinging to the hopes of good news, pushing crumpled papers with their loved ones' photos and descriptions into our hands as we waited to be waved through the barrier. It was heartbreaking to see their pleading faces look up at us, and I tried to memorize the pictures, knowing full well that the chances of finding their loved ones, or anyone else alive at that point, were slim to none. With a sense of reverence, I smoothed a flyer over my legs. The black and white face of a young woman wearing a graduation cap beamed at me from the paper. I folded it in half once, smoothing out a creased corner, then folding it again and sliding it into my jeans pocket, my only place for safekeeping.

Over the course of the following days, those faces near the roadblock changed. The realization that their loved ones were probably not coming home drew the grieving families into the safety of their homes. Now, when our truck stopped, we were not given any Missing Person posters. Instead, people handed us water bottles, food, or just held out their hands for a moment of connection. There was less grief, more love, and something close to defiance. They waved flags and held up posters with messages painted in bright, big letters: "*May God bless you, First Responders,*" "*We will prevail,*" "*You are our heroes.*" These people showed up FOR US! As I write these words, the memory alone sends a cold shiver down my spine again. Instead of feeling the love, I felt extremely uncomfortable. Those words were not meant for me! They were meant for all the Firefighters and Police, who worked tirelessly every day, who ran into burning buildings, saving the lives of thousands of people. I, on the other hand, felt like an impostor. Who was I to accept their gratitude? Who was I, but a girl who happened to be on a truck, carrying supplies from A to B? I had not been directly affected by this attack, had not lost a loved one or friend. In my mind, I did not deserve any of it. So, I shrank, eyes fixed on my dirty sneakers, or picking at the layer of dead skin around my blisters, making them bleed, focusing on a pain I could control.

"You are good to go." A soldier with a clipboard waved us through. We drove past armed military, several police cruisers, and armored vehicles parked along the roadblock. I was glad when we passed the checkpoint, and my shoulders dropped with a sigh of relief. Lower Manhattan looked like a scene from a movie: Papers and trash danced like post-apocalyptic tumbleweed down the deserted roads. Stores and restaurants that used to be teeming with people now lay abandoned, and rows of dark, empty windows stared down at us as we passed. The silence was palpable. The closer we got, the denser the air felt. There was so much to do, so much to feel, that it settled on my shoulders like a mesh of iron chains that I was only able to shake once I was back home, closing my eyes in the hot shower when the water washed the dust and the images off my mind.

Friends and family checked in on us daily as more news from the attacks unfolded. Their question of how I was doing was often accompanied by an *"I cannot believe you can do this!"* That simple comment was enough to send me into a tailspin of guilt and shame, especially since I was there only for less than a week, while others went back every day for months. Leaving on day five, as I had, came with a tidal wave of guilt. I had reached my limit, both physically and emotionally. And since I was "only" a volunteer, I could quit any time I wanted.

And I did.
I quit.

I turned my back on the rubble and never looked back. Not once. In fact, I have never been back to where Ground Zero used to be. Never. I don't know if I can.

And I didn't want to talk about it. It was too complex to even attempt an explanation. There was guilt for leaving, guilt for not being able to help or save anyone, all of it smeared with the sticky residue of fear and hollow empathy beside the real pain of those who lost loved ones. Who would have known that those memories would come back to haunt me years later? And who in their right mind would have ever expected a mysterious encounter in the Seychelles to heal my scars within minutes?

If that was not bizarre enough, I remember clearly NOT telling Kanti anything about 9/11. When he placed his hand on mine, he did so without knowing about my PTSD. Once again, I had stayed quiet. Maybe he did see something when he studied the lines of my hands so closely. But I didn't believe in palm readings. Or did I? I'm not sure anymore.

That night, Andrea and I stayed up until just before sunrise. We talk through a bottle of wine, a stick of Toblerone, and a bag of chips. We talk through tears and silence. We hold hands and space for each other. As the first birds start their morning choir, I brush my teeth in the bathroom, take off my makeup, and slip into a short negligee. Before I get into bed, I open the thin jewelry drawer of our built-in closet, swipe off my stainless-steel bracelet and my watch and put them next to the folded satin paper. I put my hand on the paper, feeling the beads of the sarong underneath.

"There is still so much I have to teach you."

Andrea and I snuggle into bed together, exhausted but more united than we have been in a long time. My mind is blank. I can't even think anymore. After not speaking about any of this for years, I now feel like I've spoken all the words there are. Everything has been said. And here we are - in each other's arms. I am not clinging to Andrea the way I used to when his presence alone saved me from my anxieties. No. Now I am comfortably snuggled up next to him, relaxed and safe just being me. No fears, no regrets.

A few weeks later, I sit in the bathroom and stare at two thin blue lines on the pregnancy test in my hand. This news eclipses everything, and Andrea and I begin our journey into parenthood bright-eyed, excited, and scared. The speed at which things change inside my own body as the baby grows leaves me no time to reflect further on my encounter with Kanti. Instead of intangible questions about life and death, God, heaven, and reincarnation, I crave the realness of my current life. I focus on building a nest for our little family, on daydreaming about the little person that is about to turn our life upside down, and on the intense love that fills my heart.

CHAPTER 23
MANHATTAN BEACH 2018

As I stand at the edge of the water, my eyes scan the turmoil of waves for a sign of the driftwood. But I know that Mother Ocean has reclaimed her gift and left me with the memory of Kanti's words.

"There is still so much I have to teach you."

It is strange - that memory sat deep in my brain for more than ten years, patiently waiting. I know deep down that staying with Kanti wouldn't have been feasible. As tempting as it was, it was not the right time. It was a time for healing and for growing. Starting a family and moving to Dubai kept me busy, my attention elsewhere.

Guilt breaks one of my fingernails and niggles the broken edge. But what if ...? Should I have been more aware? Did I let a huge opportunity pass me by? Maybe my life would've taken a different turn had I accepted Kanti's invitation that day.

Another set of waves rolls towards the shore; their backs break against the pillars of the pier, and white foam explodes into the sky before the whitecaps have time to whisper their secrets. I walk down the beach, where the waves' crests are unencumbered by concrete, and listen - maybe they'll hint at what to do next.

Had I stayed with Kanti, would I have learned how he healed my PTSD? Knowing what I know now, I am convinced that whatever he did was some sort of energy healing. That jolt of ice and fire, followed by the emotional release, felt like the industrial-strength version of the energy I work with during my Reiki sessions. My index finger with the broken nail scrapes more guilt against my thumb. If only I'd spent more time with him.

"Don't go there." My shoulder critic's voice is in my ear, but I see him standing in a tree pose on a tiny yoga mat a few yards ahead of me. He has one foot resting against his thigh, the knee sticking out at a flamingo-esque angle. His arms are stretched up towards the sky, and his eyes are closed. His features are relaxed, serene-looking, but I catch him peeking out at me from underneath one half-closed eyelid. "Don't go where?" I frown at him. "Down the What-if-road," he replies and brings his palms together in a prayer pose in front of his chest. "It doesn't lead anywhere." He is wearing leopard-print leggings and a tight-fitting zipper jacket with a neon pink *Beach Please* printed along the sleeves. A portable coffee cup is stuck between a pair of rhinestone-studded flip flops next to his yoga mat. I swear, he is turning into a Manhattan Beach mom in front of my eyes, if it weren't for his pale, hairy feet and the five-o'clock shadow he's sporting. "When did you become so wise?" I hate to admit it, but he is right. "I have my moments." He replies, pleased. Without acknowledging the satisfied smirk on his face, I lower myself into the sand next to him and look out over the waves.

"You know," he continues, as he comes out of his tree pose and pretzels his legs into a lotus seat next to me, the bottoms of his feet facing up, "sometimes it helps to just sit quietly with your own thoughts and trust that the answer will come to you." I chuckle. "Trust? Where'd you get that from?" He grins out at the ocean. "Kathrin, well Mona, ... eh, Kathrin. Whatever. Well, she was right. Trust has brought us this far. Let's see where else it can take us."

Warmed by his words and feeling closer to him than I have in a while, we both let our eyes wander towards the horizon in comfortable silence. The ocean has settled into a deep gray, breathing gentle swells against the shiny stretch of sand in front of me. A small shell rolls with the lacy edge of foam before tumbling back into deeper waters and out of sight. Schhhhhhhhhhhhhhh, schhhhhhhhhhh, the ocean whispers. She seems to agree with my shoulder critic. I need to trust. I smile up at the clouds above us, hoping for a sliver of blue sky, a window that would offer a straight line to Kathrin, reminiscent of the imaginary door in the ceiling of my childhood room. But the clouds are sociable today, bunched together, thick as thieves. She is not up there anyway. I smile to myself, to that memory of her that I always carry in my heart, more tangible than imagining her up there somewhere.

"So, what do you think I should do with my Reiki?" I speak without looking at my shoulder critic, but I know he is listening. "I feel that I have to do more with it than I am doing now. Working on clients in Gia's room is okay, but ... I don't know. Should I open my own Reiki studio, or join an existing one? None of these options feel right. Treating digestive issues, insomnia, anxieties -it's all nice, but something is missing."

"You are asking someone who, until recently, didn't even believe in any of this stuff." He exhales a little grunt. "I don't know. I just think a lot has happened over the past few years to bring you here. Right here, right now. And if I have learned anything from all that weird stuff," he turns, looks at me, and I meet his eyes, "it's that you already know the answer. I think what you need is a purpose. What brought you here, where does it take you, and why?"

Those are a lot of questions, but they make sense. I know deep in my heart that a path laid out for me, and it is not along any traditional route. I have learned so much these past years. Death has walked beside me for a long time now and has taught me to move through grief, not to shy away from it. Grief and I have become close. Everything in my life has been about healing that pain, facing the reality of death, and not turning away from it. So, where I can use that? Is there somewhere where I can soften grief with Reiki?

A thought forms on the next wave, and I watch as it gathers strength, rises with the next swell, and breaks onto the beach and into my subconscious.

"Hospice! I think Reiki is leading me to hospice!" I turn to my critic. Words, like glowing strands of glass inside my mind, fuse in sparking connections to other strands: loss, grief, energy, reincarnation, soul, emotions, death, fear, trust, and spirituality all merge in one word: hospice!

The clouds above us break apart to throw a spear of sunshine into the ocean. A blinding reflection of light sends diamond-crusted ripples along the coast just long enough to bring a huge smile to my face before the clouds join forces again and the ocean settles into the muted gray of winter. I have learned to pay attention to signs.

A few weeks later, sitting at a red light, I spot a large blue-and green-logo on a building along the road. I recognize it immediately - the logo of one of the largest hospice services in the South Bay. After the beach epiphany, I researched local hospices. But something held me back. Who am I to just show up at a hospice and volunteer my services as a Reiki practitioner? I was still new to all of this, my confidence wavering. Was I really ready? Maybe I should practice Reiki for a while longer with my small pool of clients until I feel more prepared. The truth was that I was still dealing with my own grief, and working with patients who were at the end of life might reopen barely scabbed wounds. I decided to put a pin in it and wait for the right moment.

Without second-guessing myself this time, I flip the turn signal and pull into the parking lot. Apparently, today is the day to take the next step. "Whoaaaaa! Where you going?" The sudden change of direction catapults my shoulder critic off my shoulder and onto the center console, where he disappears into the cup holder, his legs kicking in protest.

By the time the sliding glass door pulls away with a soft whoosh, he has composed himself and runs after me, his skinny legs and Converse-clad feet tapping a hurried tap, tap, tap on the asphalt. His purple satin bomber jacket flutters in the air behind him, but he still isn't fast enough. The glass door slides shut before he reaches the building, and I suppress a grin as he bounces up and down in front of the motion sensor without success. Without paying him much attention, I enter the reception area of the building. Photos of smiling people, larger-than-life, line the walls with brass name plaques underneath. A poster with a dreamy willow tree and an elderly couple on a bench reminds me to "plan ahead." The air smells lemony-clean, probably because of a diffuser I spot in the corner behind a fake potted tree.

I don't know what I was expecting. Maybe more of a hospital setting? The only experience I have with anything hospice-related is the palliative care center where my mom died - a different wing of the same hospital where she'd spent the prior weeks. This is just an office building. No patients.

"Hi. Can I help you?" an elderly lady with white, wavy hair smiles at me from behind pink-rimmed glasses. "Um." I turn to her. "I was wondering if you have volunteer opportunities here." My words - and my feet - hesitate as I approach the reception desk. "Of course, we do, dear!" She sounds like someone's grandma, and her loving air of kindness puts me instantly at ease.

"Let me get you Jordin. She's the Volunteer Coordinator," she says in an apple-pie-scented tone and picks up the phone next to her. "Wait over there, dear." She points towards a waiting area behind the reception desk. There is a plush couch with an antique writing desk along the wall and stacks of books everywhere. A small brown teddy bear is perched up on the desk, his shiny black glass eyes smiling at me as I look around. Instead of the couch, I opt for one of two formal leather chairs next to a round glass table along the window and watch through the vertical blinds as the traffic passes by outside. The traffic light I had just been waiting in front of a few minutes ago turns green, and I wonder what I am getting myself into. Me and my spontaneous ideas. I sigh. I hear the whoosh of the glass door as a delivery guy carries a heap of packages into the building, and a few seconds later, my shoulder critic jogs into the waiting area, visibly flustered. He slows down and adjusts his jacket when he sees me and makes a beeline for the couch, where he plops himself onto the plushest cushion in the corner, a deep frown creasing his face as he studies me.

"Hiiii! I'm Jordin." A bubbly voice pulls my gaze away from the couch. Her brown eyes sparkle, and she extends a slender hand in welcome. She is shorter than me and younger by maybe fifteen years. Her long brown hair is pulled into a ponytail that dances down her back. "I am so glad you caught me. Usually, I am in and out of the office," she pulls the other leather chair out and sits down across from me. "We have patients all over the Los Angeles area and another office on the other side of town, so I am all over the place." Her laugh paints her words with dapples of sunshine.

"Um, where are the patients?" I ask and feel unprepared. I know the hospice is affiliated with the nearby hospital, but her remark makes me wonder.

"Some patients are at the hospital," and she shrugs in the general direction of the building a few blocks away. "But most of our patients are in their own homes. Our team of nurses, social workers, chaplains, and volunteers visits them." Jordin puts her hand on mine and smiles. "No worries, you'll learn all about that later. Tell me about yourself. What brings you here?"

An open window rustles the blinds behind me, making the streaks of sunshine on the carpeted floor sway. Their movements are mesmerizing, and I find myself drawn to their dance as I gather my thoughts. I tell Jordin about Reiki, my journey through grief, and the move from Dubai to LA, and some more about Reiki. Jordin listens with unusual focus. She is fully present and engaged, and her genuine interest makes me feel seen in a way I have not felt in a while. I'll learn later that this is common among hospice workers - and a skill I cannot wait to practice myself. Jordin is curious about Reiki and what it could offer to patients since I would be the first practitioner to join the team. "To expect physical healing is probably unrealistic, but Reiki works on an emotional and spiritual level as well. It can help with pain, soothe fear and anxiety," I pause, feeling like I am swimming in very deep waters here. I can sense that I have barely scratched the surface with Reiki and all it can do, but this is uncharted territory for me. "Be right back." Jordin chirps and disappears in a nearby row of cubicles.

A choir of voices whispers *trust* in my ear - Kathrin, Mona, my shoulder critic, even my mom.

A heavy thud jolts me out of my thoughts, and I am faced with a severe-looking stack of papers that Jordin drops in front of me with an apologetic smile. Bureaucracy demands an obscene amount of paperwork, background- and medical checks to become a registered hospice volunteer. With the patience of a saint, she answers all my questions as I fill out the forms, explains the process and any wording I am unfamiliar with. My shoulder critic has made his way over to the table and reads through the papers I sign, thick horn-rimmed glasses on his prominent nose.

"What do I check here?" I look up from the papers and point at two boxes. One is marked *PHS*, and the other *HS*. "Oh, that depends on where you want to work. Do you want to work with adults? Then check HS, for Hospice Service, or if you want to work with our Pediatric Hospice, then check PHS."

"Pediatric!" I blurt out immediately, without thinking, and I set my checkmark on PHS. My shoulder critic's face freezes in a mask of incredulity. His eyes bulge from his skull, and his mouth forms a silent "Oh Shit! Kids?"

Unaware of his presence, Jordin's face lights up even more, and she passes me some additional papers to sign. My gaze sinks onto the forms in front of me. The letters bounce and blur on the page, and I hope she does not notice my trembling hand.

Why on earth did I say "pediatric"?
Shit!

I look back at the black checkmark I had just made. Can I erase it? The pen in my hand is a regular ballpoint pen. Not erasable. Damn! My hands start to sweat, and I put the pen down for a moment, wipe my palms on my jeans, and stretch my fingers. The teddy bear winks at me from the desk, his stitched smile carrying a level of understanding that had escaped me earlier.

I need a minute. My heart is fluttering in my chest, and I excuse myself to go to the restroom; my shoulder critic follows at my heels. As soon as I close the door behind me, I sink onto the toilet seat and bury my face in my hands. I feel cold, and small patches of sweat appear under my armpits.

"What the heck did you do?"
"Children?"

My shoulder critic's voice moves back and forth on the other side of the stall, and I can hear him pacing.

I did not even know that Pediatric hospice was even a thing!

The tiled walls close in on me, the straight lines of the grout dancing in front of my eyes like the blinds in the other room. I get up and walk to the sink, my hands still shaking. My shoulder critic sits on the edge of the sink, his head resting heavily on his arms, elbows on knees. I cannot see his face, but his head shakes in disbelief or frustration. I splash my face with cold water and pull a rough paper towel from the dispenser.

Since I get no support from him, I look in the mirror and give myself a pep talk. "Okay. Take a deep breath. Remember to trust. This is not a mistake. You are meant to be here. You got this!" One more deep breath, and I head back to finish my application paperwork.

What I feared would be a jump into the deep end turned out to be a welcome slow start. I stretch my legs towards the flames of our gas fire pit in the garden as I reflect on the last nine months.

I remember being so scared when I signed up to volunteer with the pediatric hospice. After I met Jordin, a couple of weeks went by, while we waited for my medical- and background checks to clear. I was grateful for the reprieve, as those weeks were filled with ups and downs as I questioned my ability and my sanity. I sought advice from friends and family, who offered little, as I fought my way through doubt and insecurities. "I could not do that," was the only response I got, and I feared that they were right. Maybe I couldn't do it either. But every time doubt filled the space where my confidence used to reside, I got support from the most unlikely source: my shoulder critic! He started wearing a leather biker jacket with a large patch with the word TRUST in red flames sewn across the back. If he wasn't wearing his jacket, he had a couple of new T-shirts with TRUST printed across the front. He even had several pairs of brightly colored socks with TRUST written between two white stripes. He never said much about it, and he did not have to. His silent support was all I needed in those moments.

It took a while to visit an actual patient. First, I joined a few workshops where I learned everything I needed to know about bedside manners, do's and don'ts, responsibilities of each team member, and how the hospice process worked. I realized that working in pediatric hospice did not mean you could tell that a child was dying just by looking at them. Sometimes it was all too obvious, but often the truth was hidden under a simple pallor or physical limitations. And sometimes not even that. Children are children. They laugh, they are silly, they want to play, they watch TV, and they love art and books. Focusing on that makes it easier to forget they're counting their future in weeks or months - not in years.

I wriggle my naked toes towards the warm flames of the fire pit. They dance over the shiny glass pebbles in the concrete bowl, and a deep sense of relaxation spreads from my feet along my legs and through the rest of my body. I lean back in my chair and soak in the late afternoon atmosphere of our garden. The gurgling from our neighbor's water feature behind the wall carries my thoughts towards the setting sun on the horizon. I had just helped a family paint a sunset with Legacy Art. That was another workshop I had taken earlier on. Even though my initial purpose as a hospice volunteer was Reiki, I fell in love with Legacy Art. Often, families ask for it during the last days with their loved one when the realization has hit that this is it - their time together is running out, and they are longing for something to hold on to, something that will bridge the rift death is about to tear through the family. That's when Legacy Art comes in. I bring a big tote bag of supplies with me - paints, paper, and brushes - and together we create art using the patient's and their family members' hand- and footprints. I help them create a piece of art that becomes a last memento of their loved one to hold on to. And just yesterday, that was a sunset.

Pink-streaked clouds fluff across a tangerine sky on the horizon, and the blue above our house deepens. The chill in the air is palpable despite the fire, and I scoot a little closer to the flames. I let my arm drop to the side of the chair and snip off a leaf from the Blackcurrant Sage bush, crush it between my fingers, and inhale the crisp scent of berries. When we moved here, I had planted a few different sage plants, and they flourished into thick bushes. Sometimes I would tie a few branches of the White Sage into bundles to dry and then burn them as incense. I was still waiting for inspiration on how to use the Blackcurrant Sage and the Pineapple Sage. Cocktails seem to be the obvious solution. I close my eyes and smell the leaf in my hand again. Moments like this are priceless - this is the gift my little patients have given me: an appreciation for small pleasures.

One of my biggest fears had been to be present during a child's death. But Jordin had assured me early on that in all her years with hospice, that had never happened. "The children usually choose to leave when they are alone, or with their parents," she explained. I like the thought that we can choose our time of death. I wonder if that is true. And if it is, did my mom choose her time? And what about Kathrin? Surely not. Maybe it is different with accidents.

The challenging thing about the visits wasn't the children. Every time I met a new patient, a sense of peace and calm enveloped me as I entered their home. I met families with babies as young as a few days old to teenagers. Feeding tubes and oxygen tubes were no longer threatening; they were simply tools that supported life. None of the visits was traumatic. I braced for heartbreak but found only a deep sense of connection. The homes were filled with palpable love and care for the children, and Reiki only deepened this feeling of warmth and comfort.

But it was the depth in the parents' eyes that strung searing threads of compassion over my heart. It's the acute awareness that Death sits nearby, pulling a veil over smiles - and with it, the silver lining of living each day with intention. Every moment becomes precious. And that was the gift my patients gave me: they showed me life's small astonishments - the marvel of a flower petal, the alchemy of a leaf's scent, the miracle of breath, and the simple lift of a smile. And that was just the beginning.

CHAPTER 24
MANHATTAN BEACH 2018

Without taking my eyes off the road, I turn down the radio to see better through the constant onslaught of rain. "Really? You are one of those people now? Turning down the music to see better?" Mocking laughter rises from the backseat. My shoulder critic is curled up, snuggled inside one of my daughter's sweaters, a leftover from the dance carpool last night. "I can focus better without the music - or your constant complaining," I retort, feeling called out. The weather should've been a sign, but I am oblivious as I focus on the short stretch of road ahead. The sheets of rain marching down the highway turn the air into a solid wall of water that my wipers, even on their highest setting, can barely clear. Muted red lights are the only indication of the drivers ahead as they slow to a crawl. My whole field of vision is painted in a watery gray, dotted with blinking sparks of red and the continuous threads of bright white from the oncoming traffic to my left. I can't even remember the last time I drove in rain like this. Southern California isn't known for its torrential downpours, and this one won't quit. Still, I feel oddly calm on this drive from Manhattan Beach to Hacienda Heights. The drumming of rain weaves a cocoon of tranquility around me, interrupted only by the occasional snore from the backseat. Without the annoying commentary of my shoulder critic, I feel peaceful as I drift like a submarine through a watery world. Even the golden Buddha on my keychain in the cupholder smiles serenely, undisturbed by nature's unrest outside. I am wearing my thin black hoodie under my jean jacket today and am grateful for the soft, warm fabric cozying up against my skin. Without looking, I feel for my Yeti cup wedged into the second cupholder and sip the strong, hot espresso, sweetened with a dash of coconut sugar.

Usually, it would take half the time, but today it's ninety soggy minutes to Hacienda Heights, a small city east of Los Angeles. I have driven through this part of the city once or twice before, but never had a reason to stop. The streets are deserted as everyone hunkers down to wait out the storm. Huge puddles of water stretch from one side of the street to the other, yielding to the occasional car that throws up a dramatic splash. I squint - I have trouble finding the right house; the puddles to the left and the right completely obscure the house numbers painted on the curbs. The rain is coming down so hard now that I can't make out the numbers on any of the one-story houses that nestle close to each other along the street.

I drive up and down from one cul-de-sac to another until I finally pull over and call for directions. Gabriela, the mother, answers the phone, her voice shaking slightly as she directs me to the driveway of their home. Judging by the number of cars parked in front, it looks like family has already arrived.

I take a slow and deliberate breath and pull my jean jacket close before leaving the warmth of my car.

I am here today to meet nine-year-old Miguel. I cannot help it, but the thought flashes through my mind that my little Giulia is nine too. Just for a second, I allow a deep sense of gratitude to swell - both my daughters are at school and healthy. Just as guilt stabs my heart with cold fingers, I push the thought away. I need to be present without distractions, so I let go of the image of Gia and Giulia and keep only the warm embrace of gratitude. I take a few deep, grounding breaths and rest my hand on Kathrin's bracelet at my wrist. It calms the jittery feeling in my stomach. Jordin told me Miguel wasn't conscious and likely didn't have much time left. How much, no one knew. My stomach is in a knot. Walking into the home of a dying child is never easy. I never know what to expect: who will be there, what the mood will be, and what has changed since the last update I received from his hospice nurse. Each visit is different, and they all leave me with a deep appreciation for the people I am meeting. Strangely, the sadness I feared rarely materializes.

Another deep breath, and the anxiety gives way to a warm feeling of trust. As scary as it is, I know that the moment I walk into this house, something deep inside of me will take over.

I know why I am here, and I know I can do this.

I open the car door and step out, huddling under my umbrella as I dash to the front door. Managing a large portfolio with poster boards and paper, a heavy tote with paints and supplies, as well as a handbag is a challenge on the best of days. Today, the rain makes my approach to the house almost comical, as I clutch the umbrella handle with one hand while trying to squeeze the rest of me and my bags under the small shelter it provides. A sudden gust of wind turns the umbrella upside down and blows me onto the front porch of the house. Those two steps leave my hair wet and my bags pelted with raindrops. I shake the water off the portfolio and accidentally shake the umbrella arm as well, showering me with more drops. Definitely not the dignified entrance I had in mind. The corrugated awning that juts out from the house is leaking streams of water onto the concrete floor of the porch. A brown doormat with the word

"Bienvenidos[41]" nestles up against the threshold, trying to get away from the ever-growing puddle that's taken over the floor. As I follow the water with my eyes, a dark figure at the far end of the porch startles me; I almost drop everything. Embarrassment flushes my cheeks. A middle-aged man with jet-black hair and a large mustache fades into a wall of cigarette smoke a few feet to my right. His stocky physique is camouflaged against the gray wall of the house. His expression bears a resigned emptiness, and he makes no sign of acknowledgment as he faces the rain without a word. I try to be as inconspicuous as possible, as I disentangle myself from my bags' various straps and handles. I struggle to close the umbrella with one hand while trying to contain the avalanche of bags with the other. For a second, I pause and glance again at the figure to my right. The smell of cold cigarette smoke resuscitates a buried memory of my mother. Cold smoke is sticky, so I hurry the last step toward the front door before it clings to me.

I received the request for Legacy Art just last night, and - as with most of these calls - there is a certain sense of urgency, and action must be taken quickly. Time is the one thing that is not guaranteed for my patients.

The front door stands a few inches ajar, open to the weather. Having composed myself enough, I give a brief knock and step inside the dark opening, bringing with me a swell of cool, rain-sodden air and an unwelcome hint of cigarettes. After just a few steps, the short hallway opens into a large living room. I can't tell whether it's the dark clouds creating a gloomy light or the fact that the room is filled with at least fifteen people that make it seem small despite its size. The energy is heavy, and the first thing that hits me is the absence of conversation. Hushed voices accompany a flurry of hands preparing sandwiches in the open kitchen to the left, while everyone else sits or stands quietly around the living room. Four or five kids

---

41   *Bienvenidos - Spanish. "Welcome."*

crowd around an iPad on the floor near the window. A chocolate Lab pushes his nose against the glass of the garden door from the outside. He looks wet and sad, but nobody notices the poor animal as he slinks away, head and ears hanging, toward a dog bed under the cover of the roofed terrace.

I look around, my eyes searching for the person in charge, trying to make out the parents among the faces turned toward me. Weary eyes meet mine with the smallest glimmer of hope. Every time the door opens, hope blossoms against all logic, against all reason, that whoever stumbles into the quiet of the living room will offer relief and escape from the inevitable. I recognize those faces, not the people per se, but their demeanor. I'm sure I had the same expression when I was waiting by my mom's bedside, and the door opened to a doctor or nurse. I know what it's like to be there for someone you love at that last stage of their life. Those last days in limbo, when all you can do is be there and wait while you cling to every breath.

"Hello," I say into the room, my eyes searching for any clues about who the parents might be. I keep my voice low, afraid to disturb the precarious balance of energy in the room.

The house is dense with emotions. Propped up on the table to the left is a large image of Jesus, surrounded by the golden glow of a halo. Various other saints jostle for space among flowers and small bottles of Holy Water. Large votive candles hold vigil; their tall glass is marred by hours of black soot and melted wax, hiding the frantic flame at the very bottom. Smaller, fresh candles are crowded around a cross, timid in their pristine whiteness and clear, calm flames.

The crumpled edges of the tablecloth speak of prayers and tears shed, of people kneeling before the altar, clinging to it for hope, for answers, for relief. Outside of hospice, I don't see many altars in people's houses. The rush of everyday life relegates God to the backseat, to the occasional crucifix, icon, or religious sculpture in a quiet corner of the house. But when Death comes around, these small symbols of faith take on a deeper meaning and a more prominent position in the household. I always find it comforting to know that people have something to lean on - a belief that gets them through the dark times and allows them to shift hope - or blame - onto something larger.

A woman pacing near the open kitchen on the left looks up. She sets the plastic water bottle in her hand on the kitchen counter. I notice that the bottle looks misshapen, marked with white streaks where the plastic had been repeatedly squeezed and bent - the torn label waves from one stubborn glued edge in resignation.

The woman walks toward me, hesitates for a moment when a sound from the depths of the house reaches her ear, and she cocks her head, her eyes fixed on the empty space above my head as she listens. Deeming the sound inconsequential, she focuses on me again and takes a few steps to greet me. Her large, dark eyes eclipse her small stature. Her brows are furrowed in a pleading expression. She does not seem to be walking on solid ground but teetering on a tightrope between reality and hope.

"Alexandra? I am Gabriela, Miguel's mom," she says, with a hint of a Spanish accent in her voice. I introduce myself, wavering between a handshake and a hug, taking in her body language and subtle cues, and decide on the latter, taking her into a warm embrace. How else can I greet a mother who is preparing herself to say goodbye to her only son?

I feel how much strength it takes for her just to be here.

"I am here for the art project." I glance at my bags and portfolio as explanation, which I am still holding, avoiding the words "hospice" or "Legacy Art. " "Is there a place where we can chat in private? I would love for you to tell me a little about Miguel and your family."

Gabriela looks around the room as if seeing it for the first time. There are no empty seats on the couch or at the kitchen table. I drop my bags in the crevice behind the couch, where they would not bother anyone, and follow Gabriela as she guides me toward her bedroom, the only room in the small house where we can sit down

and talk for a few minutes. The room is crowded with piles of clothing and toys stacked against the far wall. The air hangs heavy around
our shoulders and smells the way most bedrooms do when the beds
are not made, and the windows have not been opened in a while.

A queen-size bed on the left takes up most of the space, with
narrow strips of tiled floor along the three sides. Two cushions still
bear the imprints of recent use. With an apologetic gesture, Gabriela
swipes a few discarded T-Shirts and pants off the bed, smooths
down the blanket, and gestures for me to sit. This is not the time for
meaningless small talk, and the elephant in the room looms, waving
his trunk from side to side, as if urging us to address him. I get the
hint and go straight to the only subject saturating the home. "To
create a meaningful piece of art, I would love to find out more about
you and your family," I begin.

Without even thinking about it, my voice drops to a soft timbre,
reaching out with all the love and compassion I have. "Tell me about
Miguel," I ask, as I sit across from her on the knitted bedspread.
I don't ask about the cancer or how he's doing. She has probably
answered that question countless times already; her universe has
orbited his illness. For a moment, she's silent, her eyes linger on a
group of picture frames arranged on the sideboard.

"He is the most beautiful boy you'll ever meet."

Her voice echoes from a time in the past, a hesitant version of
what she might have sounded like a few years ago. She plays with
a loose strand of dark brown hair that has fallen into her face and
continues, her eyes lost in the depths of the memories.

"He loves to play on his Nintendo. Oh, how long did he beg us
to buy that stupid thing until we finally gave in. And for weeks, we
could not get him off it. He was completely obsessed."

She smiles at the memory, her hand caressing the bedspread as she
speaks. Her fingers follow each loop of the loose knit, trailing the
curves, exploring an unseen path of comfort along the soft fabric.
A single feather sticks out between the threads, and she picks it up,

smoothing the disconnected barbs back into their natural perfection, lets it rest upon her fingertip before blowing it into the room.

Rain falls in glassy sheets from the gutters above the window. The weather shows no signs of slowing down. Battered by Mother Nature's continuous onslaught, the broad-limbed tree outside the window bows its branches low to the ground, looking dejected, some of its green leaves tumbling from heavy limbs too early in the season. I wonder if he mourns the premature loss of his leaves.

"He loves the color green. It is his favorite," she says, smiling up at me. Suddenly, she looks like a young girl, vulnerable and small. Her eyes are looking at me, but not really seeing me. She is in a world of her own.

"His room is filled with green. Even his stuffed animals. He has a lot of stuffed animals," she laughs. "Way too many. But what am I to do? He just loves them so much. So, his friends keep bringing them. And his sister, his *tia* and *tio*, his *abuelos* and his *primos*[42] - they spoil him so much."

The strand of hair has fallen stubbornly back into her face, and she blows it away with a determined huff. She gets up, walks over to the pictures, straightens them according to some invisible order, caresses the frame of a larger picture, then places it back down. It shows a handsome boy of about six years, with sleek black hair, sides shaved in a fade. He is wearing a green-striped shirt and looks up from whatever he is doing with a smile that fills the whole picture. His velvety brown eyes sparkle with life. Before coming back to sit on the bed, Gabriela picks up a lonely child's sock from the floor, turns it the right way around, and folds it in half. She places the sock on the wooden sideboard next to the photos, rather than the nearby hamper and runs her hand over it as if it were a precious possession.

---

42   *His tia and tio, his abuelos and his primos - Spanish "His aunt and uncle, his grandparents and his cousins"*

"He loves to play with his Legos. Recently, it's been hard for him, but sometimes we put his Legos on his bed, and he plays until he gets too tired. He sleeps a lot these days."

With something that sounds like defiance, she adds, "He is sleeping now."

"That's okay," I reply in a lighthearted voice, walking along the path of hope with her. The hospice nurse told me earlier he wasn't sleeping - he's unconscious.

"Let's not wake him then," I continue. "But can I go see him? We'll be quiet. We can even start our art project while he's asleep."

This prospect seems to shake Gabriela out of her memories. Her eyes light up as she leads me a few short steps down the hallway toward Miguel's room. I pop into the living room on the way, grab my bags of art supplies, and follow her. Just a few paces down the hallway on the left, we reach a door, decorated with stickers and six wooden letters hung in topsy-turvy angles, spelling M-I-G-U-E-L. She says a few quick sentences in Spanish as we walk into the bedroom, and several family members squeeze their way past us out of the door. With an apologetic smile, she scoots past a pile of medical supplies that encroach on the narrow space between Miguel's bed and the mirrored closet along the wall. For a moment, I pause in the doorway.

There he is.

He is lying on a large bed that occupies most of the room. There are posters of soccer players on the wall, next to another one that must be gaming-related - I don't recognize the characters or loud graphics. Miguel's head and arms are the only parts of him visible under a mountain of blankets, which have been straightened and tucked in on the corners of the mattress. An audience of stuffed animals surrounds him in undulating waves, holding its breath in anticipation. Someone has taken great care to place his favorite animals in a precise formation into his arms, so they all face him. There is a chubby frog with large eyes, a brown teddy, whose fur looks matted by hugs and sticky hands. There's even a Hulk figurine, with bulging green muscles and tattered remnants of a shirt, leading the troupe in their devoted vigil.

"Miguel, mi amor[43]," whispers Gabriela as she caresses her son's hand. He does not move or react in any way. His mom gestures for me to come closer. Without disturbing any of the stuffed animals, I sit next to him on the other side of the bed and place my hand on his. It feels small and very warm under my touch.

"Hi Miguel, I'm Alexandra." I caress his hand with my thumb. No reaction. "You go ahead and rest. I will be doing some artwork with your parents and your sister. I heard you love the color green. We'll make sure to use that. I warn you, it might tickle your hands when we paint them," I say with a wink meant for his mom.

He bears little resemblance to the handsome boy from the photo. The long battle with cancer, strong medications, and the final stage of his journey have left him visibly altered. His eyes are half-open, and his breath labors with a soft rattle on every inhale. All sounds around me fade away as my world shrinks down to just the two of us. This simple touch contains everything that would normally pass in a conversation between two people over the course of a few minutes: the introduction, the getting-to-know-one-another, the small talk. Today, speech, body language, and eye contact are replaced by the simple flow of energy through touch. This isn't a Reiki thing - it's something born from empathy (and maybe a dash of Reiki, too). But I am not here for that today.

I turn to Gabriela. "I think it would be nice if we could have your husband and Miguel's sister here. We can start the artwork together, just the four of you, and then - if you want - we can include everyone else outside as well."

She lights up at the suggestion.

---

43   *Mi amor - Spanish, "My love"*

"That is a great idea. We have hardly had any time alone with him. You know, just us. You saw our big family," she nods toward the wall separating the bedroom from the living room. "They all want to spend time with him ..." she trails off and, without further explanation, leaves the room to get her husband and daughter.

Alone with Miguel, I try to figure out where to put all my supplies. There is no room. The narrow space between the door and the bed along the wall is taken up by two plastic carts filled with medical supplies, various bottles, syringes, and a large medical device now sitting unused under a layer of towels in the corner. There are shoes of different sizes scattered across the floor and plastic containers with loose Lego bricks. I decide to set up everything on the floor and start making space.

A thumb-sized Lego tree rolls out as I move the shoes aside. I pick it up and twirl it between my fingers. It's little geometric branches tickle against my memories of hours spent with bent backs and interlaced legs, building small cities, and racing tiny cars on imaginary roads. I can hear my daughters' laughter as it peels off the walls of our living room, my legs tingling with sleep as I finally disentangle my limbs and unfold myself from the floor, tiny Lego-brick imprints on my bare thighs.

Grateful for the memories that ground me in the strength to carry on, I put the little tree on the bedside table next to Miguel and know what we will paint. From what I have seen here today, Miguel is surrounded by all his family. They are the branches that lift from him. He is the center, the trunk that holds them together - *un árbol de familia*[44].

Gabriela walks back into the room, accompanied by her husband, Javier, and Miguel's older sister, Bianca. Javier is a tall, strong-looking man who walks as if gravity has a stronger pull on him than on the rest of us. His thick eyebrows lean against each other in a con-

---

44 *Un árbol de familia - Spanish. "A family tree."*

stant sorrowful embrace. Bianca, who looks like she is about 14 years old, nods a brief hello in my direction before turning her attention to her little brother. She is wearing an oversized sweatshirt and red-and-black plaid Pajama pants. I never understood this trend of middle school kids wearing PJ pants to school - my daughter does it too - but now I am almost envious of the comfort they offer, like a safety blanket wrapped around her legs. As if to point out the fact that I am not the one in need of comfort, my own jeans pinch the backs of my knees as I bend down to finish setting up the paints. Bianca scoots onto the bed without disturbing the sheets and breathes a kiss onto Miguel's cheek.

After the crowded living room, this intimate setting of a small family surrounding their son feels sacred. "He is sleeping!" Gabriela tells her husband as if to convince herself. Javier stands like a statue at the end of the bed, his hand resting on the bump in the blanket, caressing Miguel's feet. He sways from side to side. I worry that this might be too much for him until I hear him hum under his breath. A faint melody emanates from under his resigned mustache.

I don't recognize the song, but it has the undulating pull of a lullaby. I continue to set up the supplies, pulling out bottles of paint and brushes. Bianca looks up at her father for a long moment, then her voice tiptoes along his hum, gaining confidence and rising in volume and emotion. I don't understand the words sung in Spanish. Gabriela joins until her voice cracks and she looks out the window, blinking away her emotions. They are serenading him. I let the comforting melody wash over me as it bathes the room in the peaceful warmth of evening ritual, soothing the sting of fear and anxiety. My heart fills with awe, and I feel humbled to witness such an intimate and sacred moment.

I start mixing a bright apple shade of green on a small paper plate and add a few dollops of blue, yellow, orange, and pink near the rim. With a large poster board in one hand and the improvised mixing palette in the other, I climb onto the bed near Miguel's right shoulder.

"Gabriela, there is a blue cloth over there. Could you spread it over Miguel and the blankets? I want to make sure we don't make a mess." Gabriela pulls the cloth out of my bag, spreads it out, and climbs on the bed as well.

I try to melt into the rows of stuffed animals against the headboard. I am here to facilitate this process, bring the supplies, give gentle instructions, and help create art, while the same time remaining as unobtrusive as possible. I wish I could be spirit - a steady, invisible source of strength and direction, a warm, guiding presence. Images of brushes and mixing palettes floating through the air on invisible hands pop uninvited into my head, and I smile at the notion. I wish I could share this thought with Miguel - I'm sure, at a different time and place, he would have laughed too. I give his shoulder a gentle squeeze, as if acknowledging a little joke only the two of us share.

This is the first time that a patient of mine has not been conscious while we paint their hands. The simple act of pressing hands onto paper when their arms are heavy and uncooperative can become a challenge. But I consider it not only a privilege, but a gift. A gift from the family to me for allowing me into their home at this special moment, but also a gift to them; what we create today is something they'll cherish forever. It's not only about the finished piece, but about the process of creating.

Right now.
Right here.

There is something transcendental about it. It quietly triggers the brain, transporting them to a carefree moment of their childhood, where they had the ability just to be, to let the paint flow onto the paper in a pure expression of creativity. It speaks to their senses.

The smell of the paint as it squeezes out of the tube, all shiny and full of promise. The feeling of the brush bristles under their finger as they fan them out, that dry, prickly feeling of anticipation, laden with the weight of endless possibilities. The languid clouds of paint blooming in the water jar when a brush is dipped between colors. And then there's that moment when the first paint meets paper - hesitation flickers, before it flows into an abundant, carefree stream of color and expression. It's that little instant, when all other worries fall away, even for the blink of an eye. Bringing art to a family at this pivotal moment lets me lift their veil of sadness for a short while and create a new happy memory - just when they thought they'd run out of happy moments altogether. And they'll be left with a tangible memory of their son - something that lasts beyond today.

The singing stops, and the family turns to me, waiting for instructions. "Miguel, we're going to get started. It might feel a bit cold and ticklish on your hand," I say to Miguel, a smile coloring my voice, before I turn to his sister. "Okay, Bianca. Why don't you start by painting Miguel's left hand with this green here?" I point to the plate. "I will help you press it onto the paper. Right here in the center. Javier and Gabriela, you can paint your son's other hand."

They hesitate for a moment, so I explain further. "Miguel's hands will be the center of your family tree. Your own hands will surround his, and the rest of the family will create the other branches, reaching all the way up and filling the page. We'll paint the trunk later." The three faces look at me. Gabriela's hair is hanging loose down her back, a small hair clip glistens just above her ear, keeping the stubborn strands from falling into her face. Her skin creases around the eyes in wrinkles that haven't had time to settle yet. Bianca's face is smaller, still carrying the soft edges of youth. But her eyes look older than her years, as they speak of a burden no teenager should have to bear. Her nose is more like her father's, broad at the base. Her lips are full and a little chapped from a nervous habit of biting them. Javier's hands are still resting on his son's feet. They look strong, toughened by years of hard labor. His face carries a few days' worth of black stubble under his mustache; a muscle in his jaw twitches every so often, giving him a chiseled look as shadows pool along his sunken cheeks.

Gabriela smiles. "Oh, Miguel, this is going to be beautiful!'

I pass the plate to his sister, who takes Miguel's hand in hers with the tenderness of a mother holding her newborn. It is a quietly special moment to watch this connection between brother and sister, intimate, gentle, and full of love.

"Okay, let me help you here." With some difficulty, we manage to put Miguel's listless hand on the large poster board, leaving a perfect print. I take his hand in mine, as if it could break at the gentlest touch, and wipe it clean with a wet wipe as his parents start painting the other hand. I marvel at the power of art as I notice the burden of weariness lift from Javier's shoulders as he paints his son's fingers, while Gabriela reminisces about his childhood.

"Miguel, look how beautiful this looks." She coos. "Remember when you did finger painting in kindergarten? I think we still have those somewhere. You used to make such a mess all the time." Gabriela smiles through teary eyes. Javier joins in with what I think are a few memories as well, though I cannot be sure, since he speaks only Spanish to his son. But from the tone of voice, I hear memories flowing out of him, lifting him ever so slightly in their sweet melancholy. Meanwhile, I keep a close watch on Miguel's breathing, which has grown shallower, with long silences in between breaths.

No, no, no! Not now!

I rest my hand again on his shoulder and let my pinky casually wander up to his neck as if by accident, sensing the subtle pulsing of his heartbeat without drawing his parents' attention. As his heart slows, mine picks up speed, and I hold on to his shoulder to hide a tremor in my hands.

"Please, Miguel! Not yet!" I beg him without words, putting every ounce of persuasion in my silent touch.

Javier lifts his son's hand onto the paper, and Gabriela presses it gently to make sure it touches the paper evenly. We did it! Two perfect handprints ...- preserved. Normally, we would now do the same for Javier, Gabriela, and Bianca, but intuition tells me to go a different route. I move the brushes, paint, and paper off to the side.

"How about we hang out with him for a little bit? Come, sit. Hold his hand. Keep talking to him. I think he really likes it."

The energy has shifted once again, and a heavy cloak of finality settles over us.

Bianca sits back down on the bed next to Miguel, holds his hand, and leans over to whisper in his ear. Gabriela and Javier are on his other side, Javier's hand on his wife's shoulder as she caresses her son's arm with one hand, while holding his hand with her other; all connected through love and touch. I place my hand on Miguel just where the hem of his T-shirt meets his arm. Before leaving the room to finish the artwork with the rest of the family, I want to take a moment to connect with him. The hospice nurse had told me how unsettled he had been just a few days earlier - beyond the obvious pain from cancer, it must be scary for a child to see his parents, friends, and family so obviously distraught. I know that Reiki can help ease his fears.

Javier sits in silence, while his wife and Bianca speak sweet words of love and affection to their boy. I try to make myself as invisible as possible, so as not to disturb the family, and I breathe in deeply, close my eyes, and quiet my mind. With a tingle, I sense Reiki flowing, and with this simple touch, I feel a connection that words alone cannot convey.

It is like stepping over the threshold into a dark room of comforting energy. While I am sitting next to Miguel, my mind is in a space filled with emotions, as if the air I breathe, the atmosphere I move in, has been replaced by a solid energy I can feel in every fiber of my body. I am expanding outward, searching for that fear, that pain, that sense of impending loss I would expect to find. Yet all I feel is comfort, contentment, and love. What is normally conveyed with words, and what takes seconds to move from thought to speech to ear to brain, is felt in an instant. The moment a thought, or a message, forms in my brain, it is already conveyed and heard.

"Miguel. We are all here with you. Your parents, Bianca ... You are surrounded by love and moving toward love and light. All is well."

I don't know if it is through Reiki or just pure intuition, but I feel a shift in his energy. The dark space my mind is visiting hums with a soft vibration, and waves of warmth and light pulse through me. He is content. There is no fear. And all I sense from him is love. A love so pure and warm that it eclipses my earlier worries.

The darkness recedes, and I blink myself back into Miguel's bedroom. We sit for a few moments, his mother whispering to him, his sister crying as she holds his hand against her cheek. I feel a tiny prickle under my hand, as goosebumps rise on Miguel's arms in response to the Reiki. Silence settles over the room. He slips away. We are bathed in stillness, carried by the love he exhales with his last breath. Then nothing. There is not a sound to be heard as the reality sinks in.

He is gone.
Just like that.
Time stops in our room-sized world.
Nobody moves.

The rain plays its sorrowful tune on the roof of the house and drags its long fingers in resigned streaks down the windowpanes. The soft fibers of the blanket covering Miguel reach up to cradle his family, to catch them before they realize his absence. The only movement comes from the rhythmic waves of a tiny golden Chinese cat on a shelf near the window. It perches half-hidden behind a tissue box and paperbacks with broken spines and bent corners. Its smile under a thin layer of dust is frozen in disbelief as it waves in the stillness that spreads like mold from our corner of the room. As Miguel's soul drops below the horizon of our reality, a subtle change of temperature announces his departure, bathing us in the first timid tendrils of loss.

Gabriela raises her head to me in slow motion. Her eyes linger on her son's face as long as possible before she pulls them away from the features she loves so much. Our eyes meet. I feel the scars of my own heart vibrate in recognition of the grief that is about to descend on her. Breaking the silence feels like sacrilege, so I only shake my head in a movement so subtle I wonder if it was even visible. A shuddering breath deflates Gabriela, and she keels forward until her forehead connects with her son's chest. Her brown hair, shot through with worried streaks of gray, fans over him like the wings of a willow tree.

Outside the window, in the pouring rain, the family's chocolate Labrador stands and looks at us. I had not noticed the dog before. He shares this moment with us, aware of what has happened. He drops his ears and his head and trots away, glancing back at the window one last time before disappearing out of sight.

I disentangle myself from the bed, place my hand for a second on Gabriela's shoulder, lift the poster board and my bag, and slip out of the room, closing the door behind me. I go to the living room, trying to avoid eye contact with the rest of the family members.

I cannot tell them.

Leaving Miguel's room, leaving the comforting warmth of the energy he shared with me during those last moments, feels like jumping into the churning waters of an ice-cold ocean. I am adrift. Lost. I am filled with a grief that is not my own, as I feel it clawing at my insides. The thought of having to be the one to break the news to the family is making me physically sick. Yet that burden is taken from me, as a low, almost primal wail from Miguel's bedroom announces his passing to everyone present. I watch the raw emotion on their faces as they rush down the hallway, taking that uncontrolled creature of grief inside me with them.

I stay behind. The couch still holds the imprints of the people huddled here just a moment ago, and their body heat lingers on the worn brown leather. The only things left behind are a tissue peeking out, crunched up between the cushions, a lifeless jacket clinging to the armrest, and a half-eaten cookie on a paper plate. They look the way I feel as the desolation of the now-empty living room spreads through my body.

I gaze through the window at the crying clouds. I had never faced a patient dying right under my touch. *This never happens.* I look down at the poster board I am holding, with two small green handprints on it. What do I do now? How can I fill this paper with art? How can I ask someone to paint their hands and press their palms next to his, when they have just lost a son, a brother, a nephew, or a cousin? The whole point of Legacy Art is to create an artwork of handprints TOGETHER with the patient. To create one last memory TOGETHER.

And now ….?
Now I stand alone in the empty room.
And I have no idea what to do next.

I lean my forehead against the cool glass of the terrace door and see the dog sitting just a few feet away. He is not under the cover of the roofed terrace but a foot or two outside of it in the pouring rain. Water rivulets stream down his back through his wet fur - his body language a perfect expression of my feelings.

Music pulls me out of my thoughts as it drifts out of Miguel's room. First one voice alone, stringing one note after another as if testing their vocal cords for the first time. Another voice joins, deep and soothing. Its warm intonation invites others, and soon every member of the family is lifting their souls in song. The melody swirls and spirals all around me. It dances with the shadows, sways like a breeze through the sheer curtains, sending shivers down my spine as it rises through the window and into the low-hanging clouds. Everyone is united, woven together in what sounds like a Spanish church hymn, full of emotion and sorrow. I have never seen grief become song, but it lifts my spirits and the corners of my mouth into a smile, defying the gravity of my sadness.

As the song fades, a small tug at my jeans draws my eye, and a two-year-old beams up at me, blissfully ignorant of what's happening next door. He wears a white long-sleeved T-shirt with juice-colored stains dribbled down the front, tucked into a pair of baby-sized jeans. His jet-black hair is shaved at the sides, and the long hair on top gelled back, making him look like a pint-sized teenager. His chubby hand reaches up to the poster board, and he points at the handprint. Thankful for the distraction, I bend and fish some markers and papers from my bag, and sit on the floor. We're at eye level as he peers at me with curiosity. He plops onto his bottom with a soft squish of his heavy diaper. We spend a few quiet minutes drawing and scribbling together on the paper between us. One by one, the older children of the family leave Miguel's room to join us. Some are crying; others are swaddled in silence as they sit down, forming a loose circle around the paper. Without talking, they reach out for the markers. I take out more papers and hand them to the older ones.

"Draw something that reminds you of Miguel, a happy memory maybe, or write a letter - anything you want to share with him."

We're all glad to have something to focus on, and again, I see how art shifts the energy as hesitant smiles spread across the little faces.

One by one, the adults come back into the living room, huddled in small groups, crying, lamenting, shoulders heaving, arms locked around one another, as if to borrow strength. I feel guilty as tears blur my vision. The grief I feel fluttering against my skin like tiny razorblades is not my own. It is theirs. It makes me feel like an intruder in this house that is covered in a fresh coat of sorrow. My heart breaks wide open for this family. And here I am, standing in the corner between the makeshift art table and the open kitchen counter, trying to be invisible. I blot my cheeks with my sleeve, rushing the movement. My tears are just a mirror of their pain. Theirs are born from years of love and affection, shared laughter, spilled popcorn, and tight hugs. Their tears have merit. They have been earned and paid for with love. Mine feel shallow and false in comparison. Who am I to cry right now? I have just met this family, yet my tears burn hot down my face, leaving flaming streaks of their pain on my skin.

I bend over the papers, dissolving into the group of children, my insecurities bleeding with every scribble. *"Trust, Alex!"* I think to myself in Kathrin's voice over and over. She is with me. Maybe not in person, maybe not even in spirit, but her words resonate within me.

Trust.

As I relax into "Trust," a thought knocks - timid at first, then insistent. I straighten and make my way back to the bedroom, where Miguel lies, surrounded by his family, who lean in to caress him, hold him, and say their farewells. The paint supplies are off to the side, where I left them, and I tiptoe in, gather everything up, and carry it back to the livingroom table.

"More paint!" a little girl exclaims as she sees me approaching. With a proud smile, she holds up her drawing for me. Flowers and hearts dance around the bottom of the page with a big "I love you,

Miguel" floating towards the blue line of the sky above. "That is beautiful! He'd love that!" I put my hand on her shoulder, bend down until our eyes are level. Her dark hair bounces in tight curls around her face, one big strand pinned back with a purple beaded hair clip. In an exaggerated gesture, I glance around, place a finger on my lips, and whisper, "I need your help!"

Her eyes light up, and she listens intently as I explain my plan. "I can do that," she replies with a small air of self-importance, then runs off - squeezing through the legs of the grown-ups in the room and out of sight. While she's gone, I gesture to the other children to help me clear the table and set up the paints around the edge, with a few paper plates as palettes. The poster board with Miguel's handprints is the last thing I place on the table, as carefully as laying an infant in its crib. Just as I finish, the little girl is back with Miguel's grandparents in tow. They approach with hesitation, their faces drawn.

This is it - the crucial moment.

If they participate, the rest will flow ... or so I hope.

Their English is hesitant, but we manage well between my broken Spanish and my little messenger's excited translations. My heart swells with gratitude and joy at how this little girl takes charge. She won't let them back out and pulls her *abuelo* closer, a paintbrush with a vibrant red held high. Her little tongue sticks out of the side of her mouth in concentration as she paints her grandparents' hands with great care and determination. I guide them to the right spots on the paper surrounding the two lonely green prints already waiting there. For a few seconds, I rest my hand over theirs, letting the soothing energy of Reiki flow with this simple touch, before handing them a wet wipe and a grateful smile.

Before I realize it, the children take turns pulling the adults to our table. One by one, hand by hand, our art piece takes form. More and more family members gather around the table, choosing colors, mixing them, and having their hands or fingers painted by the little ones. Smiles mingle with tears; people pull me into hugs, leaning in to see the tree grow before their eyes. I stand back, watching in awe as the Legacy Art takes on a life of its own, propelled by the love and determination of the children - Miguel's cousins, and friends. There is an empty circle around Miguel's hands, a place of honor reserved for his parents and sister. They are the last ones to emerge from his room, and a hushed silence falls around the table as all eyes turn to them. I hang in a breath of apprehension, searching their faces for a sign, an emotion, anything to tell me I haven't overstepped an invisible boundary.

In silence, people give way, opening a path through the living room to the table and the tree, its center a circle of white space around two small green handprints. As they step close, Javier wraps his arms around Bianca and Gabriela in a gesture that speaks in equal measures of comfort and of drowning. The tide of family closes in behind them, hands reaching out in support and yearning for connection.

A smile climbs from Gabriela's lips to the outer corners of her red, swollen eyes as she looks up at me. "I want my hand to be green. Blue-green," and she says, extending her open palm to me.

CHAPTER 25
MANHATTAN BEACH 2019

It's been an unremarkable day; busy and hectic, but unremarkable nonetheless. I am always surprised by how I can run around all day without accomplishing anything of substance - just the usual school runs, after-school activities, chores, and cooking. But now, with the kids in bed, and the house finally quiet, I have the choice: vegging out in front of the TV or using the quiet time for a meditation. The latter seems not productive, but at least beneficial.

The last three months since my visit with Miguel and his family have been uneventful yet strung with a subtle new frequency that sharpened the edges of daily life. Wherever I went, or whatever I did, the air around me was still, yet dense with energy, as if a lightning strike was imminent - the silence before the proverbial storm.

Miguel's death was a miracle to me. He had chosen his time, just like Jordin had told me all these months ago. Instead of dying alone or amid the bustle of family members, he had chosen that very moment when it was just the four of them. I do not know what role Reiki played, but I know it did something - not only to him - but to all of us. It was a beautiful death, if there is such a thing.

I pull my purple yoga mat into the middle of our bedroom, close the curtains, and dim my bedside lamp to a soft glow. With a flick of my feet, I catapult my flip flops toward the shadowy corner of the room, fold my legs underneath me, and settle into a comfortable seated position. I have always loved sitting cross-legged on the floor. For years, during my college days, the floor was where I did all my schoolwork, where I bent over books and papers, where inspiration or frustration hit me one after another. I don't know if it was the years of cross-legged sitting or the abuse my knees take during CrossFit, or maybe the plain fact that I'm not getting any younger, but my knees now sound like a bowl of snap, crackle, and pop. To make sure my knees won't distract me from my meditation, I reach for the bed, pull my cushion out from underneath the comforter, fold it in half, and slide it under me. Propped up like this makes me feel like I mean business. I am serious about my meditation. Like a yoga studio that is equipped with bolsters, my makeshift solution gives me an air of authority.

I know what I am doing.

I am a professional meditator.

I do this all the time.

None of that is true. In the grand scheme of things, I consider myself a meditation novice. I can do it. I enjoy it. But I lack the discipline of daily practice. I incorporate short meditations before all Reiki sessions, and I do see the benefits: relaxation, inner peace, and an opening of perception. Sometimes I almost understand something that was previously hidden from sight - almost. As if I crack open a door to a deeper understanding, but before I can grasp it, the very thought of the door slams it shut. I have to approach every meditation without an agenda to find my way back to that door. The mere thought of the door makes it impossible to find. So, I try not to

think, not to have any expectations, as I turn on my favorite soothing background music, pop in my headphones, and close my eyes.

Usually, my meditations are quite deep and very relaxing, but
rather uneventful, apart from occasional lights, colors, or short
images that pop up in my mind without leaving a trace once I
come back to reality. I am rarely left with a thought, an image, or a
message of enough significance that I can recall it afterwards. But
tonight would shape up to be quite different.

One deep exhale, and I let my shoulders drop. A long inhale, and
I feel myself grow lighter, letting go of worries and distractions with
the next exhale. The deep, sonorous hum of the music carries me
deeper, one breath at a time. First, I let go of external distractions. I
do not hear the neighbor's dog barking anymore, don't feel the floor
underneath me, or the slight ache in my shoulders. Inhale. I do not
notice my hands resting on my knees anymore, or that one loose hair
that moves gently in front of my face with every breath. Exhale. I am
lucky today because nothing pulls me out of my meditative state - no
dogs wanting to be let out, no kids waking up from a bad dream, no
husband unwittingly banging closet doors next to me. All is quiet.
My facial muscles relax. Behind my closed eyes, I am enveloped in
a velvety blackness, suspended in the quiet expanse of my subconscious, as I let go of thoughts one by one. Inhale. I feel suspended in
gentle darkness, my mind floating in rhythm with my breath, like an
astronaut in deep space. All is still. The darkness gradually fills with
a golden glow until it reaches an almost blinding intensity and with
it a deep, thundering vibration. And then I hear it:

"Remember Gabriel." It booms in my head.

The "voice" ebbs and swells in intensity, like a deep hum. I call
it a "voice" for lack of a better word, since it feels like a frequency
shaping itself into meaning. There are no actual words - only vibration that my mind receives as a voice. My whole body hums with the

name: Gabriel. I become aware of the yoga mat underneath me, the soft fabric of the cushion against my back, the warmth of my hands against my knees. Yet, I feel disconnected from my surroundings. All my attention, all my being, is wrapped up in the booming vibration inside myself.

"Remember Gabriel."

I feel the hairs on my arms rising, moving, like a carpet of beach grass dancing with a cool sea breeze. Yet this is not my body's reaction to an outside stimulus. There is no breeze in the bedroom. All doors and windows are closed and the air is at a perfect temperature. Not too hot, not cold.

"Remember Gabriel."

The light and vibration fade back into the recesses of my mind. Usually, thoughts or memories that surface during my meditation disappear by the time I come out of it, like the delicate tendrils of a dream that linger for a few moments before you truly wake up, just to dissipate completely the moment you open your eyes. Today is different: the words are imprinted with the force of an industrial printing press, slamming down over and over again. Gabriel, Gabriel, Gabriel. The noise pushes me out of the meditation like a cork out of a shaken champagne bottle, and, with a gasp, I open my eyes to the dimly lit bedroom. With one fluid motion, I grab my phone from the nightstand and, without even thinking about it, Google the name "Gabriel."

The very first listing is Archangel Gabriel.

I pause and stare at the screen.

Huh? Why would Archangel Gabriel show up in my meditation? I don't believe in angels. To me, they are closely linked to Catholicism, which is a religion I married into, but don't identify with. Either that, or they remind me of spiritual enthusiasts who "speak to their angels" and read angel cards as a form of divination. Both feel equally unbelievable and unsubstantiated.

But the voice and light were real! And persistent. I am supposed to remember Gabriel! There was no doubt about that. The only question is why.

And who the fuck is Gabriel?

"Gabriel?" My shoulder critic wanders towards me. The light from the open bathroom door behind him casts his body in a black silhouette. If it weren't for his voice, just judging by the bizarre shape moving towards me, I would have guessed Marge Simpson walked into my room, tall hair, dress, and all. As he crosses the threshold, the light from my bedside lamp lifts the three-dimensional shape of my critic out of the black Marge silhouette. He has a towel wrapped into a towering turban on his head, another one draped around his waist, skimming his ankle. Water droplets glisten on his chest; he smells like my pineapple body scrub. His toenails shimmer in hot-pink nail polish, and he still has the toe separator stuck between them. "I know Gabriel. He is the kid in Giulia's class," he pipes up, looks at his left hand, and blows onto his fingernails that are painted black with only his middle finger in hot pink. "The one with the long blonde hair. You know who I am talking about." I had not even considered that. "He dressed like an angel last Halloween, didn't he?" I recall the white dress and the golden halo. "But, no! That is not it. The Gabriel I mean, was grander, all-encompassing. He filled up my whole being somehow." I say, more to myself than to my critic. "Wait. What?" my shoulder critic looks at me above his outstretched fingers and frowns. "What the hell are you talking about? What did I miss? All-encompassing? What the heck?"

"Never mind," I sigh as I peel myself off the floor. "It was just a thought that came up in my meditation." I try to downplay the voice I still hear ringing in my ear.

In the days to come, I realize I need to investigate this experience a bit more and see what there is to learn about Archangel Gabriel, whom I definitely do not believe in.

I Google "angels in religion." The first interesting fact I found is that angels, such as Gabriel, Michael, and Raphael, are not confined to Catholicism. Instead, they are present in almost every world religion. Judaism, Christianity, and Islam all include angels or angelic beings of some form.

But I am still unsure about it all. Why would I hear the name of an angel in my meditation? There was nothing leading up to it, no references to angels in any movies or books I was reading, nothing that might have subconsciously triggered a memory or thought about angels. It came out of nowhere.

Another search for "Archangel Gabriel" reveals that Gabriel is considered a "herald of visions" and therefore a direct messenger from God. Archangel Michael, on the other hand, is more of a protector, in charge of truth, courage, and strength. Now that sounded useful. Having an angelic protector would be pretty cool. But no, I got Gabriel - God's mailman.

"Seriously!?" I huff under my breath as I click out of the page. All these Bible references and religious scriptures are a bit much for me. My shoulder critic sits on the couch to my right, his own tiny laptop open on his knees. His hair looks like it just got a fresh cut, and even his face looks clean-shaven. There is a hint of aftershave in the air. I raise an eyebrow and look at his manicured, black-painted nails as they move across the keyboard. "Maybe," he pauses and looks at me over the top of his frameless reading glasses, "your search should focus on the most obvious explanation." He says with a tone of superiority and types "religious visions, psychiatry" in the search bar. "Jesus!" I huff. "Don't you think you are exaggerating just a bit now?" He turns his screen so that I can read the results: an article about "Religion and Schizophrenia." Dark. Let's hope my meditation didn't put me on a straight path to a psych ward. My critic adjusts his reading glasses and, with the best imitation of a professor's lecture voice, he reads:

"The relationship between religion and schizophrenia is of particular interest to psychiatrists because of the similarities between religious experiences and psychotic episodes; religious experiences often involve auditory and/or visual hallucinations, and those with schizophrenia commonly report similar hallucinations, along with a variety of beliefs that modern medical practitioners commonly recognize as delusional." - Wikipedia

He emphasizes the last word and stares at me over his glasses. Cold fingers clamp around my stomach. I breathe, press my palm to Kathrin's bracelet, and pick TRUST over the spiral.

How can I feel so normal, yet according to Wikipedia and Mr. Know-it-all, have obvious symptoms of insanity? But would it be likely to have a "religious vision," triggered by a schizophrenic episode, if I don't subscribe to that particular religious belief? And if this vision brings on skepticism instead of complete exaltation and spontaneous hymn singing, how crazy can I really be?

I walk over to the balcony and stare outside without really seeing anything, not noticing the weather or the cars driving by. The sheer curtain undulates in a breeze, and the sunlight caresses my cheek with a warm hand, as my mind wanders. The booming voice of my meditation has plucked a string on my soul, which is still vibrating; I can feel it. It has left an imprint that I cannot push aside and ignore. An echo that keeps reminding me: this really happened! There must be a reason for it. Figure it out! Remember Gabriel!

A stray feather from one of the pillows on the couch has found its way into the weave of the curtain. I pluck it out and look at the delicate structure. How perfect. How intricate and meticulous. The architecture of a feather is nothing short of miraculous. The way the barbs connect, without overlapping, one perfectly aligned with the other. So flawless. How can something so light, so seemingly insignificant lift a bird into flight? Nobody could have designed it better. Is it divinity or evolution I am holding in my hand? Such a heavy question for such a light little thing. I place the feather on my palm and blow it out through the open glass door, following its ride on the wind until it disappears over the edge of the balcony.

Contemplating the existence of God is not a sign of insanity, is it? If anything, it's human. Believing that nature's perfection is a spark of divinity is one thing. That alone does not scream "mental illness." But pondering that question is very different from "hearing an angel."

If that's even what happened.

I could solve the psychiatry angle by calling my dad and having him weigh in. But that is a step I am not quite ready to take. I can already hear it -

"Hey Dad, I had an angel visit me in my meditation, yelling at me not to forget him." I see in his office ... actually, as Freud, with a beard and tiny round glasses he didn't have before this call. He laughs, then slips into his official doctor-voice I remember from my childhood: "Tell me more about that."

Nope. Not doing that.

So, I shelve it and do as Kathrin told me: TRUST.

I take a deep breath, exhale all the way, eyes trailing over the railing where the feather disappeared. "Okay," I whisper against the curtain, "I trust that I am not crazy." I roll my eyes at myself - talking to yourself is its own kind of crazy. "And what about talking to your shoulder critic? Think that's normal?" He's hopped up on the windowsill, back against the glass, arms folded, one foot propped behind him. He is dressed head-to-toe in black: tight, ripped jeans, a turtleneck, a slick wave of hair, black-and-pink nails, and Doc Martens with hot-pink laces and pink pom-poms on the sides. I raise an eyebrow.

"Oh well - maybe I just embrace the crazy."

We grin at each other.

"No, seriously. Angel or no angel?"

H squints, lips pursed. "No offense, but that Gabriel guy should've picked someone else. Why not a priest - someone who'd roll out a red carpet for a celestial apparition?" He paces the sill, windmilling his arms. "Again, no offense. But not to a mother of two in Los Angeles. Why? Makes zero sense."

Right then, Gia bursts through the front door. "Mammmaaaaa, can you drop me off at swim? I'm already late!" Drawers slam. "Where's my swim bag? Mammmaaaaa!" Chaos pulls me into its tide. Gabriel can wait. Surface life sounds perfect.

As the days go by, nothing changes. I am still not a believer, and my tolerance for angel research is low. I poke at it, then abandon it for school runs and groceries. My critic perches on my shoulder, watching every keyboard click, arch-browed at my attempts to crack the door of possibilities just a hair. He shakes his head with an accusing "Tse, tse, tse." Beyond that heavy wooden door of doubt lies ... what? A place where angels exist? A place where I believe? I don't even ask him. For once, he is quiet.

So far, Reiki is the only thing that's opened the door to something deeper - beyond what eyes can see. But Reiki isn't about religion. It has nothing to do with angels ... at least as far as I know. So why now? And why can't I shake it? Gabriel is still resonating deep inside my thoughts.

A few weeks later, AirPods in, I'm skimming through various podcasts with no plan and stumble on a show about angels. Wow. Talk about coincidence. Fine. I click - part curiosity, part boredom. Trust the breadcrumb, I tell myself, and press play. A honey-dew voice oozes through my headphones. "You can call on your angels any time." I cringe. "I talk to them every day; it's enriched my life beyond imagination." A flashback to the "religious visions and schizophrenia" pings my brain. I picture her: long, gray hair, glowing skin, purple embroidered floor-length skirt, incense haze, windowsill crystals, angel statues in every pose.

Out of the corner of my eye, I catch a movement above my head. My shoulder critic, dressed in a white, flowy robe, cradles a miniature golden harp in his arms and floats in a circle around my head. A glitter halo on a wire bobs in his unruly hair. He even sports a set of fluffy white wings and trills a "hosanna" in imitation honey-dew flavor. Annoyed, I swat him so that he thuds against the window and glowers at me, his halo crooked.

It is all too weird for me.

I come from a family of academics. Parents, grandfathers, aunts, and uncles - mostly physicians. Logic, knowledge, proof, and science are things that I grew up with. Believe only what can be proven. Science is the bedrock upon which my understanding of the world is built. Reiki already stretches it further than I'm comfortable with, yet here I am researching angels.

Funny how life can change.

But before I turn the podcast off, the angel lady says something that catches my attention: "It is normal to be skeptical. Just ask the angels for a sign. It can be anything, really - a feather, a certain animal, a song on the radio. Be as specific as possible and wait for it."

I click out of the podcast and grin at my own foolishness. "I am going to ask angels for a sign. Are you joking?!" It isn't Gabriel that drives me crazy, it's the hunt for answers. I decide to treat this like a trust experiment - curiosity without commitment. "Hmm, might not be the worst idea," my critic says, twirling the crooked halo like a miniature hula hoop. "Just saying. Might be a good way to put this stuff to rest. For good."

I swing my legs onto the desk, blocking my critic as he saunters along the edge. He pauses, jumps onto my legs, tiptoes along my jeans, and stops at my knee. "Ask for a sign and wait for it NOT to come," he says. It's a solid plan. In fact, as I think about it, it seems like the perfect plan! "Ok, so what sign can I ask for that would be absolutely impossible to just show up by accident?"

My chair creaks as I readjust my position and ponder the question. My shoulder critic pulls a street sign out of nowhere and waves it at me. I don't think he grasps the meaning of "signs." I ignore him. Asking for something mundane as feathers, songs, or coins would be too easy. You can find those anywhere if you're looking. I stand. My gaze travels through the window again, along the trees and rooftops of the neighboring houses, searching for ideas. It is another sunny day in Los Angeles. The Crayola blue sky is so crisp and fresh, I almost expect it to smell minty. Instead, the breeze carries with it hints of ocean and eucalyptus - not a cloud in sight. And then it hits me!

"A rainbow," I say. "Let them try to conjure that." I whirl around and grin at my critic, who is rubbing his hands together, a mischievous grin on his face. He does a tap-slide on my trackpad until the Manhattan Beach weather forecast fills the screen: no clouds all week. Perfect. With a challenge in my voice, I look up at the ceiling (where else do you address angels?) and say, feeling rather foolish: "Ok, angels! You are on! Show me a rainbow today. Then maybe - maybe - I'll consider believing."

My shoulder critic peers up at the ceiling, then back at me, and raises his tiny hand towards me in a high-five gesture. I tap his hand with my index finger and shake off the feeling of complete absurdity. Time to seal the deal with TRUST, move on, and leave this all in the rearview mirror, since nothing will come of it anyway.

A glance at my watch reminds me that I have to go. I volunteered at Giulia's elementary school to lead a rock-painting project. This will be fun. We will paint rocks in bright colors with inspirational messages and pictures. Once they are dry, I will varnish them, and the kids can hide the rocks in the community for others to find and enjoy.

I prepared everything last night, and the trunk of my car is filled with boxes of paint tubes, brushes, trays of rocks, and plastic table covers. By the last bell, more than fifty kids swarm the tables, eager to start painting. For an hour, we're a happy mess: paint on hands, paint on tablecloths, paint everywhere - perfect. When the crowd thins, I rinse the brushes, restock the trunk, and walk the quiet yard like a proud curator. "Have a wonderful day," "You are great," "Dream big," "Be kind." Hearts, ladybugs, butterflies, and emojis - even the poop emoji. And then: rainbows. So many rainbows.

Seventeen to be precise.

On a larger rock, a bright arc over a blue sky with BELIEVE underneath in wobbly kid letters. I laugh out loud. Well. There's my sign.

Damn it!

But still, there is no way I can accept this as legit! I mean, kids love rainbows, no? Odds were good I'd see at least a few of them among the rocks. But seventeen? Seems like quite a large number to be a coincidence. Maybe I should have been more specific and asked for a rainbow "in the sky." Still, I asked for a rainbow. I got seventeen! Seventeen rainbows!

Still grinning, I pull the tarp with the varnished rocks under the awning of the 5th-grade building, where they will dry until tomorrow, when the kids pick them up. I climb into my car and once again, speak to the air above me:

"Fine. You got me."

Not a believer yet - just a truster-in-progress.

The short drive home is a blur. Even my shoulder critic is quiet, stunned into temporary good behavior. This is all just too bizarre. I mean, seriously?! Angels? Signs? I wish I could pick up the phone and call Kathrin. We would have a good laugh, and then we'd change the subject. And under the laughter, I hear her again: Trust.

"Pfffhhhhh! Rainbows." I murmur under my breath as I pull the car into a spot in front of our house. I should feel tired after managing all the kids, the painting, and the cleaning, but I am still buzzing with energy. I unlock the door and sprint up the stairs, taking two steps at a time. After washing the last traces of paint off my hands, I drop into my desk chair again and pop my laptop open. The podcast window is still open, and the funky angel lady's icon is waiting like a dare. I drum my fingernails on the side of my laptop, lost in thought.

Rainbows or no rainbows, I still don't believe it. My critic has found his way back and is making himself comfortable on my shoulder once again, stretching his arms, cracking the knuckles of his tiny fingers. His discarded wings, halo, and harp lie in an untidy heap on the edge of my desk. The words of the angel lady drift back: "Just ask the angels for a sign."

Alright. Let's try this once more.

What to ask for - anything can just show up by coincidence - even rainbows. I pause, listening. The house is quiet; the kids are with friends, and Andrea is at a meeting. Good. I swivel around on my chair, face the living room, and speak to the empty air: "Ok, angels - one more time. I'm just not there yet. Rainbows are one thing, but I need more. Show me something undeniable, something that I can't explain away. Up to you. Convince me"

What exactly "more" is, is unclear to me at this point. I just need another nudge to believe in something as far-fetched as angels. I mean, who believes in angels anyway? According to the internet, plenty of people do. But I'm not one of them. Or am I? Nah! I just can't. I think back to a childhood drawing in a box in my dad's cellar: a Christmas scene with Jesus, Mary, and Joseph, donkeys, sheep - plus a giraffe for good measure. In the right corner was my interpretation of an angel: triangle dress, circle head, and two polka-dot butterfly wings. I remember feeling very proud of this particular work of art, and the existence of an angel floating up in the corner did not strike me as strange at all. Back then, angel belonged. So, when did I actually stop believing? Did I chuck angels in the same category as Santa Claus, the Easter Bunny, and fairy tales?

I push the whole angel business to the back of my mind and carry on with my day, my shoulder critic happily nestled into the crook of my neck.

Two days later, it's Saturday, and the weekend is off to a glorious start: a late pancake breakfast and PJs until just before noon. Lazy mornings feel like such a luxury, hours slipping through our fingers like silk. Humming along to Ed Sheeran's *"Perfect,"* I dance between the kitchen counter and the dishwasher, sneaking the last cold pancake from the plate. Later, I'm taking Gia to the beach to meet her friend Zack. I pack towels, sunscreen, a box of brownies, Gia's boogie board, and some snacks, and with it my promise not to "bother them". Apparently, parental supervision is starting to be embarrassing. I sigh, all too aware of how fleeting childhood is. Soon enough, she will be a full-fledged teenager with mood swings, arguments, and fights for independence. She will tiptoe heavy-footed on the balance of boundaries and freedom. And I'll have to trust that the roots we gave her will be enough to steady her as she spreads her wings. A constant tug-of-war between staying and going, holding on and letting go.

I throw the beach bag into my car and slam the door on my worry. She's still only eleven. Let me enjoy that.

We arrive at the beach 10 minutes later and pick a spot near the pier. The beach is quiet today, with only a handful of people nearby and a small bob of surfers out beyond the break. The afternoon is sunny but cool, and an army of goosebumps marches over my arms. Gia steps in front of me, gathers her long curls together, and with a shrug asks me to zip up her wetsuit. I lean down and kiss the back of her neck before pulling the zipper up and securing it under the little flap of neoprene. Out of the corner of my eye, I see Zack slinking towards us, backpack casually thrown over his shoulder, his boogie board surfing the sand behind him. His brown hair is windswept, and he meets us with an open smile. A beat of awkwardness, as the kids greet each other, then they're sprinting for the water, boogie boards, and sand flying in their wake. I manage a quick, "Stay where I can see you!" before they are out of earshot.

I lean back on my towel and look out at the glittering water, Gia and Zack small shapes in the foam. To our right, the proud Manhattan Beach Pier struts out into the ocean, a string of people leaning onto the railing like barnacles, watching the surfers below. At the end, looking longingly towards the horizon, sits the famous roundhouse with its orange roof and cheerful green windows. Inside, the Roundhouse Aquarium Teaching Center, with over a hundred species of marine life, typically found in the waters all around the California coast. I always found this concept heartbreaking: creatures meant to swim, float, crab, and crawl their lives happily below the surface of the ocean are now stuck in aquariums, destined to be eternally suspended above their natural habitat, without ever being able to reach it. I guess the benefit of the teaching moments is supposed to outweigh the sadness of it all.

I dig my toes into the warm sand and flick a small shell with my big toe - a twisted snail shell, white with a pink blush. I pick it up and peer into its tiny opening.

Anyone home?

Obviously not; it was buried in dry sand. Still, it was a habit I retained from my childhood vacations at the German North Sea, where I had spent hours tossing stranded shells with "tenants" back into the churning water. What happened to the little creature that had called this shell its home? Had it died or just moved on? I roll the little thing absentmindedly between my fingers and land on the obvious: hermit crabs switch homes; snails don't. I've done the crab thing for years - every time I moved, I made my home in a "new shell," while grief built its own armor around me; one I carried with me wherever I went. I stay in my shell, where it is safe, where I don't have to worry about feelings or attachments or loss. Maybe that's the reason I've not yet made any significant friendships here. Maybe it is Manhattan Beach, or maybe it is me, burying myself in my hospice work and parenting duties without allowing relationships to grow. No attachments, no pain. I flick the little shell as far as I can. I think it is time to embrace my new life in LA. Time to trust a little and come out of my shell, even if I feel like a paler, less saturated version of the old me. Maybe Grief washes off over time, revealing the brighter me underneath?

A towel drops into the sand next to me. "Hey there." I peer up, momentarily blinded by the sun, and squint my eyes at the shadowy figure. He seems vaguely familiar. "Mike - Zack's dad," he helps me out, as my confusion must have been visible on my face. Of course! Silly me! I had not expected Zack to come to the beach by himself, had I? I had met Mike once or twice at school with his wife, Katelyn. She was one of the few moms in school with whom I had clicked immediately. She seemed very down-to-earth with an open smile and a welcoming demeanor. So, it comes as no surprise that her husband is just as lovely. He drops himself onto the towel next to me. He is wearing board shorts, an old T-shirt, and is barefoot as far as I can see, without any flip-flops or shoes in sight. His salt-and-pepper hair is shorter than his son's, sticking out carefree in all sorts of directions, and an easy grin creases his tanned face.

Growing up, I was a tomboy, a late bloomer, who thought it easier to be friends with boys than develop any romantic notions that would not work out anyway. My mom always joked that I'd rather punch a boy than kiss him. True. Boys were uncomplicated, straightforward, and without the nuances and bitter undercurrents often seen between girls. Due to the relatively remote location of my childhood home and the lack of parental involvement in organizing playdates, typical of the 80s, my social circle was defined by who lived nearby. And in my age bracket, there were mostly boys around. I was comfortable around them, and that comfort continues to this day. Since moving to Los Angeles, I had missed the company of my guy friends back in Dubai, where some of my closest friends happened to be men, and I cherished our platonic banter and easy connection.

I had not found any potential male friends in LA yet. Maybe it was due to the fact that we were still pretty new in town, or possibly because Manhattan Beach is just a peculiar little place, where men and women seem to be more segregated. Even at dinner parties, they flock into separate groups, rarely intermingling. If I happen to talk to a man at some point, the conversation rarely captures my interest and hovers, limp and lifeless on the surface.

I started to question myself. Maybe it was me! I was the issue. Maybe my grief had marked me somehow, like the black version of a scarlet letter. Working in pediatric hospice is not making the matter any easier. I have learned to dodge the questions about my work because nothing can turn the vibes at a dinner party faster than the thought of dying children. But I have become quite adept at finding ways around the conversational tarpits of death.

So, it comes as a surprise that talking to Mike is effortless! Our conversation flows without a hitch and quickly moves from the superficial to the more substantial subjects of where we grew up, how we met our significant others, and what we thought about life in this quaint little beach town. He is a true breath of fresh air.

A bit later, we are joined by another dad, whose name I do not catch, who brings along his son Lucas, one of Zack's close friends. It is obvious that Mike and Lucas' dad know each other well, yet I do not feel stranded on the outskirts of their conversation. I am one of the boys, and it feels good to be completely myself. The conversation is varied and engaging. Unlike most conversations between Manhattan Beach moms, we do not talk for hours on end about our kids, their teachers, their need for growth hormones due to their small stature (I am not joking, this is a subject often discussed by mothers in this little town of ours). Neither do we talk about money, hunting, or current sports events, subjects usually favored by the testosterone-heavy side of any gathering. Instead, we speak about our childhoods, growing up in different countries, and how we ended up here. I feel lighter than I have in weeks, and time flies by, marked only by the shadows growing longer across the sand. The kids have a great time with their boogie boards, and we can hear their laughter peal from the water's edge. For the first time since moving here, I feel hopeful that maybe, MAYBE, I will find my people here.

After a few hours, we coax our sun-tired, happy children out of the water. I pack my bag, and we head home, waving goodbye to the boys as we leave. At the first red light, I push my sunglasses up and send Mike a quick text.

> "Hey Mike, Thanks for joining us today - so fun. Also, what was Luca's dad's name again?"

I felt awkward asking while we were still at the beach, especially since he had introduced himself and I had promptly forgotten. Happens to me all the time - I am terrible with names. But I want to make sure that I can introduce him to Andrea next time without fumbling.

> "We had a good time too." Came the reply. "And his name is Gabe."

Gabe? Wait a minute! The thought takes a minute to form in my head. The traffic light turns green, and it is only the honking of an impatient driver behind me and Gia's annoyed two-syllable, "Mom," that knocks me out of my thoughts. Then it lands:

Gabe as in "Gabriel."

I burst out laughing, earning an astonished glance from my pre-teen in the seat next to me.

I had just spent the afternoon at the beach with Michael and Gabriel! MICHAEL AND GABRIEL! Not statues in church - two dads with sandy feet and good stories. The humor is not lost on me, and I continue to giggle on our drive home. I had asked for a sign I couldn't explain away, and the universe sent a joke I couldn't miss. Maybe angels belong - if only in the column labeled "possible."

I grin at the thought of what Gabe and Mike would think of the role they just played in my angel saga.

CHAPTER 26
MANHATTAN BEACH 2019

Words have power - they really do. Through their meanings, intonations, and hidden depth, they can hurt or heal, joke or forgive, distance or pray. And those are only the obvious ones. I twirl my pencil in my hand and stare at my computer screen. The notepad next to my laptop is covered in scribbles, circles, and spirals, framing three words. I have stared at these words for the last hour and a half. I flick the metal grooves of the eraser-end of the pencil against the paper, bouncing it up and down, and turn my gaze back at the screen. The cursor blinks in the Google search bar.

I cannot remember life before Google. Adjusting to life in a new country is a million times easier when everything is just a single search away - after-school activities, restaurants, shops, even German chocolates. But today, Google disappoints. I typed the three words in every possible spelling, every possible pronunciation I could come up with.

Nothing.

I drop the pencil, rest my chin on my hand, and stare at the note-pad until the lines blur. Maybe I wrote them down wrong. Maybe it was not an 'n' in the second word, but an 'm.' I try that.

Again, nothing.

My pencil recommences its rhythmic pounding. Jackhammer down, eraser-bounce up, little dust-rolls everywhere, as if this could dislodge a memory. Three words. Not words. Sounds. They hit me last night out of nowhere. I'd gone to bed at my usual time, snuggled up next to Andrea while we watched another episode of *Suburra*[45], the tips of his fingers caressing my back in familiar tracks and patterns. When I was finally ready to drift off to sleep, I did a short self-Reiki session to wash away the show's residual anxiety. Within minutes, I was asleep. I don't recall any dreams. Then I am thrashed against the shores of wakefulness with a sudden intensity that startles me. As the tides of the night recede, I am left splayed against the sands of consciousness. The sounds cling to me like seaweed. Still fresh on my mind, their vibrations fill me, echoes that were not melodious but rather the intonation of something sounding like words. Three words. Vowels stretched in a deep, sonorous hum that rolled over my skin. Half-awake, I knew I had to hold on to something too precious to lose. As the tones ebbed, I imitated them as best I could with the limited means of the human body. The sounds I felt were not words as we know them, but frequencies entwined with knowledge and wisdom. It didn't feel like a dream but like a connection - waves received on the antenna of an open mind.

This was similar to the voice months ago telling me to remember Gabriel. Then I had an actual word. Today, there was only the all-encompassing sound my brain tried to translate. My mouth tried to recreate the intonation, as if speaking for the first time. I could

---

45 *Suburra - Italian crime drama TV show, centered around organized crime in Rome*

not get it quite right. I did not dare to break the connection by opening my eyes. I lay there, letting the last waves of sound wash over me, trying to catch them between my bare hands like water.

When wakefulness finally overcomes me, three approximations remain: *Sulatha mana etha*[46]

Eyes still heavy with sleep, I pull the drawer of my nightstand open, feeling for the notebook and pen I keep there. With sleep-clumsy hands, I scribble the sounds down and collapse back into the comfort of my bed, relieved that I'd captured their elusive nature but clueless as to why that would be important.

All day, I feel the imprint these words left on my soul. I think about them as I make breakfast, as the warm water of my morning shower washes away the last remnants of sleep, leaving only the hum of three words behind. I know they are important. I can feel it. But Google brings none of the answers I hoped for - no known language, nothing associated with them in any way. It leaves me baffled, but not worried. I've relaxed into Trust. Trust has become my security blanket, catching me whenever my world tumbles this way or that.

But still ….

I am curious.

I draw a rectangle around the three words on the page. The lines start light, and as my frustration grows, they grow thicker and darker as if the box can give its content some justification for existing. The pencil flutters again, tapping the paper with stern impatience.

It is a cool evening. The girls are in bed, and Andrea is on a late-night conference call. I love those quiet hours. Dante is sprawled out on the floor next to me, his legs periodically nudging me for belly rubs. The room is dark, lit only by the desk lamp casting its warm arc over my laptop and a corner of the desk. I cuddle deeper into the

---

46   *These are not the actual "words" I heard. Until I understand them fully, I am using this as a placeholder.*

oversized sweater, wrinkle my nose to slide my reading glasses into place. I close my laptop with a sigh and pad over to the kitchen for a piece of chocolate. The floorboards creak, a reminder that the rest of the house is asleep, except for Andrea, whose muffled voice reaches my ear through his closed office door downstairs.

Days and weeks pass without any further insights, and the words are shuffled under the sheets of new priorities, collecting dust in the back of my mind. Life settles into a predictability challenged only by the demands of raising a nine- and a twelve-year-old. Their little childhood problems - friendships gone sideways, quizzes looming on the horizon, or tantrums when screen time has met its limits - keep me firmly grounded in the realm of motherhood. The only time I shed this skin is when I am visiting my hospice patients. Legacy Art and Reiki sessions are welcome interruptions that require presence. I have to leave it all behind - the worries, the schedules, the to-do lists, whatever emotion is ruling my day. I never know what to expect when I enter a patient's home. I cherish the fluidity with which I must adapt, and hold on to Trust's hand to guide me through it.

A month later, I wake to the vivid images of a dream and the vibrations of *Sulatha mana etha* still ringing through my sleep-heavy body. They sound exactly the way they did when I first felt them. But this time, the dream that accompanied them lies like an open book on my nightstand, vivid and clear. There is a family: a mother, a father, and a child on her bed. She is pale and thin, one hand on the door to another realm. We are gathered around her and, as always, I place my hands a few inches above her heart, close my eyes, and let Reiki flow. It seems like something I have done a million times before, yet this time the energy feels different. I am not the only one holding my hand over the child. The parents have both their hands touching their daughter as well, eyes closed in meditation. *Sulatha mana etha* lifts from my lips, spooling a web of light and energy around us, a cocoon so bright that it startles me wide awake.

This is it!

I jolt upright and jump out of bed with an intense burst of energy and excitement. That is what it's for! *Sulatha mana etha*! I need to use it during my Reiki sessions! But not just any Reiki session. It is meant for something new: a form of Reiki at the end of life, woven with the family's hands - an End-of-Life Family Reiki.

My shoulder critic yawns, stretches, and brushes a strand of my hair out of his face. His hair sticks up in all directions, making him look like a nutty professor in his striped silk pajamas, naked feet on spindly legs. He doesn't even need to look at me with his sleepy, reproachful stare. I know what he's going to say.

I know that getting messages in a dream is mad, and getting a continuation of that dream is even crazier. Maybe I should be used to it by now - life has thrown me a few unusual curveballs these past years. But how can I take something as fleeting as a dream and try it on a dying child? This is nuts! I do trust Reiki without question. Energy work cannot harm, since it draws directly from "the source," as some people call it, the universe, or God. I have felt it - its warmth, its depth, and its connection to something wiser and grander. It has opened the door to deeper understanding, introduced me to angels, and allowed me to feel part of something bigger. It does not have any negative side effects; that would go against the definition of Reiki. *Rei* means "universal," and *ki* refers to the vital life-force energy that flows through all living things. And mantras are part of my practice too. So, there is nothing strange about using words to help me with my work.

But still ....

Believing in something given to me in a dream puts me squarely on the side of the spiritual mumbo-jumbo people. If I do this, there is no turning back. (Breathe. Trust.)

Nothing can be rushed. Not even the use of a dream-given mantra. A few hospice visits go by without any incidents. I tell myself I'll know when to use the new End-of-Life Family Reiki, but so far, nothing stirs me to do so. Legacy Art and Reiki - sometimes one visit, sometimes several with the same patient - which I consider a special gift. Time is precious toward the end of life, and spending more than one session with one of my kids is a true blessing. I call them "my kids" because no matter how short the time is that we spend together, they leave a trace on my soul: little faces, smiles, spirits that I can sense so clearly despite the decline of their physical health. In terms of energy, none of them is attached to any negativity. Once you look beneath the surface, beneath the façade of a failing body, the ugliness of death - all I see is beauty. I know the love the parents wrap around their child, I see the soul already detached from what we perceive as pain and suffering, yet holding on a little longer. And I see time as a velvet-lined box, containing the most precious possession they can share ... a sparkling jewel of minutes. Sometimes, just a splinter, a tiny fragment of a life filled with games and imprints of love left behind on the hearts of the people they meet. Sometimes a row of pearly hours - one per week - that we spend together. All precious and miracles in their own right.

And then I met Jack.

CHAPTER 27
MANHATTAN BEACH, 2019

I have been called for a Reiki session. Osteosarcoma. Bone cancer. He has not been responsive for several days now. The family of four lives in a tiny garden house in the back of Jack's grandparents' home. I walk down the cracked concrete driveway towards the back of the property, past kids' bikes, scooters, and toys strewn across the ground. The tassels on the handlebars of the bike wave a sad Hello as I pass. The lawn in the patch of garden between the two buildings is brown and withered. The door of the garden house stands open, casting a warm rectangle of light across the dark concrete, pointing the way. It is the beginning of January, and I pull up the collar of my padded jacket against the wind whistling around the corner from the back of the house. Before I can knock, the light is eclipsed by a large man, who fills the frame, grunts, holds the door, slips past without a word, and disappears into the dark. Inside, the heat hits like a wall. I take a breath and feel it gliding down my lungs with the viscosity of oil, and I hurry to shrug off my jacket before breaking into a sweat.

I stand alone in a tiny living room with a three-seater couch to my left, a kitchen corner ahead of me with a small dining table, hugged tightly by four bar stools. To my right, a large TV on a glass sideboard and two narrow doors. One of them opens to a dark room and a man, a woman, and a girl of about four spill into the living room, instantly crowding the small space. The girl, Jack's sister, is dressed in Christmas PJs and hides behind her mom's legs, peering up at me.

With few words, I introduce myself and am welcomed into their home. We skip the small talk. They know why I am here, and the air is heavy with a sense of urgency.

Before I meet Jack, I ask to use the bathroom to wash my hands (hospice protocol), and I am stunned by how miniature everything is. Four toothbrushes share a cup on the lip of a salad-plate-sized sink, the toothpaste curled over the drain. I wonder what mornings look like for a family of four getting ready here.

Mom and Dad guide me to the only bedroom, shared by the parents and the sick child. Despite the heat, the room feels cozy, lit by a carousel nightlight casting bunnies, bears, and stars across the wall. Jack is under several layers of blankets; only his little face is peeking out. His hair stands up in wild defiance against a pale, emaciated face and sunken eyes. He's unresponsive and clearly doesn't have much time left. Hours, possibly days? His grandmother perches on a little stool, holding his hand and whispering softly to him. She wears a pink muumuu, her silver hair neatly pulled into a bun at the nape of her neck. She is soft. Soft curves, soft skin falling in gentle folds along her neck, hiding her jawline, soft voice, and I can only imagine how soft her hands feel on her grandson's skin.

The queen-sized bed fills the whole room. Makeup and hair products line the windowsill, and a lingering scent of aftershave hangs in the air, mixed with the sickly-sweet smell of whatever is about to claim this life. Two adult-size bathrobes cling to a hook behind the door, holding sleeves, their belts snaking along the floor as if trying to reach the child on the bed. Mom and Dad hover by the door, looking in. At my invitation, they slip off their shoes, climb onto the bed next to their son, and sink against the wall, as I prepare myself for the Reiki session. Jack's little sister scrambles over her dad and curls against her mother's lap, never taking her eyes off me. For a moment, the trivial question of where she sleeps at night crosses my mind. I cannot imagine that all four of them would fit on the bed, cuddling around the dying child, but there was no other bed in the doll-sized house. The couch, maybe? My heart stirs, uncomfortable with the pain that is cracking along its surface. There is not much space to move or sit, so I stand by the bedside and reassure Grandma with a gentle pat on the shoulder that she can stay right where she is.

I don't plan to use the "new Reiki" mantra. In fact, I haven't used it yet. I trust that I'll know the right moment, so I go with the flow. I close my eyes, soften my breath, and place one hand a few inches above Jack's forehead, the other where I sense his heart beneath the blankets. The room is stifling, and I wish I could crack the small window. Instead, I turn my attention inward and begin.

One of the first things I learned studying Reiki was that I had to get "out of the way" for the energy to flow freely. My personal intentions for the session, and my wishes for specific outcomes or goals had to be checked at the door. Reiki goes where it's needed. I focus on my breath - slowly, in and out. The warmth of the room fills my lungs. My hands feel hot, and I don't know if it is the heat radiating out from Jack or from within. I am on autopilot. My thoughts are swaying to the rhythm of the Reiki mantras that I am silently reciting in my mind, and I lose myself in the gentle tingle I feel in my hands. Time blurs. A soft strain between my shoulder blades and in my lower back is the only indicator that time is passing and that I have been standing in the same position for a while now. I completely forgot about the new mantra until I sensed a shift. Even though the room is still hot, the air beneath my hands feels cool and thinner. My mind is completely relaxed and offers little doubt or resistance to the idea of using the new *"End-of-Life"* Reiki. It is the most obvious thing to do. Guided by intuition, I invite the family to join me by placing their hands on their son, brother, and grandson. *Sulatha mana etha* hums in my mind, eclipsing everything else. Jack doesn't move.

Minutes pass. A giggle starts to work its way up from my stomach. My mind is yanked out of the meditative quiet, shocked by the inappropriate timing. What on earth is going on? It is unmistakably a giggle - one of those hard-to-contain, full-body laughs that starts as a bubbly feeling in my stomach and works its way up until it nearly bursts out of me. My eyes fly open. Thankfully, Jack's family has not noticed anything amiss; they all have their eyes closed and seem to be in their own silent prayers, Mom now crying freely, while Dad remains composed, his arm protectively around his wife's shoulders.

I steady myself and return to the new mantra, breathing slowly again - in and out, in and out. And again: the small, impossible rise of laughter. I feel mortified and lose the thread.

Why on earth would I feel a laugh at the bedside of a dying child? Guilt crumbles in ice-cold clumps in my stomach. I tried a mantra without knowing its meaning. I trusted blindly and now ... I want to run.

What have I done?

My shoulder critic sits in a comfortable lotus pose on my shoulder. He is wearing lime-green harem pants with an old Care Bears T-shirt. His hands rest on his knees, palms up, thumb and index finger touching, with thick silver rings on his hands. His face is completely relaxed. But something tips him off, as he opens one eye, like an owl, and looks at me.

"What's going on?" he mouths silently.

"Nothing," my lips form the words without a sound, and I pinch my eyes shut, against their struggle to pop open. Only a tremor in my hands betrays my panic. From what I can tell through half-closed eyelids, no one - besides my shoulder critic - has noticed anything.

Okay, maybe I can salvage this.

I need to focus.

I run the familiar Reiki mantras like prayer beads. Their rhythm steadies the scramble in my head. No more End-of-Life Reiki. Back to basics.

"What happened?" my critic hisses near my ear. "I can feel your hand shaking!"

I shrug him off. It's hard enough to concentrate without his buzzing. I'm still scolding myself for trying something new. At this point, I feel the Reiki session is a complete failure, but maybe Reiki - the real Reiki - can still help Jack somehow.

"Trust. Just trust." My shoulder critic has a hand on my cheek, as he leans closer to my ear and whispers, "You got this. Do not be scared. Breathe!" His voice - unexpectedly soft - lets the tension between my shoulders melt into the floor. His small hand feels hot against my cheek, but the warmth washes through me, allowing me to relax. My hovering hand steadies. Minutes pass, my breathing evens, and my mind unclenches. Silence spreads out into an inky black lake in my mind. Lights sparkle above, dabbing glittering reflections onto the water. Drops of reality mix into my meditation, as the illuminated shapes of bears and smiling stars from the carousel nightlight orbit across my internal horizon. Silence ebbs and flows with each inhale.

A scene takes shape behind my closed eyes. The dark waters recede, and I find myself next to Jack's bed. Grandma holds his limp hand, forehead pressed to his fingers. Her curly hair shimmers blue and pink in the night light. Jack's sister is asleep, her head still resting on her mother's lap while Mom cries silently, her lips moving without a sound. Dad leans his head against the wall, his face is pale, and there are dark crescents under his eyes. I know my eyes are closed, yet the scene is very vivid in my mind.

Suddenly, a little boy pops up behind Dad. He must be around six. He's wearing a red-and-blue flannel; his black hair is short, sticking up in the back, giving him a mischievous look. His brown eyes sparkle, and I notice how thick and long his eyelashes are. He gives me a sheepish look, yells "Peekaboo!" and vanishes. My eyes fly open, and I look around in shock - no boy in sight! The room is exactly as before - dark, quiet. No boy, apart from Jack, under his mountain of blankets.

Am I dreaming?

I glance at my critic, and our eyes meet. His head is cocked to the side, eyebrows knitted. I can tell he is trying to read my expression. He didn't see him. Of course, he didn't.

I close my eyes once again and take a deep breath. Within seconds, he is back: the little boy pops up behind Mom this time. "Peekaboo!" Gone. And there it is again - the laugh trying to rise, the same one that threatened to crack the session earlier. I am not sure if I am now laughing at the boy and his shenanigans or at the absurdity of it all.

At this point, I'm sure I've failed. My pulse skitters, and I focus all my attention on suppressing the giggle that is still bubbling up in my throat.

What the frog is going on?

As a mom of two girls, I have trained myself to say "frog" instead of the other F-word, but this situation requires a full-force "What the FUCK!!!???"

My shoulder critic is now visibly flustered. "Are you ... Do you have the hiccups?" He presses his ear to my shoulder, listening. "That sounds like ..." he listens again. "You're LAUGHING!" he hisses, scandalized.

I shoot him a look that says, "Shut up, not helping!"

I clear my throat softly to signal to the family that the session has ended, wipe my palms on my jeans, and roll my shoulders. I am so glad this is over!

Mom sighs deeply and looks up at me with tearful eyes. "Oh my God!" she whispers. "That was incredible! I could feel him!" The hint of a smile softens her face. "He was …like …like before …" her voice breaks. Dad pulls her close, nodding his thanks. She strokes her sleeping daughter's hair. "Remember when he wanted to wear your sweatshirt to school?" she asks him, watery smile returning. "He was what - six? Seven? It hung to his knees. But he didn't care. He was so proud." A sob slips under her smile, and her husband exhales a short, sad laugh through his nose.

Not knowing what else to do, I turn to Jack, lean over his bed, and cup the side of his pale little face in my hand. His skin is cool and damp, his eyelids flutter, then still. Grandma hasn't moved. She is cast in anticipatory grief, her hand glued to his.

I am at a loss for words. How can his parents experience these profound, intense sensations, while I feel like a complete failure? Reiki didn't work! The new End-of-Life Reiki was a complete and utter disaster! "Bye, Jack," I whisper and brush a strand of his dark hair to the side.

While Mom dislodges herself from the bed without waking her daughter, I grab my bag and slip into the living room. I feel disheartened and empty. This visit did not go as expected. Guilt shudders within me, and I try to release it by shaking out my arms and rolling my shoulders. My eyes fall on several family photos in frames along the wall that I had not noticed earlier, and I step closer to have a look: Mom and Dad with a baby; a black-and-white wedding picture (Grandma maybe). Four kids at a baseball field and one official studio shot with Mom, Dad, Jack's sister, and …

I blink and step closer.

There he is! The Peekaboo boy! He is dressed in black trousers and a white shirt, looking sharp. His hair is brushed out of his face, but in the back, a few strands defy gravity and stick up, just the way I had seen it tonight.

"That's our last official family photo before Jack's diagnosis two years ago," Mom says softly behind me. She kisses her fingertips and presses them to Jack's face in the picture.

"That's Jack! Oh my God! Look at his cheeky grin!" My voice sounds more surprised than I intend to. I had not recognized the boy in my "vision" (for lack of a better word) as Jack, whose small, sunken face was barely a shadow of his former self. My mind reels - Peekaboo boy WAS JACK, the way he had been before the cancer!

Mom picks up her daughter's pink hoodie from the floor, where it lay crumpled and discarded, and folds it over her arm as she walks me towards the door. "Thank you so much for coming tonight," she glances over her shoulder at me, the edges of her mouth try to form a grateful smile against the heaviness of anticipatory grief. "I am not sure what you did, but I felt it in my heart." She unlocks the door, pulls it open, and cold air rushes in.

Should I say something?

I feel torn. There are still remnants of guilt pulling on my emotions, but now there is a new undercurrent of timid excitement. A subtle thought that is barely there emerges out of the realization of what happened tonight.

But what did happen?

And what am I supposed to say?

There are only a few steps to the door, not enough time to really think this through. Before stepping over the threshold, I gather my courage and turn to Mom: "What does Peekaboo mean to you?" We lock eyes, and she just stares at me.

The cool air of the evening beckons me as I stand one foot out, one foot in. I am suspended between two realms, two realities: One is the impressionist's night painted in blues and blacks, shimmers of golden light dancing on the metallic frames of the bikes sleeping in the driveway. And then there is the inside, golden warmth, where time stands still. The air is so heavy, it refuses to be the last breath. I hear a metallic clunk from outside somewhere and a cat meowing in response.

"How do you know ..." Mom stops herself, swallows hard.

"Peekaboo is his favorite game! Even just a few weeks ago, when he was walking around on crutches, he would hide behind every tree, every car, every piece of furniture, and yell 'peekaboo!' Of course, we had to pretend to be scared, even though we saw his crutches from a mile away." She smiles at the memory. "And then he would drop his crutches and roll around on the floor, laughing like crazy. It scared the hell out of me. I always thought he would hurt himself. But it was ... is his favorite thing to do." Her voice drops until her last words almost slip into the night unheard.

"How do you ...?" Her voice trails off again.

"He showed me. During the Reiki session," is all I can answer. Without another word, she crosses the short distance between us and draws me into a long hug, before releasing me into the cool evening air.

When I arrive at my car, I throw my handbag unceremoniously onto the center console and plop myself into the driver's seat, start the engine, and lower the windows - all of them! The cool evening air is laced with the scent of someone's cooking nearby. After being in the tight confines of the sweltering, dark bedroom, I crave the cool, refreshing air, inhale deeply, and wait for my mind to clear.

What had just happened?

My shoulder critic is clambering up onto the dashboard, where he paces back and forth. His naked feet make faint slapping sounds as they hit the top of the dash. The nearby streetlamp transforms his dirty blonde hair into shimmering strands of gold amid a wild sea of dark waves rising in every direction. "Again?" he wrings his hands. "Why does this keep happening to you? First, the angel, then you get messages in dreams, and now this - And I am not even mentioning all the other crazy shit, like ghost-Kathrin in your car or all this stuff with the dude in Seychelles. I did not sign up for this."

He is right! My thoughts precisely. Of course, he is voicing my thoughts verbatim. In some strange way, we are one. Even though he is usually the grumpier one of the two of us. Despite the absurdity of it all, I laugh.

I look back at the house. The garden is still and black, illuminated only by the golden rectangles cast from the windows. From the outside, nothing betrays what is going on within.

I wonder what they are doing now, Mom, Dad, and Grandma. I am sure Jack's sister is still sleeping next to her brother. And Jack ... after "seeing" young Jack pop up with so much energy and cheek, I have a hard time consolidating the image of the dying child with the one that interrupted my Reiki session.

Did I imagine him?

"There is no way you could have imagined him exactly the way he used to look," my thoughts race. I could have seen his picture on my way in. I don't recall having seen any photos, but possibly my subconscious ...

"And how would you explain the Peekaboo?" Mr. Know-it-All interjects.

"I cannot!" I answer out loud, shake my head, and snap on my seatbelt with an unnaturally loud click. As I pull away from the curb, the air whips around my head, cooling my flushed face. My critic looks like he's touched an electrical outlet; his hair is flying in all directions, smacking him in the eyes and obscuring his vision. I only hear a faint "We still need to talk about this!" then a soft pop, and he is gone.

A big sigh escapes my chest as I settle into the quiet of the car, grateful for a moment alone to sift through the whirlwind in my mind. The vision has rattled - not because no one else could see it, but because it arrived unbidden on the heels of that unfamiliar Reiki technique I'd embraced in a surge of trust. Was the Reiki the catalyst, or did it coincide with the vision by chance? I've learned there are no true coincidences in life - only alignments waiting to be understood.

Without my inner critic to spar with, I find myself debating both sides alone, circling the same questions without resolution. How could I be certain it was Jack? The figure matched the boy in the photo, down to the playful peekaboo gesture his mother later confirmed. Yet what had I truly witnessed - his soul, some echo, a memory surfacing for his parents?

I stop the car at a traffic light. It dawns on me then: the new Reiki had unlocked a deeper channel, one I'd never accessed before. That peekaboo wasn't for me; it was a bridge to his parents, a silent message transcending words. And perhaps that was its true purpose - to facilitate connection at life's end, when words fail, a thread thrown across the gap. The realization leaves me in awe, suspended between wonder and humility.

A loud Harley Davidson with a bearded biker in a leather jacket pulls up next to me. He looks over and gives me a courteous nod, roaring off down the street when the light turns green. Before he disappears into the traffic ahead of me, I see the back of his black jacket. It is well-worn, and the design is patchy and scratched off in some areas. There are white swirls on the top and bottom of two words, of which the latter I can barely make out as *Daniels*, but the first one stands out sharp and clear: Jack.

I got the call the next afternoon: Jack had died peacefully just four hours after my visit.

CHAPTER 28
MANHATTAN BEACH 2019

"Okay, so this is a tricky case," Jordin, the volunteer coordinator, exhales on the other side of the line. "We are pretty much at the end of our rope here and not sure how else we can help this family." It is 2:15 pm on a Monday afternoon, and I sit in my car in front of Giulia's school when I take the call. The school lies in one of Manhattan Beach's dead zones, where cell reception is less reliable. Static rattles through my phone. "Jordin? Are you still there?" Word fragments crackle in reply "Mom's expec…" - silence - then a crackle again "Reiki …n you go this week or nex…" more static until I can finally hear her voice clear again: "I sent you an email with the patient's details. Let me know how it goes." And with that, the line goes dead. I put my phone back on its magnetic holder on the center console and look out the window towards the school gate. The courtyard is still deserted, apart from a few parents lingering around the entrance to wait for their little ones.

LEARNING TO SAY GOODBYE

One thing that fascinates me about my Reiki work in hospice is that I never know who I will encounter on any given day. Before visiting a new patient, I only get the basics: the names of the family members and the patient, the patient's age, and sometimes a diagnosis. That's it - not enough to get a complete picture. Googling the diagnosis does not help much since I do not know what that translates to: What state is the child in? Is there anything I need to watch out for? Is he conscious? There are just too many variables. And a diagnosis doesn't change the one thing that matters: he is dying. But I do know this: I am about to meet a family who is facing the impossible situation of having to say goodbye to their child - maybe not today or tomorrow, but the goodbye hangs in the home like the pressure system before a storm. I look back at the school gate and check the time on my phone. The bell should ring in a few minutes - enough time to check my email. I click on Jordin's message and the attached patient sheet.

Gavin, 16 years old
Diagnosis: Lennox-Gastaut Syndrome
Caregivers: his parents
Location: Long Beach, CA

This is not much to go on. I read the few sentences that accompany the fact sheet. Gavin has been in hospice for over a year, and despite all efforts from nurses, doctors, and his loving parents, he is stuck in a stagnant decline. The word "stuck" catches my attention. I am not sure what it means to be stuck at the end of life, but I can imagine it must be very hard for everyone involved. I never want to feel stuck in any situation. To me, being stuck means that I cannot move, neither forward nor back. I am stuck waiting for something to resolve, open up, and release. But being stuck also means a lack of control, a helplessness, a waiting for something or someone. I do not know what catalyst could bring about a change for Gavin and his family. Still, Reiki is known for getting things "unstuck," for allowing trapped energy to flow freely, which in turn often causes a shift in the emotional or physical state. Maybe Reiki is precisely what Gavin and his family need.

A few days later, I pull up in front of their house. It is a gorgeous March morning. Tufts of clouds chase each other across a sparkling blue sky, and the wind is rustling in the nearby trees. Gavin's family lives in a peaceful neighborhood of Long Beach, where old, majestic Eucalyptus trees line the streets, and the sun paints a beautiful, ever-changing mosaic of light and dark on the road. As I park in front of the meticulously kept mid-century bungalow, a shimmering green hummingbird zips around my car. I love hummingbirds and always consider them a good omen. My shoulder critic arrives dressed in a safari outfit complete with tan-colored cargo shorts, a matching shirt, and a straw hat, and swipes a butterfly net towards the bird. "What are you doing?" I roll my eyes at him. He jumps onto the roof of my car, and a heavy assortment of gold chains clinks around his neck as he waves the net. The hummingbird hovers at a safe distance, its black eyes sparkling with what I would call amusement. The wings blur; my critic sulks. "Whatever!" I shrug and turn towards the house, glad he is too distracted to follow.

The front door is painted a bright green, which matches the house's overall design and the landscape of the desert-themed garden, giving the home a lively, inviting character. The door opens almost immediately after I ring the bell, and Mom greets me. She is a vibrant woman, approximately my age, with wavy auburn hair, sparkling green eyes, and a dewy complexion. A welcoming smile washes over her face, making her freckles dance as she invites me into their home. The energy inside is airy and intentional: modern open plan, clean lines, layered textures. It looks like the home of a family with an appreciation for design and attention to detail, which feels both familiar and comfortable.

Mom leads me to the dining area, where Gavin rests in his reclining wheelchair next to the table. His nurse, sitting nearby, greets me with a friendly smile as I approach, but she quickly retreats into her phone, creating the illusion of privacy. Gavin is impeccably dressed in a pair of jeans, with a neatly pressed shirt collar peeking out from under his sweater. His eyes are half closed; his tongue peeks out partially between his lips, quivering occasionally. I am not sure if he is awake or just dozing, but he makes no sign of being aware of my arrival.

Not to disturb him, Mom and I go to the nearby sitting room to chat. The room envelops us in soothing brown and beige tones, and I feel I have entered an Architectural Digest spread. An oversized couch divides two moods: one wall warm and inviting in textured raffia; the other, exposed brick softened by a fireplace and a black-and-white cactus photo in a gold frame. We sit on the couch, and a whiff of room fragrance rises from an elegant bottle nearby, beckoning me to relax as Mom starts to talk about her son.

Framed family pictures on a mirrored built-in bookshelf already tell part of the story I am eager to hear. Background helps- not just the health, but how a family carries it. It's obvious to me that Gavin is surrounded by an incredible amount of love and attention. Despite his declining health, he is very integrated into their everyday life. They went on road trips together in a van completely adapted to his needs. They took him to his sister's volleyball games and other outings, created elaborate Halloween costumes, and showered him with as much love as possible. Over the past year, he had been declining steadily, requiring more and more medical attention, each crisis adding another tube, vest, or tweak in meds meant to keep him comfortable. It is a tricky balancing act for a family to weather the storms such a diagnosis brings. When do comfort measures become too much? How do you read pain in a nonverbal child? Hospice teams help, but the choice still lands in a parent's hands. When is the right time to let go? How can they be expected to hold back the measures that have helped sustain their child's life in the past? It is an impossible situation that no amount of support from hospice doctors, nurses, or chaplains can alleviate.

After a few minutes, we move back into the dining area, and I pull one of the chairs out to sit next to Gavin. He has not changed and still seems to be sleeping. I turn to the nurse, who watches me with curiosity. "Please, if Gavin needs anything while I do Reiki, feel free to interrupt." She nods and slips back into her phone. "Ok," I say with a breath, indicating that all my attention is now focused on him. "Hey, Gavin." I soften my voice as I lean closer and place a hand on his arm without expecting a reaction. His face is relaxed. His glasses make his eyes look large on his face, and his eyelashes are as blond as his hair as they rest against his cheek. The only movement is the gentle quiver of his tongue that peeks out between his lips. I wonder if he is dreaming.

"How does this work, exactly?" Mom's words startle me as she pulls up a chair on the other side of Gavin and looks at me, curiosity glowing on her face.

"Well," I pause, and my gaze wanders out into the garden, where a large Chinese Elm hangs a swing low from its majestic branches. My shoulder critic has found his way into the backyard, is sitting on the bottom of the swing, and trying unsuccessfully to get it to move. His thin legs are too short to achieve any momentum. The butterfly net lies discarded in the grass, and the hummingbird flits in and out of the elm's dense canopy. I close my eyes for a second to gather my thoughts. "Reiki works with universal energy, flowing all around us and within each person's energy field. Some say it is just a natural occurrence, others see it coming from "the Source," or "God" … that part can't really be explained." I shrug my shoulders with an apologetic smile, aware of how little we truly understand the invisible energies all around us. Reiki just scratches the surface. "And that's pretty much what I am working with. I will hover my hands over Gavin, following the different energy centers in the body, and then we'll see what happens. Sometimes I can sense my patient's energy quite clearly; other times, I don't, and they just reap the benefit of experiencing deep relaxation. But it can also help on an emotional and spiritual level."

"Ohhh, that sounds like I could use some Reiki, too," Mom muses as she pushes the chair back and gets up. "I'll let you get to it. I'll be right here if you need me," she points to the kitchen behind me and walks away. I return my attention to Gavin.

"Okay," I take a breath and readjust my position in the chair. It is important that, even though he is not awake, I tell him what I am about to do. After all, despite having the physical appearance of a younger child, he is a teenager, and I want to respect his space. "Gavin, you can just relax, and I will hover my hands right about here. It might feel a bit warm or tingly, but nothing else. You can sleep right through it." I stretch out my hands a few inches above his chest; still, no reaction from Gavin. Mom busies herself in the kitchen behind me as I hover my hands over her son. I exhale, soften my shoulders, trusting the quiet to show me where to start.

Every time I do Reiki, I am in awe at the build-up of the energy flow. Sometimes it happens rather quickly that my hands tingle, and the energy builds in intensity until they feel hot, as if an electric current is running through them. Sometimes I feel absolutely nothing. It is pretty unpredictable. Today, I can feel the energy immediately and move my hands from his chest to his forehead and back down. Near his throat, the air feels denser - near the throat chakra. I have learned that the throat chakra is responsible for communication. When talking to my patients about a session, I avoid the term "blockages" because it always has a negative connotation. But when Reiki flows, I sometimes encounter spots on the body that feel "denser" than others, as if the energy cannot flow through them easily. Usually, that is a sign of unresolved issues, such as health problems, inflammation, or sometimes even remnants of emotional trauma, which we carry in various parts of our body. Reiki can often dissolve these blockages, but sometimes they just serve as a way to pinpoint trouble spots to revisit throughout the session or in follow-up sessions. I pause and move my hands back and forth, feeling the density again. Then suddenly, it is gone. Not gone, as in dissolved, but gone as in gone. Completely. I cannot feel any energy now. This is strange. Something is missing. Gavin's energy is missing!

Where did it go?

I open my eyes, but nothing has changed around me. The nurse across the table is still hidden inside her phone, and I can hear Mom potter away in the kitchen behind me. My shoulder critic stands outside next to the floor-to-ceiling windows, his hand cupped against the glass above his eyes to get a better view. He gestures at me and raises his arms in question. I shake my head at him, simultaneously saying, "I don't know" and "Go away." I close my eyes again and imagine my awareness expanding outwards like a balloon filled with light. It only takes a few seconds for me to sense Gavin's energy off to the left, outside of his body.

I had experienced a similar sensation several times before, usually with unconscious patients. It makes sense to me that their spirit, or soul, if I want to call it that, is not permanently attached to their failing bodies. Instead, they explore outside the confines of their physical beings, leaving the stillness and sometimes even the suffering behind, to roam close by in their spirit form. But they never seem to venture far, as there is still a strong bond to their physical body. I cannot explain that knowledge. It is just something I feel in this space where the distance between life and death shrinks with each breath. It is the same today. Gavin's spirit is not a vision, as I had experienced with Jack. Instead, I feel him with something like a sixth sense. The hairs on my arm closest to him prickle in recognition. It seems that he is standing behind his wheelchair, eying me curiously. I get a strong sense of his personality, which feels very different from the boy lying motionless in front of me. He is skeptical, as most teenage boys are, but also quite funny in how he appears to question my presence and actions. I can imagine him with his arms crossed in front of his chest, glaring at me with an expression so typical of boys his age. Restless, he shifts his energy from one place to another, like the flitting of a dragonfly - now on my right, now on my left, then next to his mother, just to appear right behind me the next instant. The goosebumps on my arms and back serve as a reliable location detector.

"Okay, Gavin. You are distracting me here - let me focus." I silently reprimand him, taking on a loving yet determined tone. But I have a hard time suppressing the smile on my face. I am here for a reason, but it feels like Gavin wants to goof off and be silly.

As I continue the session, I do not feel that his death is imminent. He seems to be in a stable condition, but not in the best state; his chest appears to have some trouble spots, energetically speaking, and I also sense a reduced energy flow in his legs. Just as the hospice staff had expressed to me, it all seemed a bit stagnant, and I am not sure why. Is it a physical issue, or is Gavin holding on for a particular reason? The way his energy keeps appearing next to his mother suggest that there might be a message here that I have not yet understood, or that possibly is not meant for me. It is strange to read emotions from energy, but he gives me the strong impression that he is very protective of her and her feelings. I understand that this sounds crazy to most people, but I have learned to trust my intuition in that regard and don't even question it anymore. With the same conviction, I know I have to use the new Reiki again. The strange feeling near the throat chakra makes me think that communication is something Gavin is looking for. And from what I have learned with Jack, that is precisely what End-of-Life Family Reiki can help with.

As always, I use an audible breath to mark the end of the session before I turn to Mom. "Okay, I am done for now."

"Great. How was it?" She looks at me, and curiosity saturates the green in her eyes to a brilliant sparkle, but she interrupts herself before I can answer. "Can I get you something? A glass of water or a coffee?" She already has a carafe of water and a glass in hand as she turns toward me.

"I'll take the water. Thank you." I take a grateful sip. "Gavin surprised me. He has quite the attitude," I smile at her, and she nods.

"I am glad you could see that. You wouldn't be able to tell just by looking at him," a laugh colors her words as she puts the glass carafe back on the countertop, and we chat a little bit about the insights of the session.

"I think we should try this Family Reiki I sometimes do with my patients, if you are up for it." I omit the "End-of-Life" part of the name on purpose.

"How is that different from what you just did?" Mom pulls up a chair on the opposite side of Gavin and takes his hand as she listens. "It is quite simple, really. Before, I worked on Gavin's energy centers. Just as we are made of energy, so are our thoughts. Thoughts are energy, and we can communicate through energy, which is what this form of Reiki does." Guided more by intuition than experience, I continue. "Just place your hand on Gavin's heart and think of anything you want to share with him. Anything at all, put it in your heart, and imagine it like a light flowing from your heart through your shoulder, your arm, your hand, and directly connecting to Gavin. I will anchor the flow with Reiki." I smile at her encouragingly as she puts her hand on Gavin's heart. "And then we listen." I pause, trying to figure out how to best explain the next part. "Not with your ears - your heart. Look out for sensations, thoughts, memories, images - anything that comes up. And we'll see ...." My voice trails off as I look at Mom. She is ready and rubs her hands together like she had seen me do before the first session.

She reaches out to Gavin, places her hand on top of his sweater, right above his heart, and closes her eyes. This connection between mother and son is intimate, and I try to recede in the background, turn my focus inward, and follow the ebb and flow of my own breath. Once again, I can feel the energy swirling in synergy with the new mantra. It feels different from the first session - lighter and more connected to the boy in front of me. It is a peaceful sensation, profoundly relaxing and filled with warmth and tangible love, even though I cannot tell if it emanates from Gavin or Mom. Minutes tick by, interrupted only by the shuffling of chair legs behind me, when the nurse readjusts her position. Time places tension between my shoulder blades from the strain of holding my arms out in front of me, and a sudden energy shift announces the end of the session.

Cool disappointment wells up within me as I pull my hands back into my lap. I have nothing to report; no vision, thoughts, or other signs that Gavin had received Mom's energy. My failure sits heavy on my tongue as I try to find words to break the silence, but Mom's smile rises across from me before I can even take a breath. It lifts and radiates over her face with such brilliance that I am stunned for a moment.

We lock eyes, she gathers herself, then shakes her head in disbelief. "I was so connected to him!" Her voice starts soft, then steadies. "I kept telling him, *you are loved, you are loved*, and images flashed - like a movie projected onto the garden. Right over there," she gestures through the window towards the tree and the grass beyond. "I saw images from his childhood, memories of times we spent together, birthday parties, special moments we shared, from when he was small up until now. It was so vivid, so real." I look out at the garden again and then back at Gavin, unchanged between us. "And all of it was tangled up with the constant *You are loved, you are loved*." She wipes a tear from her eyes and smiles. "Maybe he heard me. Maybe he wanted me to know he remembers."

The tingling I had felt on my skin earlier has returned, and I know immediately what Gavin was showing her: his Life Review with her! Having read a lot of literature about the end of life and near-death experiences, I am quite familiar with the concept. Many people who have had a near-death experience report this phenomenon, in which they see a rapid succession of images encompassing much or the totality of their life experience, seeing their life "flash before their eyes". I think this is what Gavin had shared with Mom.

I catch sight of my shoulder critic pressing his nose against the window. His eyes are wide, and he brings his fists to the side of his face and makes an explosion gesture. I grin at him, thrilled that I have someone to share this moment with. His mind is blown as well. Today I was not the one receiving a message; it was Gavin's mom. And in that, it is even more of a confirmation that my new End-of-Life Reiki had once again done something miraculous. She rises and hugs me, freckles bright with emotion as if even they're trying to make sense of it.

It is pretty clear to me what Gavin was trying to tell her: he showed her his favorite moments to say that he was ready to go. His short life had been full; he was surrounded by his family, who loved him deeply and shared many precious moments with him. His heart was filled with love and gratitude, and he wanted Mom to know. He was ready to move on. But this is just my interpretation, and I don't feel it is up to me to share this with her right now. She would have to come to this conclusion on her own. Or maybe that was not even necessary. Energy communicates more clearly than words ever could. No need to put a label on it, and it is not my place to influence her opinion on what she has experienced. My job is to witness. So, I stay quiet and return the hug, happy to have been allowed to witness this special moment.

Before I leave, I squeeze Gavin's arm. "Bye, Gavin. You did great. I'll see you soon, ok?" Mom walks me to the door, and we agree I'll return for a session with Dad.

Nearly two weeks later, I park in the same spot. Another bright morning; a hummingbird zips past my car like a déjà vu. I pause and breathe in the sweet, oxygen-rich air. I feel the sun's warmth caressing my skin, chased by the cool touch of a breeze that ruffles my hair in an invitation to play. Everything is identical to my last visit - apart from the fact that my shoulder critic has swapped his Safari outfit for tiny tiger-print Speedos, a towel is draped over his shoulder, and he carries an inflatable unicorn floatie under his arm. He winks as he walks past me towards the door. Not difficult to guess what he wants to do during the Reiki session. My heart swells with love for my little weirdo; for the hummingbird that shoots out of the red flowers of a nearby bush; for Gavin, whom I am about to see again; and for his parents. The moment passes and leaves me with an echo of gratitude as I cross the last few yards to the green door.

Mom opens before I can ring the bell, and a feeling of familiarity embraces me like an old friend. Just like last time, her freckles dance along with her smile, and we hug before she walks ahead of me towards the kitchen. Her voice rises in a singsong of introductions moments before I lay eyes on Dad, who is walking towards us from the dining room and greets me with a warm handshake.

Dad is a tall man in his forties; his short blonde hair is swept up with just the right amount of product without overdoing it. Like his wife, he has a very open, inviting demeanor, and his bright, gentle eyes twinkle at me from behind a fashionable pair of dark-rimmed glasses. He is wearing a blue short-sleeved shirt printed with tiny colorful palms, which adds a hint of whimsy to his wardrobe. I set my handbag on a barstool and, on impulse, pull out a small amethyst heart Gia had given me as a gift a while ago and slip it into my hand. I am not well-versed in crystals and their mystical properties, but I like how they feel in my hand, and Gia's little heart makes me feel connected to her and grounded in the moment.

My eyes scan the dining room for Gavin. "He is in his room," Mom catches my eye, and her smile mellows at the corners, where her freckles pause for a tense moment. "He's had a low fever on and off. Not much, but there might be an infection brewing." Dad's glasses mirror Mom's concern, then turn toward the hallway that leads past the open living area to his son's room. I follow his gaze and tip my head towards the door. "Let me go and say hi to him, and then we can chat."

Gavin's room is dim. The wind whispers lullabies into the drawn curtains through an inch of open window. The soft fabric billows to the song's rhythm and dances waves of sunlight over Gavin's sheets. He does not move or acknowledge our presence in any way. There are thin red veins visible under the translucent skin of his eyelids. He looks pale. The faint quiver of his tongue is the only movement. It reminds me of the involuntary moment of a baby's tongue during breastfeeding. Gia and Giulia's image lifts out of the fog of memories, and motherly love pours out of my skin. My fingers close around the amethyst heart in my hand, and I slip it into my jeans pocket. "Hey, Gavin," I whisper as I lean over him. He is wearing a PJ shirt and is covered up to his chest with a sheet and a blanket. A pulse-oximeter is attached to his still hand, and red, anxious numbers jump out of a nearby screen, beeping for attention.

Dad teeters at the edge of an armchair in the corner of the spacious room. His body language clearly announces that, despite his open-mindedness, he is on a tightrope way above his comfort zone. I feel the urge to give him a safety net or an umbrella for balance. There is a swivel stool nearby, and I pull it closer. "Okay, before we start, let's take a breath and relax." I take one long, audible inhale so his breath can follow. Mom had told him about our session, so I do not feel the need to go into too many details. But I am relieved that the breath allows Dad to lean back in his chair, and his thoughts, bound in an anxious knot, release their coils and drop heavy on his shoulders. "Sometimes, we have a hard time finding the right words. Especially in situations like this," I soften my voice. Dad's earlier cheer and confidence wobble under the weight of anticipatory grief. He opens his mouth as if to say something, but closes it again, receding into the back of the chair, where the dim light of the room is pulling layers of shade over his features. Fear of what the future holds for Gavin chokes his words, and I see the reflection of tears in his eyes. I roll the stool over to the side of Gavin's bed to give Dad the space he needs.

"Energy makes it easier to communicate without the hindrance of words. After all, there are no words to express a parent's love. But through energy, nothing is lost in translation. Come, sit here." I pull the stool close to Gavin and pat the seat. Dad walks over and sits next to Gavin, thumb rubbing his wedding band. "All you have to do is put your hands on Gavin and imagine that you communicate directly heart to heart. You can close your eyes, and if you've ever done meditation, you can try that to still your mind. Reiki will do the rest. And then just listen with your heart for emotions, thoughts, memories … anything that comes up."

Dad wipes his hands on his jeans and gently places his palms on his son's chest. His breath shudders as he closes his eyes. As father and son merge into their soul-to-soul communion, I am alone in the room. I feel myself sinking into the calm waters of Reiki, where the energy laps against my skin. Mom's earlier vision released me from the expectation of being the one to relay information. I trust that Gavin can speak for himself. I smile, and my hands feel warm as Reiki flows. Like last time, I can sense Gavin's energy outside his body. But he lacks the speed and attitude he displayed before. Instead of flitting here and there, his presence ebbs and flows, with long moments of absence in between. I wonder if he is checking in on Mom in the other room.

Through my closed lids, the bright red numbers of the oximeter demand my attention and force me to watch as they decline, one by one, to a state of relaxation. Gavin's pulse had been high due to his fever, but is settling now as he senses his father's energy. But the numbers' grip on me is relentless, and soon a beep shatters the silence, then another, then quiet again. My breath follows the fluctuations on the screen, tied to every changing digit. They are not announcing drastic changes. The beeps and the twitchy numbers are the rhythm that has dominated this family's life for years. I cannot imagine living under such tyranny.

The beeps rush time, and before I realize it, the flow of energy changes, and the session is over. Dad lifts his head, and his softened features are startled at the rush of emotions they have to display. "Just take a few moments," I whisper, and now it is my turn to recede into the back of the armchair in the corner as I watch Dad gather his feelings around him like a soft blanket. When he is ready, he turns to me, his face channel-surfs between expressions. He does not need to explain. I can sense that this exchange has had a profound effect on him.

As if on cue, Mom tiptoes into the doorway, her eyes on her husband. "How did it go?" she whispers. A deep exhale carries her husband into her arms, and they stand united in a hug before he pulls away. "I don't even know where to start." His voice is raw and splinters at the edges. I feel the conversation about this session has to happen between the parents alone, so I get up. "I'll leave, so you guys can talk," I whisper and nod towards the hallway. I am unsure why I lower my voice, but a comforting silence has settled over the house. Mom walks me to the door and embraces me long and hard. "Thank you! You do not know how much this meant to us." I smile against her shoulder and hold her for a second. I feel a deep connection blossoming beyond what I have felt when visiting a patient. "Call me anytime." I pull back from her hug and make sure she understands my sincerity. "Any time! When you or your husband had some time to digest today's session and want to talk about it, I am here."

As I walk away from the house, I pull the amethyst out of my jeans and feel its warmth in my hand. It is the closest thing to a hug from my daughter that I can get right now. I turn around and wave at Mom one more time before getting into the car.

My shoulder critic sits in the passenger seat already, his hair wet, the unicorn floatie, and his towel in a heap on the floor mat. "You ok?" he looks up at me, and I can see a touch of sunburn on his shoulders and nose, despite the scent of sunscreen that fills the car. I look back at the house as it holds its breath. Life goes on around it unflinching. Specks of clouds race high above the roof, the tree branches whisper, and two birds chase each other near the gutter. I gaze back at my critic, stretch out my hand to him, and he places his hand on top of mine. "Yeah. I am good."

Three days later, I got a text message from Mom.

Hi there, I just wanted to let you know that Gavin passed away peacefully this morning with us right by his side. He never woke up after you left. I am confident that the time you spent with him and us allowed him to release from his body. Sad but filled with peace and gratitude.

CHAPTER 29
MANHATTAN BEACH 2019

I turn my chair away from the table to face the ocean. Tonight, I wanted a drink - just me. I did not want or need company. Sometimes silence feeds the soul, and mine wanted my silence with a side of sunset and a dash of Pinot Grigio. The waiter places my wineglass on the table with a smile. "Anybody else joining you?" he asks with a look at the empty chairs next to me. "No, just me." He nods and collects the unnecessary cutlery and glasses. Before turning back towards the other guests, he pauses to look towards the horizon.

The vast evening sky above Manhattan Beach drapes the sun in folds of orange and pink as she prepares to settle into the dark comfort of the ocean. Couples, silhouetted in love, walk hand in hand along the edge of the water, where the receding waves have cleansed the sand of any footprints, leaving brief illusions of solitude. Enamored long shadows follow at their side and lean into one another, just as the sun kisses the horizon.

Despite the soothing song of the waves and the bustling of the restaurant behind me, my thoughts are bathed in stillness. Very little truly shakes me anymore. Looking back at the years since Kathrin's accident, I realize that my life has not taken the most predictable route. If someone had told me years ago that I would use Reiki to help parents say goodbye to their dying children, I would have scoffed at the thought. Back then, death felt only threatening - something to be feared and avoided at all costs. I turn around and let my eyes wander over the people at nearby tables. I see laughter, smooth skin, perfect white teeth, cocktails, and designer handbags. Death is ignored in favor of everlasting youth. People strive to look younger, be healthier and stronger, and live like Death is not their constant companion. But he is mine. He sits on one of the three empty chairs at my table and gazes out at the darkening sky, where the blue is still too bright for stars.

Three months ago, when Gavin was able to say goodbye to his parents with the help of Reiki, I felt overwhelmed by a deep sense of gratitude and purpose. It all started to make sense: the dreams, the visions, the intuition that guided me with every patient. Since then, the subsequent visits have been softer in nature. I learned that sometimes the connection is so intimate, so profound that asking parents about it afterwards felt like an intrusion. On those nights, I slipped out quietly, leaving the bubble of energy unbroken. Not once did I start a visit with the intention of using the new mantra. I was there for Reiki - the "old" Reiki. But occasionally, the new words emerged from within without being called forth. They opened like a night-blooming flower only when conditions were right.

It was a communication tool between parents and their children at a time when words were not sufficient to express the depth of their feelings. So much needs to be shared at the end of life, where words fail us. A parent cannot say goodbye. How could they? That would mean giving up, letting go, and admitting to what they perceive as the ultimate failure of protecting their baby. Yet deep inside, the soul understands that there is no such thing as failure when confronted with Death. But we do not have words for that. Yet, the new Reiki does just that. It is a literal heart-to-heart, feelings carried as energy from one heart to another - nothing lost in translation. This is what the new Reiki is all about: Learning to say goodbye. I had no idea that I had only scratched the surface.

Everything was about to change.

Two weeks later, I grab a thin sweater and my handbag, and kiss Gia and Giulia goodnight. My lips brush the hair on top of their heads; one is silky smooth, and the other tickles my nose with bouncy curls. They throw a casual "Bye Mama," over their shoulders while keeping their eyes glued to the TV. I know Andrea is indulging them with a few extra minutes of screen time while I am out, but that is the price I pay for leaving him alone to take the girls to bed. The quiet hours when time stretches and yawns after a busy day are perfect in their stillness for visiting my hospice kids. Either that or before noon, when the sun and the energy are high and the girls are in school.

Rush hour is over, so it only takes me 30 minutes to reach Francisco's home in Gardena. His house sits like a glittering snow globe at the end of a cul-de-sac, where the neighbor's houses scooch in for company. Even though Christmas is long gone, there are rows of fairy lights strung above the driveway, all joining in one spot over the front door, guiding the way towards the house. The soft light casts a magic spell over the home, hiding cracks in the exterior paint and the traces that time left on the pavement and windows. My shoulder critic walks next to me up the driveway, mesmerized by the twinkling lights that sway in a soft breeze. He's wearing a pair of jeans and black-and-white Air Jordan 1's with a gold sequin bomber jacket that reflects the lights and makes him look like a miniature disco ball. A wrought-iron gate stretches protectively over the front door. I ring the bell, and a harmony of gongs announces my arrival. An elderly woman, who I assume is the grandmother, in a velvet tracksuit, opens the door and greets me in Spanish, fully expecting me to understand her fast staccato. At my confused expression, she just smiles, opens the gate, and points me down the hallway. My footsteps echo off the tiled floor as I enter a dimly lit living room. The space is illuminated by just a few small lamps whose warm cones of light deepen the shadows around them. There is a dining table with eight heavy wooden chairs with carved armrests off to the right. Instead of a bowl of fruit or flowers as a centerpiece, a large illustrated Bible is propped open at one end of the table. An invisible pendant light hangs from the ceiling above and casts a mystical glow onto the pages. My shoulder critic pulls himself up onto the tabletop and tiptoes over to the bible, a magnifying glass in hand. With one nimble jump, he hops onto the open page and examines the intricate illustrations with interest. His jacket scatters golden flecks across the ceiling.

A woman walks out of the shadows towards me. Mom is about my age - mid-forties - and her brown hair is pulled back in a tight bun. She wears jeans and a black silk blouse that shimmers as she moves toward me, determination in her step. Her light gray eyes sparkle with life, and her outstretched hand is soft yet speaks of strength and confidence. "Thank you for coming at such a late hour. With work and everything, I rarely find time earlier." She motions for me to sit down on the ornate couch in the corner. "You met my mother." I don't know if that was a question or a statement, so I just nod as Mom gestures towards the elderly lady, who is now as silent as she was chatty before. I take a seat. The tufted velvet upholstery is deep purple, but every weight shift causes the fabric to glow golden, reflecting the light from the nearby floor lamp. I smooth gold back into its calmer purple tone with my palm, remembering my grand-mother's green velvet couch - soft at first, then prickly if you lie the wrong way. I cross my legs and settle, the fabric needling lightly through my pants.

"Let me get you some water," Mom says, and I take a moment to look around while she disappears into the kitchen. The room is heavy with ornate design elements - swirls, gold leaf, and thick curtains - somewhat not what I was expecting. Across from the couch is a crystal cabinet with decorative plates propped up in wire holders, small glass figurines, and assorted memorabilia that glitter and shine, illuminated by ceiling spotlights. There is a photograph of a family with three kids printed on a ceramic plate. Judging by the design and the fading of the picture, it must be from the 80s. Maybe Mom as a child.

Grandma busies herself wiping the Bible-free side of the dining room table and gathering stray napkins and knives, restoring everything to its spotless pre-dinner order. "Here you go," Mom puts a beaded coaster on the wooden side table and places a glass of cold water on top, condensation beading on the outside. She sits next to me, scoots a bit closer until our knees almost touch, and lowers her voice. "Jordin mentioned your Reiki." She looks up at her mother, who is putting placemats into a cabinet on the far corner of the room, and continues sotto-voce, "I know about Reiki. I have not had it myself, but my acupuncturist told me about it." Again, a furtive look at Grandma. I raise my eyebrows in a silent question. "She is very Catholic. Old-fashioned, you know?" I nod and clear my voice. Some assume Reiki conflicts with religion, even though, in reality, it is simply energy that does not require belief in any way. But I get it. Many people fear what they do not know and cannot understand. "Why don't you start by telling me more about Francisco?" Mom nods, and her voice rises in confidence as we enter a territory she is comfortable with her mother overhearing. I wonder if Grandma understands more English than she lets on.

Francisco was born with Cerebral Palsy, which demands around-the-clock care. He cannot speak, walk, or even sit up without help and is partially blind. He's nearly fifteen now, but his condition is deteriorating fast with seizures and heart complications. Time is slipping away. To add to the burden, Raoul, Francisco's dad, lost his job after an accident, and the family was forced to move in with the grandparents. So now the aesthetic dissonance makes sense: this is the grandparent's home. Mom lowers her voice again. Recently, another bad news hit home with the cancer diagnosis of her dad. But despite all of that, Mom sparkles with life and positivity. She is the engine that keeps everything running. Her optimism is not a front; it radiates in how she talks, moves, and smiles. She is a remarkable woman. "He has been sick before," she explains. "Very sick even. There were many times the doctors told us he would not make it. But he did. Every time, thank God." Her left hand touches a gold cross pendant that hangs from a delicate gold chain around her neck. "And now he is almost fifteen," she smiles, and a pause stretches between us like tea and honey as she follows her thoughts in silence. Releasing my need to fill the void with words, I just sit back and simply watch her face soften.

Suddenly, I feel the prickle of someone's intense gaze on me. The couch I am sitting on is against the wall, with the living room ahead of me, open and empty, except for Mom, still lost in thought. Grandma has disappeared somewhere into the depths of the house. We are alone. Goosebumps rise on my arms, and I turn towards my glass of water. Shadows collect at the feet of the side table and billow up behind it, almost obscuring a face just a few feet away, staring at me with an unmoving expression. I jolt back, spilling the water. My shock catapults my shoulder critic backward as if shot out of a cannon. He scrambles in a backward crab crawl along the top of the couch until his back is pinned against the carved wood trim. His eyes are fixed on the face that stares at us, unmoving. "Jesus!" The word escapes my lips before I can hold them back, and wakes Mom out of her thoughts. "… and Mary," she adds, a teasing tone in her voice. Right. What startled me was a lifelike statue of Mary holding baby Jesus in her arms. I had never seen such a large statue in someone's home. Mary stands almost 4 feet tall, and her eyes are level with mine. Her face is serene, and the dim light casts a lifelike glow onto her skin. She holds Jesus in folds of cascading fabric, with only a tiny smiling face and a naked arm and leg sticking up towards his mother. How did I miss it when I sat down? It's a few feet away in the shadows. My heart is still pounding as I wipe the water off my legs. "Let me get you a towel," Mom laughs, smile dancing around her lips, eyes sparkling. "No, don't worry. It was just a drop." Embarrassment warms my cheeks, and I laugh to release some of the adrenaline that is still rushing through my body.

My heart is still racing as a double door opens to my right and throws a rectangle of light into the living room. The room next door is brightly lit, and through the opening I can see a bed against the far wall. Before I can make out more, my view is obscured by Dad, who walks in with Francisco's gaunt figure cradled ever so gently in his arms. "Here comes my angel! *Mi angelito*[47]!" Mom exclaims as Dad sits down on the other end of the couch next to his wife. Mom scoots closer to her son, caresses his short dark hair, and kisses his forehead. Dad adjusts, settling Francisco's legs so they hang comfortably off the side, and lifts his son up to better cradle his head. Loose tracksuit pants and a white long-sleeve T-shirt hide Francisco's thin frame, but the wrists and hands that peek out of the sleeves are thin and pale, the skin stretching over pronounced joints. His large dark eyes are open, but stare up at the ceiling unfocused. I lean in until we are face-to-face and soften my voice. "*Hola*, Francisco. Hi!" A long, thin nose dominates the shadows and valleys of his face, and his eyes are framed by a curtain of long black lashes, but his gaze remains unfocused. I put my hand on his. It is soft and cool, and thin blue veins run under his translucent skin. His hand flicks slightly. I cannot tell if it was a reaction to my touch or involuntary. In his stillness,

---

47 *Mi angelito - Spanish. "My little angel*

there is something disarming about him, an aura that is ethereal, almost elf-like, that wakes an immediate urge to protect and nurture. There's no doubt that I'm here for the new Reiki. I couldn't be more sure if the boy had asked for it out loud. My shoulder critic has climbed up onto the couch behind Dad. His head is cocked to the side, and he is pulled into Francisco's spell the way I am. A softness has settled over his face, smoothing out the perpetual frown he carries, and I can almost hear him coo in affection.

Finally, I manage to pull my eyes away from Francisco and look up at Dad. "Hi. Where are my manners?" I smile as a form of explanation towards his son. "I'm Alexandra." "*Encantado,*[48]" Dad replies with a deep, sonorous voice that reminds me of campfires and storytelling. Just like his son, he is wearing tracksuit pants with white stripes along the sides and a pair of black-and-white Converse sneakers. He is tall and lean, with gentle, patient eyes that gaze at me from a thick cover of unruly eyebrows. Mom pulls a thin blanket over her son and puts her hand on her husband's arm as she turns back to me. "Okay, what do we need to do? Can Francisco stay here with his dad, or would you prefer him in his wheelchair, or on the bed?" Her voice trails off as she looks around the room for other options. "No, this is perfect here. In fact, I would love for both of you to participate in the Reiki session." I get up from the couch and drag one of the armchairs until I can sit opposite Francisco and his dad. I pull my phone out of my handbag and open my meditation app for some soothing background music. As the first gentle melodies drift out of the speaker, I explain how Mom and Dad can participate in the Family Reiki session.

A few minutes later, we sit in silence, their hands directly on Francisco, while mine hover a few inches above. To my surprise, my shoulder critic is sitting between Mom and Dad on the couch, his hands stretched out to touch Francisco's chest. He has taken off

---

48   *Encantado - Spanish. Enchanted. Usually used as "nice to meet you."*

the sequin jacket that had made him look like a walking Christmas ornament, and underneath, instead of his usual outrageous outfits, he wears a button-down shirt in bright pink, green, and yellow tartan stripes, a more flamboyant version of what my dad would wear. That connection instantly evokes a feeling of safety and warmth in my heart, and I am glad my critic is joining me. His eyes are closed, and a soft glow illuminates his face. The music matches the energy in the room. The track is called "Peaceful Journeys" and has an ethereal quality of harmonies that swirl into one another like wisps of thought. As soon as I close my eyes, the music pulls me into a weightless spiral of energy. My breath slows, and everything around me drops away. Life takes on a deeper meaning, as if fate, not coincidence has brought me here today. With the familiar tingle, I feel the new mantra flow from my hands without needing to formulate the words in my mind. I'm suspended in a velvet black void, where I lose track of time or time loses track of me. A wonderful warmth wraps around my back and shoulders like a blanket. It spreads through my body and fills me with a radiating heat that extends beyond my body, engulfing Francisco and his parents. This isn't my usual Reiki energy; it's vaster, steadier, profoundly peaceful, and I sink into it.

I can sense that the warmth has an origin. It emanates from behind me, spreading forward like a globe of soft, liquid light. As I tune into the source of the energy, I can differentiate layers - a harmony of energetic frequencies that carry feelings of love, so deep, so unconditional, and all-encompassing, that it leaves me in awe. I realize how small my own definitions of love have been. I can feel it running through my veins, pulsating in every fiber, in every molecule. Love isn't just an emotion; it is the essence of life. I know that I am not in a meditative state anymore. I'm acutely aware of my body, feel my hands, my feet on the floor, yet I have completely surrendered to the energy flowing through and around me.

In front of my closed eyes, I can see lights swirl and stretch from behind me on both sides. They start with a golden glow and form long streams of brilliant blue and turquoise ribbons of pure energy that dance like waves. Their tips arc towards one another until they almost form a complete circle around us.

Perceiving the world around me with a sense other than sight reveals itself in layers. First the feeling of peace and love as a pure sensory experience. Then the light and energy ribbons, and now, as my "vision" adjusts, images, click into brilliant focus, revealing the source and epicenter of it all.

There is an angelic presence standing just a few steps behind my left shoulder; large and beautiful - way larger than the ceiling of the room would allow for. He - for it is a 'he" I can feel - stands at least 12 feet tall, with dark hair and soulful brown eyes that look down on us with so much love that I can feel it as a warm golden wave ring through my body. His features remind me of Francisco, the way he might have looked as a young, healthy man … just more; more everything: more beautiful, intense, deep, loving. There are no words that suffice in describing the angel, for that is what I am seeing. He does not look like the angels in my imagination with feathered wings and flowing robes. He's both more and less: less solid, less defined. Yet grander, overwhelmingly ethereal. He looks like the energy-expression of what I thought an angel to be.

A golden glow surrounds him and streams out in swirling ribbons of energy that change into the brilliant blue and turquoise that I sensed earlier. The angel and the light are made from the same fre-quency, emitting a warmth that wraps all around us. I feel like I am falling backwards into weightlessness, arms wide open, into a space where light and love are all there is. Gravity ceases to exist, time falls away, brilliant dust motes float around me. I do not know how long I am suspended like this, but the ribbons of light bring me back and embrace our little circle, like wings, but without substance. Tears roll down my face as I realize that angel wings embrace us. Angel wings, I learn, are not made of feathers at all.

That thought jolts me back into my body, and I open my eyes with a start. The room is unchanged. Francisco's parents are still sitting with their hands on their son, in silent meditation or prayer. The music is still playing. The angel is gone - or simply beyond my senses; I can still feel the remnants of heat dissipating behind me. My heart starts beating out of my chest, and my palms feel cold and sweaty, not out of fear, but rather a visceral reaction to the over-whelming intensity of seeing an angel. I already miss the feeling of love and safety that held us.

I feel my shoulder critic's eyes on me. He is sitting wide-eyed on the couch, his mouth open in awe. A few tiny lights hover around him. He blinks but remains motionless. I know he has seen him too.

A few minutes later, I sit in my car, my heart racing and my hands trembling - clearly in no state to drive. What just happened? Adrenaline is flooding my body, and I am caught in a whirlwind of emotions.

I had just seen an angel!
AN ANGEL!

I let the tears run down my face while I laugh and cry at the same time. It is not so much that I doubt what I had seen. The lingering feeling of unconditional love has left a trace on my soul, a glowing fingerprint that will probably never be erased. It was so utterly inde-scribable that now, as I am back in the cool darkness of my car, I feel lost, alone, and detached. My heart is torn between pure joy and the acute sense of separation.

I am aware of how crazy I must look to anyone walking by, but thankfully, the night has settled onto the cul-de-sac, and I'm alone with my shoulder critic, who sits in the passenger seat, eyes still wide. He has not said a word since we walked out of Francisco's grandparents' home. I had brought the Reiki session to an end as gently as I could, took a few minutes to talk to the parents without mentioning the angel, packed my things, and left. But to me, it felt like I had bolted from the home.

"You should have said something!" My shoulder critic's voice is hoarse. I look at him and wipe my nose on the sleeve of my shirt, ignoring the makeup stains I leave behind. "Why did you not tell them?" His voice rises in intensity, and he stands up, his hands stretched wide in front of his body to express his disbelief. His words cut through me, and doubt rises amid the emotional turmoil. Why didn't I? Now it is my turn to stare at my critic wide-eyed. "I have no idea." The words are barely loud enough to tumble over my lips. I feel the color drain from my face and swallow hard. I was so focused on my own emotional experience that I had completely forgotten about the parents. A cold dread pushes through my bones, and for a moment, I am so shocked I cannot even think.

I should have told them!
I should have said something!

I look back at the house. Maybe it is not too late. I could go and tell them now. It would be awkward, but maybe they need to know. "Not maybe, they DEFINITELY need to know!" My critic jumps onto the center console and gives me a push. I take a deep breath, put my hand on the interior door handle, and look up at the house. Just at this moment, the lights behind the sheer curtains of the living room go dark, and the house settles in for the night.

Damn!

By the time I get home, my nerves have softened their tingle to a subtle hum. The dogs greet me with wet noses and wagging tails, and soon curl up in their beds next to the couch. The girls are asleep downstairs, and Andrea lies on the couch, snoring softly. The TV has switched to the Apple screensaver, and aerial views of Dubai glide across the screen. I turn the TV off, but hesitate to wake my husband. I can't sit still. I pace in the dark living room back and forth. The moon shines straight through the window and dips Andrea's features and the furniture in silver. The black silhouettes of the palm trees across the street catch the moonlight on the sword edge of their fronds, where it balances for a moment before dipping into the inch of black ocean visible between our neighbor's houses.

As soon as we walked in, my shoulder critic grabbed a small notebook and is now pacing next to me, scribbling incessantly, filling page after page. The scratching of the pen on paper, together with Andrea's deep, even breath, is the only sound in the room. "What are you doing?" I whisper. "I am writing it all down. This shit is crazy!" He pulls his wire-rimmed glasses down to the tip of his nose and looks up at me. "Do you even realize what happened?" he hisses with a slight tone of mania in his voice. "You … we … saw an angel! A friggin' angel!" He continues to pace. "You should have told them."

With a sigh, I plop myself onto the carpet in his path and lean against the armchair. "Come here." I stretch my hand out on the floor, palm open, and nod my head in invitation. He closes the notebook onto the pen, pins it under his arm, and climbs up onto my shoulder, where he settles down, legs crossed. We both take a deep breath and, with the exhale, melt into one another. The afterglow of our shared experience settles down on us. "Trust," he mumbles. "We need to remember trust." The moonlight softens his tense features and soaks both of us in a deep feeling of contentment. "It is all right. It all happened the way it was supposed to. If they're meant to know, I'll get a sign," I smile. He leans his head against mine, and we look out at the night sky for a long time.

Five days later, the sign arrives in the form of a phone call. "Alex?" Jordin's voice shines as bright as she does, even through the phone. "Could you go and visit Francisco again? His parents really enjoyed the last Reiki session and asked if you could …" This is exactly what I was waiting for! "Of course!" I blurt before she has a chance to finish the sentence. We settle on Thursday afternoon. I get an enthusiastic thumbs-up from my critic, who is pruning my houseplant with tiny silver scissors, dressed in green gardening overalls and matching daisy rain boots. I wink at him and hang up.

By the time I arrive at Francisco's house, the sun is laying long afternoon shadows across the street. Mom opens after the first ring and folds me into a hug. On the drive, my excitement had cooled into nerves - how do I start a conversation about angels? My critic rode shotgun on the dashboard, legs dangling, speaking with an intensity that was hard to ignore. "You got this! You asked for a sign, and here it is. Trust. You'll find the words" He held onto the dash with both hands as I drove around a corner, and his little body leaned into the curve. At a traffic light, he popped up in a complete cheer outfit wearing a short, pleated excuse for a skirt and a cropped tank with the letters "SC" in pink with black trim, and matching pink and black pompoms. "Give me a T, give me an R, give me a U, give me an S, give me a T! TRUST!" He spelled the letters in enthusiastic swings with his arms. The light turned green, and as I accelerated, he somersaulted into my handbag. We were both laughed, tension fizzing out.

But now, as I walk into the living room, doubt is only a far-away voice, drowned by the memory of that ridiculous cheer. He'd slipped me one of his small pompoms for luck, and I close my hand around it now, feeling connected and supported by this little guy who in recent months had become less of a critic and more of a friend.

"Francisco is still napping, but he should be up soon," Mom explains, as she sits in one of the armchairs. Her white blouse is threaded with delicate stripes of gray and pink, hair braided, pearl earrings luminous against her tired eyes. Mary smiles serenely from her corner as I slide onto the couch.

I mean to warm us up with small talk, but the story surges through me, wanting to come out. "I need to tell you something."

It pours out, one solid stream of words fills the living room, washes over the coffee table and the couch, and draws Mom and me into a gripping riptide: Reiki, the overwhelming emotion, the love that eclipsed everything else, the angelic presence that looked so much like Francisco, the wings that weren't wings but pure energy - and how this feeling has stayed. How I'd been too overwhelmed to say it then, but I kept choosing Trust, and all the signs pointed me back here to tell her now. Mom's eyes brim with tears, and she stares at me without a word, without a hint of a reaction.

"I'm so sorry if this sounds crazy," I add, squeezing the little pom-pom. "I followed my heart. I truly hope I didn't overstep." We sit, surrounded by silence. Mom fishes a tissue from her sleeve, dabs her tears that have carved soft riverbeds through her makeup. My throat is parched, and I swallow hard. "Shhhhh," I hear my shoulder critic's soothing voice in my head. "You did the right thing. Trust," A still image of his trust dance flashes in my mind, and with one deep breath, I am able to drop the anxiety that clamps my throat. Another breath and my shoulders relax. A luminous feeling of peace settles over the room, and, in unison, Mom and I breathe a sigh of relief. She lifts her red-rimmed eyes and finds mine. "Thank you," she whispers, voice caught between a sob and a smile. She looks up and wipes the corner of her eyes. The ball of wet tissue in her hand cannot hold a single tear more.

I had expected tears. I had expected disbelief. I had not expected what she said next.

"You are my sign from God!"

Sounds tiptoe through the sudden silence from the bedroom next door. A shuffling and a muffled voice, then nothing. Sun pours through the sheer curtains; the purple fabric of the couch shines with golden highlights. My brain scrambles to make sense of Mom's reaction. I must have misheard.

"No! You were sent to me by God!" she repeats, firmer now. Her eyes are dry, a new depth lighting her face. "I have to go back to explain." She touches the cross pendant on her necklace. "We're very Catholic. All my life, we have been going to church every week, often more than once. We pray daily. My faith is what lets me walk with God through everything - Francisco's care, my husband's job loss, moving in with my parents and my dad's diagnosis. We trust in God. He will provide." She leans forward, her eyes locked on mine. "But then ..." her gaze flicks to Mary. "A few days ago, I found a lump in my breast." She pauses, struggling for composure. "That day I had my first crisis of faith. I sat in my car and I cried, and I prayed. I asked 'Why do you burden us with so much? I've never stopped trusting you.'" She looks back at me, breath fluttering. "I needed Him to give me a sign. I needed to know that we were going to be okay, that Francisco was going to be okay. So, I prayed 'Dear God, show me I'm not alone. Protect us. Give me a sign that my ...'" she pauses again and looks at me with a new fire in her eyes. "... that my angel Francisco will be ok."

Her words drop into the quiet and ripple outward. It takes a beat for my mind to catch up. Then they settle on my soul like dew, soothing the worry I'd carried with me. A sudden weight pulls me deeper into the velvet-covered couch as the enormity of the situation peeks out from the cover of doubt. I curl my fingers into the rounded grooves of the armrest, grateful for wood and velvet to tether me to the room while the universe inside me widens.

Not only had I seen her son as an angel - her angel Francisco - but what I had witnessed was the answer to a prayer she hadn't voiced yet. I feel like the floor is dropping away from me, and I float suspended in awe. I had thought the angel was the miracle. I had no idea that was only half of it

I study her face to stay grounded: the smooth skin, the corners of her mouth lifted by a joy neither of us has fully grasped.

I am speechless.

Even my hastened escape from the home last time made sense now. Timing was part of the message. If I'd told her that night, the message would not have had the same impact.

Even Gabriel showing up in my meditation months ago feels like quiet scaffolding - a gentle on-ramp towards belief. And Trust - that single word Kathrin handed me through Mona - has been the rope I've held the whole way. That one word has changed my life. I trust my path, trust the messages I get, the things I see and experience, and most importantly, I trust that there is something bigger than us.

I leave an hour later feeling light as air and wildly at peace. To speak openly about angels and be met with validation - not argument, but echo - is mind-blowing. I skip the last steps to the car, where my shoulder critic is already waiting for me. He has changed into red corduroy shorts and a blue-and-white striped T-shirt, an outfit I remember him wearing when I was a child. He leaps into my arms and hugs as much of me as he can contain in his little embrace.

"I am speechless!" I say as I drop into the driver's seat. The idea that God used me as a messenger makes me giggle. "I mean, really? Me?!" I look at my critic who just shrugs his shoulder and grins. He pulls a tiny glowing halo out of the car door and throws it like a frisbee until it hovers over my head. I pull the visor down and catch my reflection. "You're an idiot." I laugh and flick the glowing circle out the open window, where it flares like a miniature supernova and disappears.

THE END

EPILOGUE

Over the past few years, working with my young hospice patients has become the center of my universe. Nothing in my life has fulfilled me as completely, saturating my soul with a deep sense of marvel, gratitude, and love. Holding space for families at the hardest hours - simply being there, one breath at a time - has taught me to be fully present. It returns me to the moment and reminds me that the present is exactly that: "a present," a gift - one precious instant followed by another.

Most of my visits bring me a deep sense of connection to something larger. You might call it the divine energy, Source, or God. Whatever name we might give it, it brings an overwhelming feeling of deep, unconditional love and, more often than not, a mystical experience. Sometimes those experiences are subtle signs, emotions or feelings that arise during a Reiki session, but occasionally they are so powerful that they force me - once again - to redefine my "normal". Just a few years ago I would not have called it normal to see an angel, or to realize that a person's spirit is standing beside their body, observing me. Now would I have called it normal to facilitate a wordless conversation between a parent and their dying child and feel nothing but love and gratitude afterward.

A lot has changed in my life since loss forced me to take a closer look at who I am and what life is all about. Just last week, drifting toward asleep, an overwhelming wave of gratitude flooded my body. Not a fleeting thought, but a warm tide that engulfed my whole being. In that instant I understood how everything in my life had lined up to bring me here: to this place, this moment in time. Every loss, every pain, every moment of soul-searching and growth led me here, where I can help others. In its all-consuming warmth, that gratitude felt like divine love - perfect, peaceful, and ecstatic all at once. It was pure love for my family, my life, my friends, my circumstances and yes, even for the losses I have experienced. It was immense gratitude for everyone who has accompanied me along my path and helped me find my way here: my husband, who - through his work - gives me the freedom to volunteer my time with my patients. For my children, who keep me grounded, for my friends who help me realize that what I am experiencing is not crazy and allow me to take ownership of who I've become, and for Kathrin, who - through all this - is, and always will be, a huge part of my life. On a metaphysical level, she remains my confidante I can still laugh with, my mentor I can turn to for support and advice, and my very own guardian angel, reminding me to TRUST.

EPILOGUE

ABOUT THE AUTHOR

Born and raised in Germany, Alexandra lived a nomadic life before making Los Angeles home with her husband, two children, and two dogs. After four losses in her closest circle, she began an unflinching journey through grief - one that reordered her priorities and changed the course of her work. Leaving a career as Director of Marketing and Operations, she first volunteered in pediatric hospice, then trained to serve families as a Pediatric End-of-Life Doula.

Her calling reshaped her understanding of love, presence, and the thresholds between life and death. She hosts Learning To Say Goodbye, a podcast "about life, death and spirituality," where she speaks with clinicians, spiritual teachers, scientists, and people who have walked through loss.

In her book, Learning To Say Goodbye, she brings the same steady gaze to the page - honest, compassionate, and practical - offering companionship through loss and a language for the tenderness that remains.